101

EXERCISES
FROM
TOP RIDERS

TOP INTERNATIONAL RIDERS FROM THE FIELDS OF
DRESSAGE, SHOW JUMPING AND EVENTING:

*Laura Bechtolsheimer, Jeanette Brakewell, Karen Dixon,
Lucinda and Clayton Fredericks, William Micklem, David O'Connor,
Sandy Phillips, Guenter Seidel, Oliver Townend, Isobel Wessels and Guy Williams*

Compiled by
JAKI BELL

D&C
David and Charles

A DAVID & CHARLES BOOK
Copyright © David & Charles Limited 2007

David & Charles is an F+W Publications Inc. company
4700 East Galbraith Road
Cincinnati, OH 45236

First published in the UK in 2007

Text copyright © Jaki Bell 2007
Photography and illustrations copyright © David & Charles,
except pages 21, 143 © Horsepix

ISBN-13: 978-0-7153-2547-6 hardback
ISBN-10: 0-7153-2547-7 hardback

Printed in China by Shenzhen Donnelly Printing Co Ltd
for David & Charles
Brunel House   Newton Abbot   Devon

Commissioning Editor Jane Trollope
Assistant Editor Emily Rae
Designer Jodie Lystor
Production Controller Beverley Richardson
Illustrators Ethan Danielson, Maggie Raynor p35
Photographers Bob Atkins (pages 67 and 69), Matthew Roberts (page 191)

Visit our website at www.davidandcharles.co.uk

David & Charles books are available from all good bookshops; alternatively you can contact our
Orderline on 0870 9908222 or write to us at FREEPOST EX2 110, D&C Direct, Newton Abbot, TQ12 4ZZ
(no stamp required UK only); US customers call 800-289-0963 and Canadian customers call 800-840-5220.

Contents

INTRODUCTION

As I write this today, in July 2006, 'celebrity' is the 'buzz' word for all areas of information – magazines, books, internet and television – and if you were to look down from Mars, society appears to be driven by a need to be famous or to imitate the famous.

In the sports arena this instinct, if that's what it is, has been used for years, but in a much healthier way: to learn from, and model ourselves upon, those who have proved themselves to be successful in certain fields. The marvellous thing about this is that, throughout all sports, whatever level a participant enters at, something can be drawn from the example of these experts.

Which brings us to this book: and once again, as happened when I compiled *101 Schooling Exercises*, I have learnt much. It seems to me that the ability of the equestrian interest to break down barriers not only of class and age but also of competence, is alive and well. It doesn't matter whether you are just beginning to understand the mechanics of training a horse or to compete, you will find almost every exercise in this book, even across the disciplines, has something that you can learn from.

If you are an experienced rider, I hope you will find that the techniques revealed here add to your bag of training tricks. If you are an aspirational rider looking to move on, some fundamental 'reminders' are included in the opening section. If you are just beginning to ride, however, this book does presume knowledge of the basics and – forgive the plug – you will be better off with *101 Schooling Exercises*.

My thanks to all those who took the time to contribute during what has been a busy time in a busy year. Many of the contributors participated in the 2006 World Equestrian Games, and, as we shall all be reading this with the benefit of hindsight, let's hope they did well. The magic is that each rider has worked on being the best they can possibly be – and that should also apply to you and me.

The fundamentals

The exercises in this book remain, as far as possible, in the terminology of the contributors, to allow their personalities to come through. There is, therefore, some discrepancy in terms. However, any unusual terminology has been clarified.

As a certain level of ability is presumed, each exercise is not ridden pace by pace with every movement described. Only crucial or unexpected positions or aids are included. It is also assumed that the reader/rider will know the aids to the basic changes of gait (a reminder of anything more complex is given here), that the horse will be warmed up before commencing work, and that the importance and use of half-halts is understood and incorporated into the schooling session.

Warming up

Each exercise should only be ridden once your horse is warmed up. Whilst it is recommended that all horses begin working long and low, you will best know how your ride responds to his schooling work, and whether lungeing is needed to settle him down, a canter to get him going, or a hack to loosen him up. As these are not preliminary exercises, and most will be incorporated into a training session and with other exercises, this will probably happen as a matter of course.

The half-halt

The half-halt is used to gain your horse's attention, although this should be constant anyway, and to signal to him that something is about to happen. If ridden well, it also helps him with his balance. Use it coming into corners, into transitions, into changes of pace and to improve collection. It can be used more than once if the desired response is not achieved.

RIDING HALF-HALT

❏ Using your lower leg, squeeze the horse into a gently restraining hand (you don't want to be blocking the forward movement of his hind legs with a 'backward' rein contact). Simultaneously, lighten your seat.

❏ Now close your lower leg again, but this time, allow the horse to go forwards.

A reminder of the aids

THE AIDS TO A TURN OR A CIRCLE

❏ Check your position.

❏ Use your inside rein intermittently to ask for an elastic contact and a slight flexion to the inside. This will also indicate to your horse in which direction you are turning.

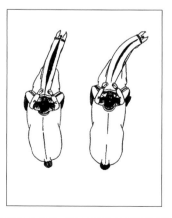

❏ Allow your horse to bend through his neck and body with your outside rein, maintaining a contact, unless you need to use the rein to control impulsion or degree of bend.

❏ Look where you are going – you will then automatically turn your shoulders in that direction.

❏ Allow your weight on to your inside seat bone and into your inside stirrup.

❏ Use your inside leg on the girth to encourage your horse's inside leg to step actively forwards.

❏ Use your outside leg behind the girth to prevent the horse's hindquarters swinging out.

❏ Use both legs and your seat to encourage and maintain impulsion.

THE AIDS TO A PIROUETTE

❏ Sit with your inside leg on the girth and your outside leg just behind it, preventing the quarters from falling out. This movement of the outside leg from the hip will also cause your weight to fall on to the inside seat bone, as desired. Turn your shoulders in the direction of the bend, and allow the outside rein to go forwards with the horse's head.

❏ Ask for a bend with your inside hand and, via contact on the bit with both hands, use gentle half-halts as required to improve your horse's attention and collection.

❏ Use your inside leg, in small rhythmic nudges on the girth, to ask for the turn, and to maintain impulsion and tempo.

❏ Your outside leg remains behind the girth, guarding the haunches and assisting with tempo where necessary.

THE AIDS TO LEG-YIELD

❏ Transfer your weight to your inside seat bone.

❏ Place your inside leg just behind the girth, and use it to ask your horse to move sideways and forwards.

❏ Your outside leg remains behind the girth, stopping the hindquarters moving too far sideways, and maintaining the forward movement.

❏ Your inside rein asks for a slight bend.

❏ The outside rein should allow this bend, but should prevent overbending and falling out through the outside shoulder.

THE AIDS TO SHOULDER-IN

❏ With your inside leg on the girth, ask your horse to move actively forwards and sideways.

❏ Your outside leg is behind the girth, preventing the hindquarters from falling out.

❏ Your inside hand initially leads the forehand in from the track and then maintains this degree of bend. Use small gives and takes of the reins to ensure that your horse is in self-carriage.

❏ Your outside rein allows this bend without restricting the horse working forwards through his inside shoulder. It also helps the outside leg to support and control the hindquarters.

THE AIDS FOR EXTENDED WALK

❏ Use as much inside leg as is necessary to generate energy and impulsion.

❏ Allow a bolder swing through your seat with the horse's paces.

❏ Allow the reins to go forwards with the movement of the horse's head and neck, but not so much that he pokes his nose out and disengages.

THE AIDS FOR TRAVERS

❏ Turn your upper body in the direction of the movement and keep your weight on your inside seat bone.

❏ Your inside leg should be positioned on the girth, supporting the bend and maintaining impulsion.

❏ Your outside thigh and knee support the bend; the lower leg asks for the horse's outside hind leg to step across the inside hind leg, underneath his body.

❏ Maintain contact with the bit with your inside rein.

❏ The outside rein controls the shoulder and allows the horse to travel forwards.

THE AIDS FOR RENVERS

❏ Your inside leg should be on the girth and your outside leg just behind it, preventing the quarters from falling out.

❏ Keep your weight on the inside seat bone. Turn your shoulders in the direction of the bend, and allow the outside rein to go forwards with the horse's head.

❏ Your inside leg will now become the outside leg as you use it to ask the horse to bend his hindquarters back towards the track.

❏ The new inside leg and hand combine to support the horse's forehand and to keep his bending position.

❏ The inside rein controls the inside shoulder, allowing the horse to travel forwards.

❏ The outside rein maintains an elastic contact.

THE AIDS TO FLYING CHANGE

❏ Establish canter.

❏ Begin to flex your horse in the new direction, retaining a light, giving contact.

❏ Bring your outside leg forward to the girth, at the same time taking your original inside leg back behind the girth with a stronger pressure.

❏ Remain light enough in the seat to allow your horse to jump through from one lead to the other. The new inside seat bone should be slightly forward.

❏ Now use your seat and legs to ride the horse forwards, keeping the inside leg on the girth to maintain rhythm.

Be the best you can be

This book is about motivation and inspiration, two key requirements to keep an equestrian going. What motivates you? A desire to win, performing to the best of your abilities, working in a partnership, training an animal, or doing something that seemed to be impossible? Whatever it might be, if you are reading this, the chances are that what makes you want to get up in the morning, or results in your social life revolving around coaching sessions, is the desire to improve your knowledge and abilities in this, our chosen field of sport. Staying motivated is what makes it happen. Sometimes this comes from within, the result of achievement following success at a certain goal, however small it may be; sometimes it comes from learning from others and benefiting from the results of their trial and error.

Quite often you hear talk of a particular sportsman or woman who has achieved their success alone or without a trainer. To have that natural ability and dedication is commendable but rare. One would also have to live in a box. Watching others perform, discussing personal development, and seeking best practice are all in themselves lessons to be learnt from. The truth of the matter is that that athlete has a physical gift and analytical ability, whether they are aware of it or not. We all benefit from studying how another sportsperson tackles a situation, and sometimes this knowledge will broaden our minds as to how goals can be achieved.

Goal setting

What is your equestrian goal? If you are reading this, the chances are that it will revolve around either competitive aspirations or a desire to improve the performance of your horse. Hold on to that thought, because so often it is easy to become side-tracked.

To keep yourself on course it is necessary to break down your end result, your goal, into manageable chunks, or short-term targets, and because the beneficial effects of goal setting are based on achievement, to bring in a time-frame on which to suspend these targets. Let's say you want to raise your game and move from being a weekend competitor to regional achievement. What is a realistic time in which that could be achieved? What would be the steps along the way that move you and your horse on towards that achievement? (And not all of these might, necessarily, be in the equestrian field, as you may need to review your income or working commitments to make this possible.) Take some time to get this planning right because you will be living with it for a while; but also remember that there has to be an element of flexibility, because life, as we all know, doesn't always go to plan, and you may find that along the way your short-term targets adjust and your goals move.

The next step is to break down your targets into action steps that can be achieved in much shorter periods, say on a monthly or even a weekly basis. Now you have a ladder of self-motivation – though bear in mind there may be occasions on which you need to bring in the help of others.

AND IF YOU FAIL?
Treat any action step that doesn't achieve its desired outcome as a learning tool. Work out what went wrong, and how you can overcome it, and translate that into future action steps.

There are five acknowledged steps to goal setting:

1. The goal must be clearly identified, not a vague wish to be a better rider, for example.
2. Your goals must be measurable in terms of both quality and time. If your target is to master flying changes before a forthcoming test, work backwards from the test, breaking down the targets along the way and giving them a time-frame; and as you progress, monitor your performance. This can be as simple as giving yourself an eight out of ten!
3. It must be practically possible to reach your goal, although in theory, this method of breaking down goals into bite-sized actions within an undefined time-frame makes almost anything possible.
4. To get a sense of achievement and to benefit from the resulting motivation, your action steps, short-term targets and final goal must have deadlines attached.
5. Your goal must be *your* goal and not someone else's.

Invest time in this plan and in keeping it up to date, even keeping a journal if possible. However well documented your analysis of your journey may be, it will help you to identify what is necessary along the way, to simplify your planning and to organize your time. Each step along the way the goal becomes closer and clearer. By seeing how you have progressed, you will feel motivated to move on, and your self-confidence will develop as you do so.

The German Scales of Training
Both Laura Bechtolsheimer and Isobel Wessels referred to the German 'Scales of Training' as their guide to training a horse and restructuring a training programme when trying to overcome difficulties.

As this is a 'training plan' that any rider can benefit from, for those not familiar with this guideline to instilling basic qualities in the horse we reproduce them here. The scales set out the three stages of the phases of development of a riding horse, and the six qualities necessary to achieve these:

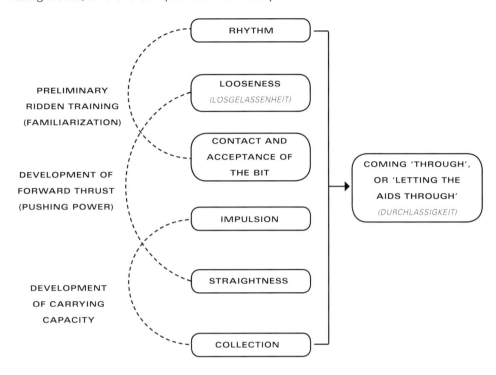

The six steps are all interdependent, and need to be worked on in a co-ordinated manner: the diagram shows how they interlink. This scale can be used to formulate a long-term training plan, but also to structure a daily schooling session and for horses involved in every discipline.

THE SIX STEPS TO SUCCESS

Use your head:
- ❏ Don't just sit there and hope that it will happen: be mentally engaged with what you are trying to achieve, and focused on the process of getting to your goals.

Keep things simple:
- ❏ Refine your aids;
- ❏ save time where possible;
- ❏ break problems down into simple steps;
- ❏ use repetition as a training tool.

Stay positive:
- ❏ Don't be dragged down by apparent failure, but use it as a learning tool to suggest further development;

- ❏ don't allow others to disillusion you; and
- ❏ reappraise your goals if they are not realistic.

Keep an open mind:
- ❏ Progress is about new development;
- ❏ watch other riders, good and bad;
- ❏ read everything you can get your hands on; and
- ❏ don't be shy of sharing your views.

Do your homework:
- ❏ Invest time in training.

Don't become obsessed:
- ❏ Keep a balance between all areas of your life, home, work and sport;
- ❏ there is more to life than horses, but it has to be good to compete with them!

LAURA BECHTOLSHEIMER

When you read through 21-year-old Laura Bechtolsheimer's exercises, her sensitivity to the role the horse plays in the dressage partnership shines through. Her contributions to this book are full of references to how the horse feels during training, and anecdotes relating her thoughts back to her own rides.

From Cirencester in Gloucestershire, Laura is big news in the British dressage world, and one of the shining lights in UK equestrianism generally. In 2005 she won the British National Dressage Championships, at the age of 20 becoming the youngest person to do so. A life-time rider, Laura began her competitive career in Pony Club horse trials, but her potential for dressage was spotted by trainer Ian Woodhead, and she decided to specialize in dressage at the age of 13. The following season she was selected to ride at the Pony European Championships in Sweden, and came home with a team silver medal. The Bechtolsheimer name is well respected in dressage circles: Laura's father is Dr Wilfried Bechtolsheimer, a renowned dressage rider and trainer. Laura is a member of the World Class Performance Programme, and in 2006 was selected to represent Great Britain at the World Equestrian Games at Aachen with her father's 17.2hh, 15-year-old Hanoverian, Douglas Dorsey; the British team came 6th and Laura came 21st in the Grand Prix Special.

Q: What's the best piece of advice you've ever been given?
Be patient, self-critical, and accept your trainer's criticism. Always blame yourself rather than the horse – it's usually something you're doing.

Q: What do you do when you hit a training 'brick wall'?
Don't let the horse feel your frustration: do other things that you and your horse are confident at – or get someone more experienced to get on, and watch what they do. By watching you usually come to a solution.

Q: How do you identify your training problems?
My feelings are confirmed through my trainer, videos, and judges' comments on competition test sheets.

Q: And what are you working on at present?
My own image and self-confidence in performance. If something goes wrong or the test isn't good you can see it in my face! I've got to learn not to give the game away.

Q: What is your training passion?
To train horses who are extremely sensitive and have very strong characters – on the verge of crazy! Most of my horses are very sensitive and I've had a few branded nut cases. But I think it is so much more fun to ride the equine equivalent of a Ferrari; they're harder to control and take longer to make up the partnership with, but it's an amazing feeling when you turn a horse like that into a real winner.

Q: Whose performance do you watch?
Andreas Helgstrand, a young Danish rider, and Hubertus Schmidt of Germany. They both ride with very fine aids and I find them very watchable when they are working in. They stick to classical horse ways, which I appreciate.

Q: And who do you most admire in the equine world?
Mark Todd. I think he's a true genius. He can get on any horse for the shortest amount of time and build enough of a partnership to take it around Badminton.

Q: What sort of horses do you like?
Hot, sharp and cheeky!

Q: And what do you look for when you get on a horse for the first time?
Activity in the hind legs, I like a horse that's a real goer. I don't like horses you have to kick or push – it is the horse that has to bring power and motivation; it has to have a workable character.

Q: Can you recall your last equine 'magic moment'?
I have that feeling most days during training when I'm riding my 11-year-old, Mistral Hojris: he's a horse that was made for me.

CONTENTS

Transitions to achieve quickness of the hind legs

'I will use this exercise during the cross-over between warming-up and starting proper work.'

TIP

Quick does not mean hectic. Your horse should not feel that he is being attacked, nor should he be confused by what you are asking of him.

The exercise

❏ Once you've warmed up, along each long side of the school ride two or three trot-to-walk, walk-to-trot transitions. Keep repeating the transitions until the horse is reacting how you want.

❏ Repetition will help your horse to understand your aids, to quicken up and to react more quickly.

❏ Whatever level of rider you are, you can implement this exercise.

What you should be looking for

This exercise sharpens the horse up and wakes him up. The aim of these short, sharp transitions is to get your horse light on the hands and quick on the leg aids. You want your aids to become finer and your horse to be reacting off very fine aids. You are looking for quickness and self-carriage. Your horse should make a quick jump into each upward change of pace.

Moving on

Your aids should become more and more invisible. This exercise can also be used before any periods of canter work (walk to canter, canter to walk), or fitted in at any appropriate moment during your schooling, wherever you may be in the arena.

What's being achieved

Quickness and sharpness are desired for collection, for self-carriage, for making good corners, to set the horse up for movements, and for coming on the centre line. If you can control these transitions, you can also control collecting up to the halt, and halt when you want to. This responsiveness is also important for later pirouettes, and for all the collected movements.

BONUS

If your horse is quick and together, it will halt square.

DOUBLE CHECK

Collection does not mean slower steps, it means shorter, quicker ones. You should make sure that:

❏ you are not using stronger or harsher aids as you train your horse to get him to be quicker – your aids are to be finer;

❏ your horse does not break pace before you ask. Think 'collect, collect, collect, and walk'. And it is the same for the upward transition.

What can go wrong?

If you are making your transitions in a harsh way, your horse will become over-sensitive and will snatch with his head, or show that he is a little uncomfortable.

Be careful not to give too harsh half-halts, because if you do, you may suddenly find yourself with an over-sensitive horse. If this occurs you will have to try to be lighter in your aids, and keep repeating and rewarding your horse until he sees that half-halts are not meant to be harsh.

RIDING AN ACCURATE TRANSITION

Before riding an upward or downward transition you should prepare your horse by riding one or more half-halts. To make an upward transition, use your weight and both legs positively, simultaneously and smoothly to send your horse on. You must allow the horse to use his neck and lengthen his frame. To make a downward transition, continue to ride forwards into the transition or your horse will fall on to his forehand and may lean on the bit instead of using his hindquarters.

'I have to do this exercise with Douglas, my Grand Prix horse, because he's such a big, strong horse and can very easily become strong and 'on the hand'. Often between advanced movements and pirouettes, I will come back to this to remind him to be quick.'

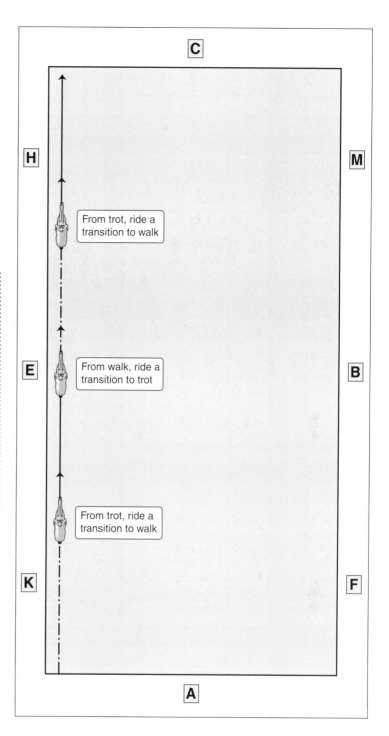

From trot, ride a transition to walk

From walk, ride a transition to trot

From trot, ride a transition to walk

Controlling the corners

'If you can't control the corners it makes it even harder to make the next movement out of the corner. The issue I have with Douglas is that on the one rein, he dives into the corner, while on the other, he won't go into it.'

'I think this is best in trot, but I find canter easier because in canter you can really collect. Generally, if a horse isn't of Grand Prix level, it's easier to collect it in canter because you've got rhythm, whereas in trot they're likely to go too slowly or almost walk.'

The exercise

❑ Using two of the arena corners and four ground poles, set up a 'mini arena' at one end of your school. The aim is that you have four corners very close together, so try arranging the artificial corners about twenty metres away from the actual corners to begin with.

❑ Choose your pace according to whether it is easier to collect your horse in trot or canter. Ride the two actual corners first, and then ride the other two corners as if they were real corners.

❑ Make sure your turns are sharp, almost like a quarter pirouette if you're riding in canter, or bringing the shoulders properly off the track if in trot.

❑ Really practise control of the horse's hind legs and the front legs as you go around the corner.

❑ Repeat on both reins.

What's being achieved

If the horse stays straight, in flexion and in self-carriage, then he is in self-balance. The corner should be used to see if you've got the horse on your aids and in control. You should be able to give the reins after the corner and the horse should stay in the same active pace and hold itself in self-carriage without tilting. If you can do this after a corner you know that you've done a good corner and that you're successful in keeping your horse in its balance.

What you should be looking for

The aim is collection and activity of the hind legs, which have to follow the exact tracks of the front legs so they don't swing out or come in through the corner. You need to keep the rhythm, and the horse should stay in its own self-carriage. The better the corner, the better you can set the horse up for the next movement. Don't let him just turn when he feels like it.

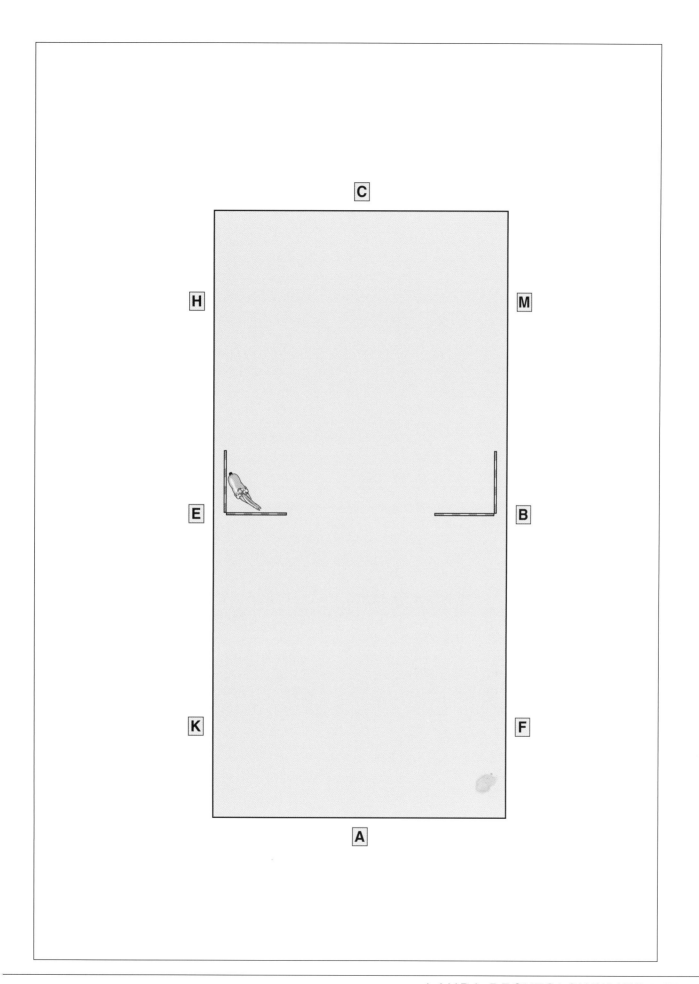

What can go wrong?

There are three obvious problems:

Your horse won't go into the corner:
If you have trouble getting into the corner, put a marker just inside so the horse has to bend around it. The marker acts as reinforcement for your inside leg. Another thing is to look for a reason why the horse might be finding it difficult. This is often something to do with us, such as we're not sitting evenly, with our weight straight in the saddle and equal weight in the stirrups. Or sometimes we fall in, so the horse falls into the corner, or we fall out a little, making it hard for the horse to go around the corner.

Your horse dives too deep into the corner:
In this case, it's good to try and ride a little bit of shoulder-fore before the corner, so that you bring the horse's shoulder in a little bit and the hind legs should follow.

You can make the horse over-sensitive:
If you try and bully your horse too much, pushing his quarters in and out, trying to straighten him up, or sending him too far into the corners, you'll find either a loss of rhythm, or you'll have too extreme an effect and you'll end up with them swinging out too far.

Moving on

This exercise is about repetition, and the aim is to improve and remain fine with your aids.

HOW TO RIDE AN ACCURATE CORNER

You need to have a fairly even contact, just slightly stronger on the outside and a little bit lighter on the inside so that the horse has a slight inside bend through the corner and you can see the inside eye just a little bit. The idea is that you can give the inside rein and the horse still stays on the inside bend through the contact, which shows that the horse has self-carriage. Use slightly more contact on the inside leg, so that your horse's inside hind leg stays active. Diagonal aids, the inside leg and outside rein, are the strong points in the corner and your legs act as a channel for the horse's body to stay straight.

Getting the horse's attention on the centre line

'I know it's really hard when a horse knows it's going to halt – it'll just splat.'

TO HELP WITH STRAIGHTNESS ON THE CENTRE LINE

In trot or canter, turn up the centre line and ride from A to C. Keep your horse straight using your legs rather than your hands. Then check on your effectiveness: give one rein away for four strides and then take it back, then repeat with the other rein. Now repeat the exercise but ask for a little neckbend for four strides, then straighten, then bend the other way, and then straighten.

What you are aiming for

Centre lines need a lot of practice and have to be treated like riding a corner. You want the horse to be collected but really active, so that you can set it up for the halt or any other movement that comes later (in more advanced classes movements are ridden on the centre line). Even just for a halt, you want it active so you can really control where the halt is. So always throw in a few centre lines. Keeping activity, and being in control, and straightness on the centre line, will make it a lot easier for you to be able to control your halts.

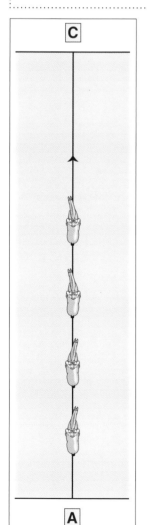

The exercise

Try the following during the course of a schooling session:

❑ Ride down the centre line and collect and go again, collect and go again, up to five times, in trot or in canter. The idea is that the horse acts really quickly on your aids. When you collect a little bit it shouldn't break into a walk or halt, and when you ask him to move forwards again, he should react really quickly.

❑ Now throw in a centre line without doing anything, so you keep the horse on his toes when he's on the centre line and doesn't always anticipate a movement.

❑ Throw in little transitions upwards and downwards on the centre line.

❑ Ride a quarter pirouette to turn on to the centre line.

❑ Finally, practise halt on the centre line, but not always where you'll halt in a test. Ride a little bit further on so that you can really control where you want your horse to be.

What's being achieved

You are working on keeping your horse really fine on your aids, and ensuring he is not anticipating the halt or the movement.

What can go wrong?

You see people swinging too far over, missing the centre line. You really want to be able to collect and control exactly where the horse's front and hind legs go when they hit the centre line.

Flexing through the body

'This is useful if you have a horse that's stiff in shoulder-in. Keep the body position but change the flexion – counter flexion.'

'Take a few strides to make the change – if you were exercising you wouldn't go from one stretch straight into another.'

The exercise

❏ On the long side of the school, from the corner and in trot, ride shoulder-in.

❏ At the half-way marker, make a transition to renvers, keeping the quarters on the track and the front legs on the inner track. Use your shoulders to maintain the angle, and change the bend by reversing your weight in the lower half of your body and flexing a little bit straighter or even to the outside, to keep the suppleness and the balance of the horse. Take a few strides to make the change.

❏ Straighten up just before the corner, and repeat on the opposite rein.

What's being achieved

Whereas shoulder-in works on the forehand of the horse, renvers is more about suppleness through the back, behind the saddle. Your horse needs to be supple and well balanced to be able to achieve the bend to the left and then to the right.

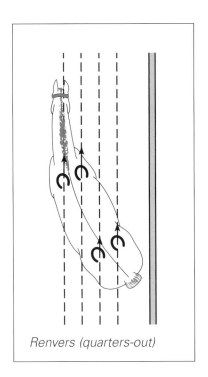

Renvers (quarters-out)

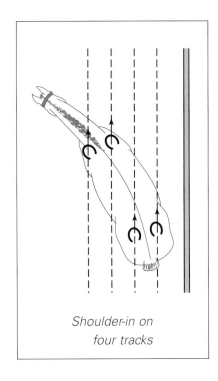

Shoulder-in on four tracks

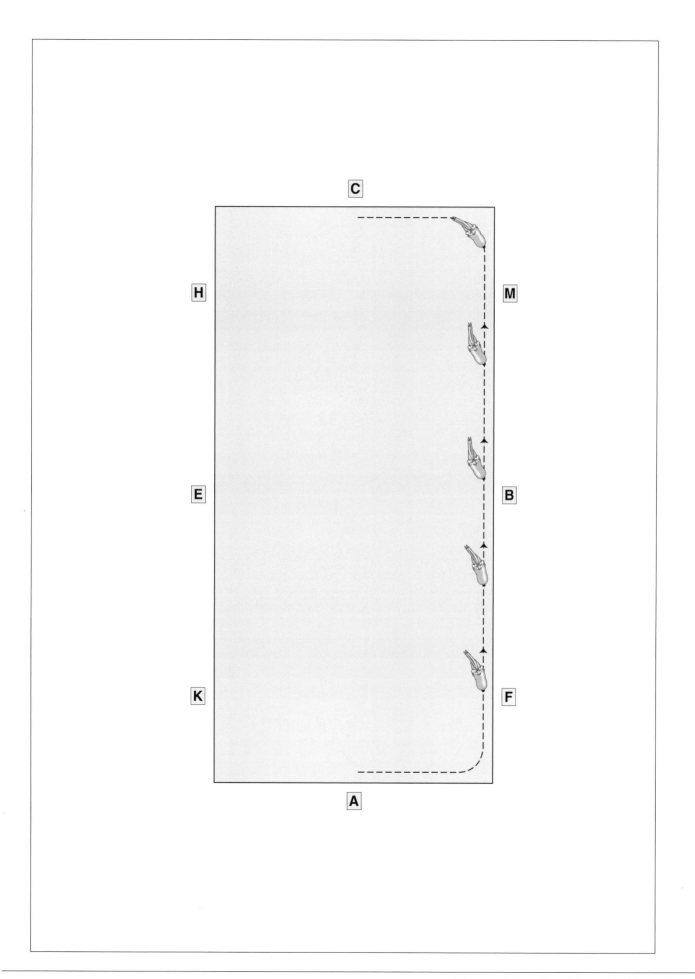

Riding a perfect halt

'Whenever you halt, whether it's to do up your girth, to check something, give your horse a sugar lump or whatever, it has to halt square because you can't expect a horse to know when it's supposed to be halting square and when it's not.'

What you are aiming for

There's no easy way to master halt but practise, practise, practise! And you'll need mirrors, or someone to look so that you can see. Always ask someone to tell you whether your halt is square: sometimes by the time you've leant over to look for yourself, you've already put the horse off balance, which is understandable. If you've pushed down too hard on one stirrup because you're looking over your horse's shoulder, you can only expect it to fall out of balance. It's important to sit in the middle of the saddle, so obviously the more even your weight and your contact is on the horse, the more likely it is to stand even and square. If you're sitting to the right, then your horse is going to lean to the right.

The exercise

To prepare your horse for halt, collection and activity are vital.

❏ Collection does not mean slowing down: your horse has to be sensitive on your aids and in self-carriage, otherwise he will pull into the halt and take far too long to stop.

❏ But at the same time, he has to go into the contact, otherwise he will just halt and go flat before you've actually asked. So you have to have a nice light contact. You have to be sensitive on your aids and your legs should be the channels straight into the halt. The horse must understand what you want.

❏ The move-off from the halt has to be quick and immediate – you want a quick immediate move into a nice clean trot.

❏ Your horse has to be straight, too, so that when you finish the centre line he can really be 'ridden' again (*see* Exercise 3), like another nice straight corner.

What's being achieved

It has to become second nature to the horse that whenever he halts, he has to stand square.

What can go wrong?

'Even when I'm stopping to get off my horse, I collect the walk and make it stop square.'

❏ If you collect for the halt and your horse starts to slow down, you know he's going to fall apart.

❏ If your horse gets really strong in your transition down, you know that he's probably got a bit long, and one hind leg is going to be out at the other end, and his head is probably going to be far too low by the time you have halted. Your horse needs to be in self-carriage and a light contact for him to stand with his head in the right frame and his hind leg under.

Working with shoulder-in

'I often use a bit of shoulder-in on the inside track if I have problems controlling a horse's front, or his hind legs moving in and out.'

The exercise

❏ From a short side, ride on to the inside track, half-halting to bring your horse on to his hind legs. Ask for flexion through the 'corner' and maintain the bend, without pulling your horse around. You should be able to see his inside eye and his mouth.

❏ With your inside leg positioned on the girth, lead his front legs on to the inner track with a strong outside contact, the inside contact being used as guidance to keep the bend.

❏ Your shoulders should be parallel to your horse's shoulders, so you shouldn't be facing down the track, you should be looking in the same direction, in balance with your horse.

❏ If he tilts his head, lower your outside rein and the outside hand, and bring the inside rein a little higher: that flexes the horse, because a tilted head is basically a stiffness.

❏ Now build in a couple of 10m circles between markers; this will test his balance out of the shoulder-in and on to the circle and back into the shoulder-in again without drifting.

❏ Ride down the centre line to change the rein, and repeat on the opposite side of the school.

What's being achieved

Whilst shoulder-in improves collection and impulsion, it also gives you much more control over your horse's forehand, and makes you aware of his responsiveness to your aids and his suppleness.

What you should be looking for

The horse should maintain activity in the hind legs, and should be in a straight line – often you see them wiggling on and off it a little bit.

What can go wrong?

'This is not a pulling of the neck in, and not a pushing of the quarters out.'

❏ Your horse can't maintain his balance on to the 10m circle, and back out of the circle into a shoulder-in. Make sure you are using your outside rein to lead his front legs on to the inner track.

❏ If your horse wants to push his hind legs out, you can bring them in a little bit on the circle, and if he wants to bring them in, you can push them out.

Moving on

You can vary the intensity of the flexion, and even go into renvers.

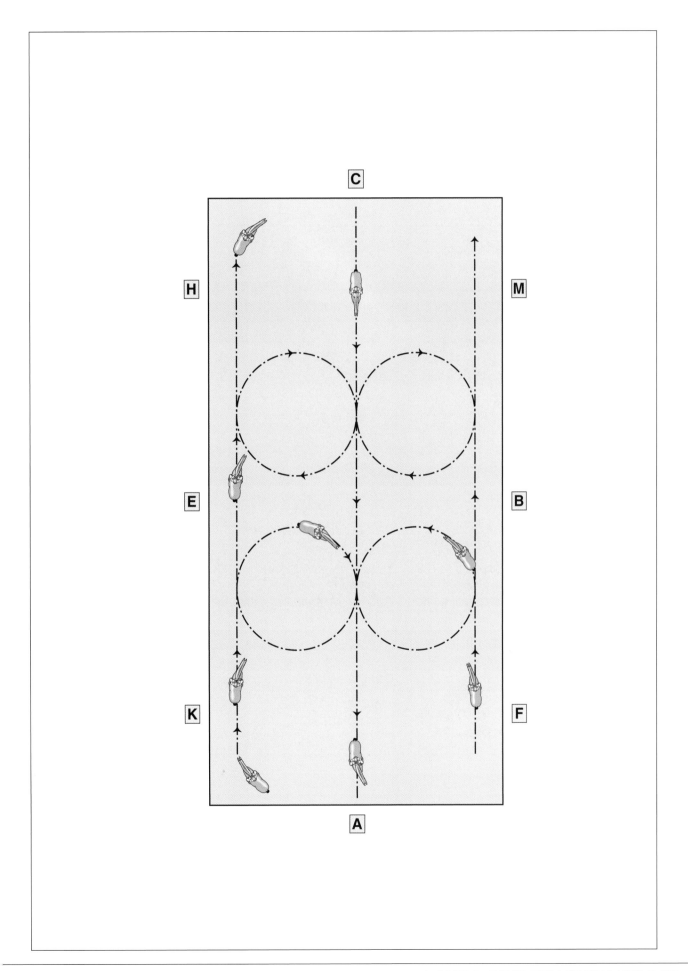

Shoulder-in and travers

'You can keep yourself entertained for hours with this one, which is good for young and old horses alike.'

The exercise

❏ Come out of the corner on to the long side in shoulder-in. After a few strides ride a small circle, 8 or 10m, and come out of the circle into travers.

❏ In travers your horse should be looking straight down the track. Put your outside leg back and, with the front legs staying on the track, ask the quarters to come in.

❏ After a few strides, go on to your circle again, and come out of it in shoulder-in. Your horse should remain active and off the front leg.

❏ Repeat on the opposite rein.

What's being achieved?

In doing exercises that involve random changes of movement, your horse not only becomes more supple and fully engages his hindquarters, he also becomes very attentive to your aids.

What you should be looking for

This exercise should be flowing, and not a battle with the horse. Sometimes they get a bit wiggly and worm-like.

What can go wrong?

The horse becomes over-ambitious and comes off track. Rather than confuse him, use a small circle to put him back on your aids. Keep flexion on the circle with your rein contact, and let your inside leg show the sideways movement.

'This is an intensified transition, the horse can't escape, and as such it is really useful, especially for increased collection later.'

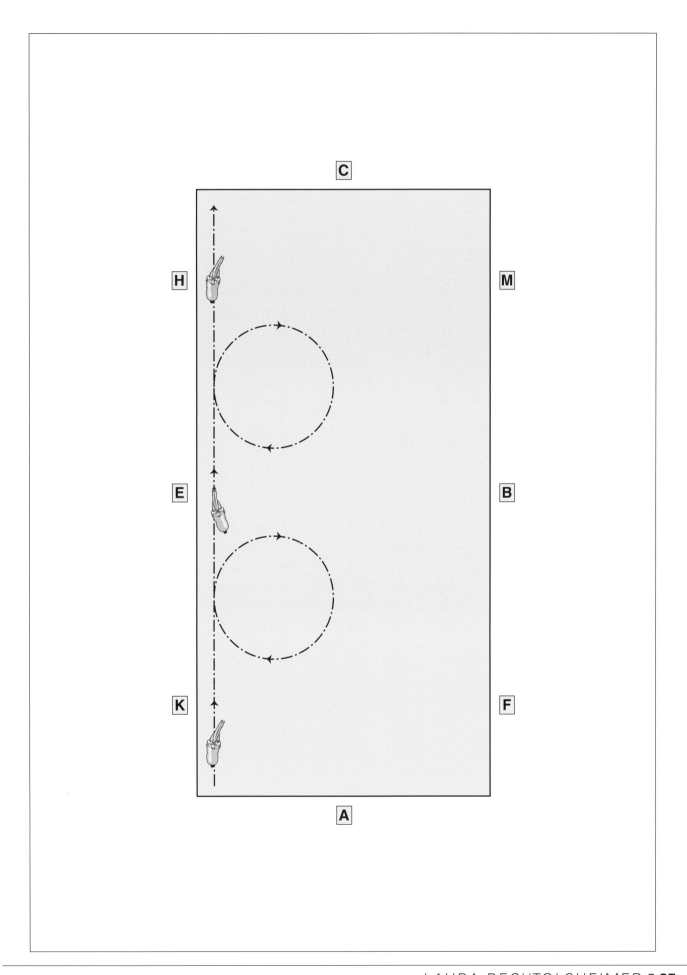

Teaching the horse to understand rein-back

'Sometimes this is a difficult thing for the horse to understand, and if you start fighting your horse you are just going to scare it.'

The exercise

❏ At suitable points in your schooling, plan in a halt and rein-back. Begin somewhere where there is some sort of natural barrier that says halt, so plan to ride your rein-back at a point on, or near, H, M, K, F, A or C, facing into a corner.

❏ Begin in trot, and with your horse collected, ride a halt at your chosen point. Ensure that your horse is standing square. Your legs should be at the girth – not behind the girth or too far back – before giving a little squeeze and catching the stride with your hands and bringing the horse back.

❏ To achieve this, your reins need to be a little shorter and held lightly. Use little vibrations of the hands to bring your horse back – don't 'see-saw'. This is not a tug-of-war!

❏ The poll should be the highest point of the horse's neck – you don't want it too low or too high, because if it is too high your horse is going to go backwards without using its back and you won't get diagonal steps or very good marks.

❏ Straightness comes with time: it is important to have the diagonal steps back first.

❏ It is also important that the horse understands what you are asking. If it doesn't understand, punishing it isn't going to help improve the situation.

❏ When you begin to train your horse in rein-back, use repetition and a specific spot in the school to help. However, once he understands the aids, you need to remember to occasionally throw in a halt without going backwards, otherwise you will find that every time you halt, your horse just wants to rein back.

'The important thing is patience, teaching your horse until it understands what you want.'

What's being achieved

The rein-back tests the horse's ability to respond to your aids, and because it makes the joints of the hind legs and quarters bend more than is usual, it helps with collection.

What you should be looking for

The horse should halt and stay still first, then it should move back on your aids, and then it should go forwards on your aids.

What can go wrong?

❏ If your horse does start to curl in, try using a little bit of inside flexion, and the horse will find it harder to come in, or a good outside contact. Usually, however, just lightening up on the side on which you have the stronger contact will make the difference.

❏ If your horse sets itself against the stronger contact on one rein and you put one leg further back than the other, you'll end up confusing the horse. Keep your legs fairly evenly balanced.

EXPERT TIP

Riders often end up looking like they are leaning forwards because the horse is going back. The ideal is to sit relatively still – not sit still as in collection, with your weight too hard back in the saddle, but I wouldn't lean forwards, either, just lighten up your seat.

WHAT IS MEANT BY DIAGONAL STRIDES?

In rein-back, your horse should step back using diagonally opposite legs. He should pick up his feet so that the strides are of equal length. Some horses find this very difficult and are inclined to swing or curl inwards.

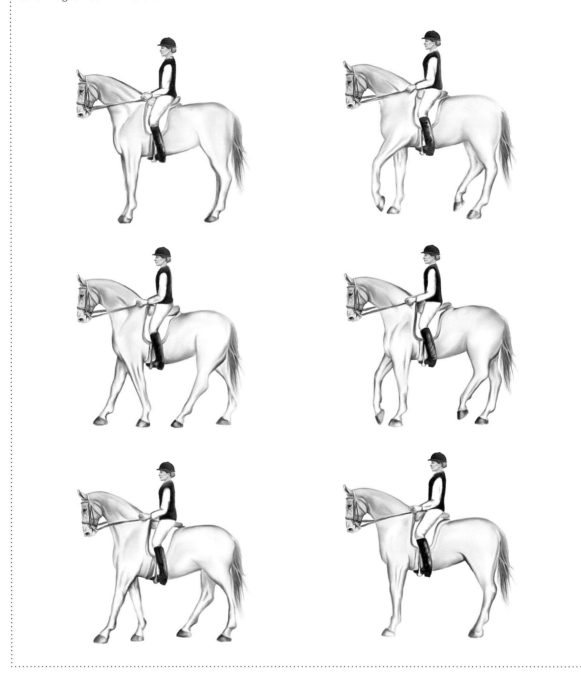

Walk pirouettes

'It is important that you have the horse dead straight because, like in travers and shoulder-in, you are positioning the horse's hind legs, and so they can start to wiggle and go against the leg.'

The exercise

❑ Pick a line anywhere in the school – it doesn't always have to be the same line – sometimes it can be on the inside track, sometimes on the long side.

❑ As you approach your spot, you should have a good contact in your reins and your legs should have a good contact on the sides of the horse so that they act as a channel for his body.

❑ Start with an inside flexion, just enough to see the horse's inside eye and mouth. Then, whilst you think inside rein and outside contact, lead the front legs round the hind legs.

❑ The rhythm should be an active four-beat walk rhythm, and it shouldn't change in the approach or during the pirouette.

❑ Have your outside leg a little bit back behind the girth, but not too far, just a guidance for the horse to come around the inside leg.

What's being achieved

The walk pirouette is about basic control, preparing the horse for canter pirouettes, and even piaffe pirouettes later. It enables the rider to control the horse's movement so that the turning point isn't the middle of the body, but the hind legs making a small circle and the front legs making a larger circle than the hind legs. As the horse has to lift his forehand and take his weight on to his hindquarters to turn, he has to make good use of his shoulders.

What you should be looking for

The horse should be stepping forwards, and the rider should be catching the forward step and bringing it around.

THE AIDS TO PIROUETTE

❑ Be sure to sit in the correct inside bend position.

❑ Inside hand asks for the bend.

❑ Outside hand uses gentle half-halts as required.

❑ Inside leg employs small, rhythmic nudges on the girth for impulsion and tempo.

❑ Outside leg remains behind the girth to guard the haunches, and uses small rhythmic nudges for tempo.

What can go wrong?

If a horse turns too fast, think of travers on a small circle with flexion, and if the horse is not coming around enough, think of shoulder-in into the circle. Take out the flexion and almost bend to the outside, so that the shoulder falls in and around, similar to half-pass, really.

A gentle introduction to half-pass

'I use this exercise for horses that are a bit keen.'

'In effect you are saying move over, and then are catching the horse again before it takes over, because you want the half-pass to be in your control.'

The exercise

❏ In a collected trot, ride on to a long side and do a few steps in shoulder-in.
❏ Then do a few steps in half-pass, and then, with your horse's body parallel with the long side…
❏ …do a few steps of shoulder-in again, and continue in this way across the diagonal.
❏ Allow the horse to straighten up before repeating this on the opposite rein.

What you should be looking for

Your horse should remain around your inside leg, and should alternate between shoulder-in and half-pass without any loss of impulsion or balance.

What can go wrong?

Common mistakes are:
❏ The horse isn't going over and the rider's outside leg goes farther and farther back, pushing harder and harder. The horse is more sensitive near the girth, and if you just push him, in the same way as if you just pull the reins, he only gets stronger, and will get more and more resistant. However, if you do little kicks and digs, and give immediately, he is much more likely to listen.
❏ Often the rider sits totally against the movement. You need to keep your shoulders parallel to the horse's shoulders. If you are half-passing right, your shoulder should be slightly towards the right and you should have more weight on your inside stirrup. You should be sitting slightly to the right of the saddle, and pushing down on the right leg.
❏ If the horse runs sideways too quickly you can build in little circles either the other way or the way in which you are half-passing, to break it up. Usually I go in the direction I am going, so as not to bring the horse out of balance entirely.

Moving on

Make the angle steeper, or try this exercise in collected canter.

EXPERT TIP: GOING WITH THE MOVEMENT

My father explained it to me in this way: when you balance a broom on your hands, if the broom starts to tip to the left, your left hand, supporting the broom, automatically has to go left to keep hold of the broom. And it is the same with a horse: if the horse is having difficulty going right, if my bodyweight is going right, too, then he has to go right to keep in balance with me. And I think it is really that simple.

HOW TO RIDE THE IDEAL HALF-PASS

This can be done either from the centre line or from the track. You need the horse to be straight, with a little flexion in the neck and the body bending around your inside leg. Your outside leg behind the girth brings the horse across, while your inside leg, with the horse bent round it, keeps the rhythm, asking him to move forwards, so that his outside legs reach across the inside legs. I think what is really important in canter half-pass is that a three-beat canter rhythm is maintained. Often horses lose that and they end up losing the right rhythm.

'You see so many people sitting totally against the movement in half-pass, and they make it so much harder for the horse to go over.'

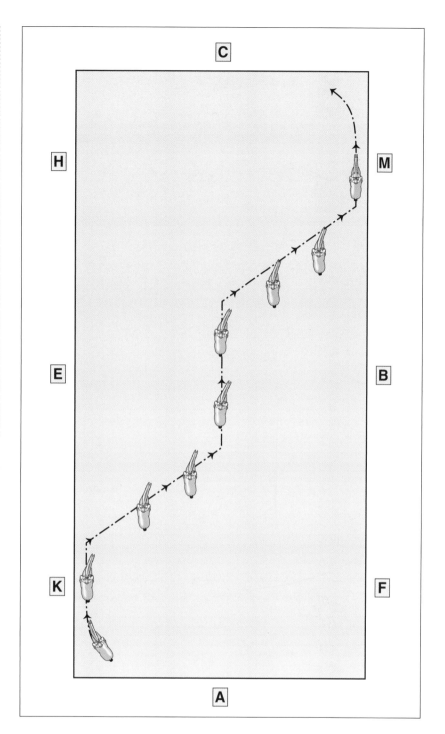

Extended walk, trot and canter

'This is my Big Thing with Douglas, and I practise the beginning and the ending of the extension until I'm blue in the face.'

The exercise

❏ In the first corner of a short side of the school, set your horse up in a good forward-going pace. Begin in trot, work through the exercise, then if your horse is not tired, move on to either walk or canter, depending on how he feels and which pace you think he will be most comfortable with.

❏ Only work on two paces at the most in any one schooling session. Be careful not to over-tire your horse.

❏ As you make the turn at the second corner, half-halt to put your horse on the hind leg, collect, and from the next marker ask for two or three strides of extension in your chosen pace.

❏ Collect your horse again and continue around the track. If your horse hasn't achieved a good extension, don't hammer away at further strides, but have another attempt on the next long side.

❏ When you are satisfied with the extension on the long side, take the next diagonal, collecting through the corner and asking for one extra stride (so if you did three strides on your first attempt, now ride four) as you cross the diagonal. Change the rein and repeat this on the opposite rein.

You must now judge how difficult your horse has found this exercise, and whether you can attempt to add an extra stride or two to those on the long side and the diagonal. If in doubt, don't over-stretch your horse, and come back to this exercise another day.

What you should be looking for

In walk, trot and canter, in extension, the rhythm shouldn't change much. The frame should lengthen a little and the length of the strides should increase, but it is not a case of getting quicker. It is important that the horse is loose in the back, and doesn't suddenly become stiff as a board. And the uphill tendency is also important.

'In extended trot, the most extreme feeling is when they feel like a hovercraft.'

❏ **In walk**, the over-track of the hind legs and the front legs is a good indication of how good the extended walk is, but it is not everything. Sometimes a horse will have a big over-track but his hind legs will be trailing in the sand – that's not good, either.

❏ **In the trot**, the elevation of the front and the hind legs should be parallel so that, looking at the horse from the side, you can see a 'V' between the two front legs and the two hind legs. Big front legs and nothing behind is not what we want, and being very active, but not coming up in front, isn't good either. You want free movement from the shoulder and active hind legs to go with it. The two-beat rhythm should remain. It needs to be an active rhythm. If a horse keeps good rhythm and has a swinging extended trot it doesn't have to have a big flashy movement in order to get a good mark.

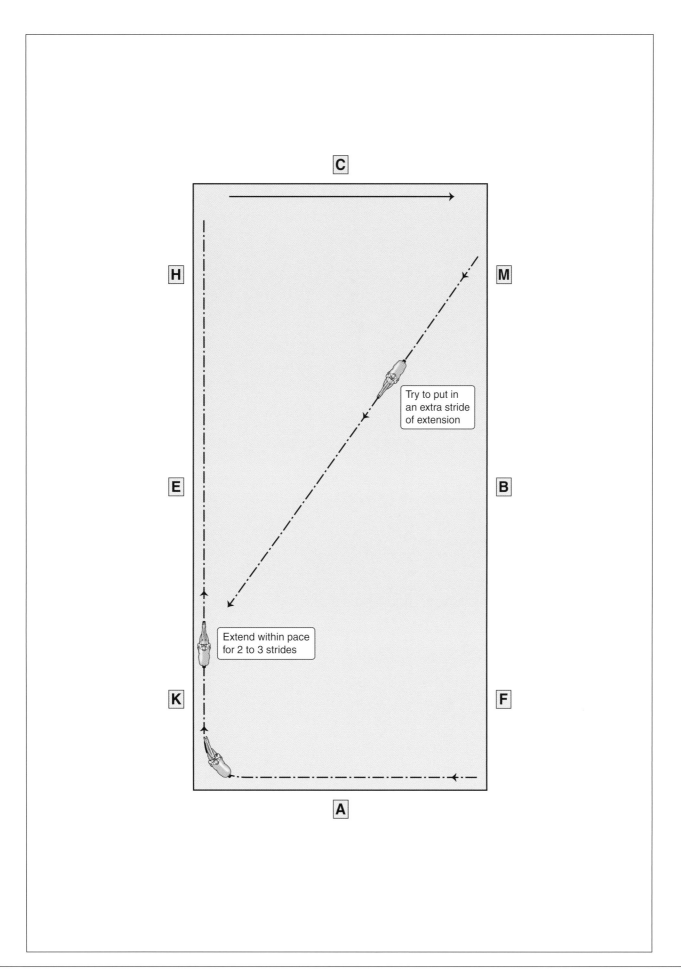

Try to put in
an extra stride
of extension

Extend within pace
for 2 to 3 strides

'My 11-year-old, Mistral Hojris, has a very active extended trot. And he swings incredibly well through his back and his backside – you can see it swinging! There is no tension. His hind legs are very active. And he always gets good marks in the extended trot, I have never had less than an 8.'

❏ **In canter**, with some people you see a very explosive transition, with others, a gradual increase of tempo – that's a matter of taste. What is important is that you prepare in the corner and when you get on to the diagonal you should be straight, and then you go. You don't want to take too long about it, but it should be one or two strides depending on how experienced the horse is on the diagonal. You should be on the seat more than the legs and hands – you don't see the top riders' legs moving – that's the ideal way to be, especially in extension. And in a canter the three-beat rhythm should remain.

What can go wrong?

❏ Some horses have difficulties with straightness in the extension so you need to counter correct. For example, bring the quarters in a bit or out a bit.

❏ Some horses, once they are more experienced, dive straight on to the diagonal and try to go for it. In this case, come through the corner, ride two metres shoulder-in, and then on to the diagonal.

❏ Build in transitions if the horse takes off with you. Some horses tend to go for it and you need to teach them to do extension on your aids. You can even try putting in circles on the diagonals. Take them a little bit by surprise so they have to think about what they are doing. Check the horse back, do a circle, and then go again, for example.

❏ If you have a horse that finds extended trot difficult, don't keep battering out long diagonals. What you want to do is a short diagonal, or trot to X, and then start the extension. Take fewer steps, until it gets a few strides, reward it with a pat, and then go again. If your horse finds it hard to keep a rhythm, and you are sending it speeding down the diagonal every time, it's going to lose its confidence.

❏ In trot, if you are having difficulty getting extension, think that you're not going faster really. Shorten your reins when you come off the diagonal, and think about keeping your rhythm. You are pushing, so you are getting more impulsion, more activity, but at the same time you need to catch your strides, so that you are bringing in a bit of elevation of the legs.

THE DOWNWARD TRANSITION

The finish is equally important because there are usually marks for the transitions. So begin by collecting, and hold on to your rhythm – you don't want to slam the brakes on. Within two or three strides, you should be back on the hind legs, light in the hands, and able to go forwards again. Often, at the end of an extended canter, trot becomes a bit of a battle. The transition shouldn't be harsh. In extension, it's easy to get flustered. You feel you have to pull to try to hold your horse and stop him – and he is pulling. People forget that it's quite easy to just let go for a second: if you give half-halts, half-halts, let go, half-halts, let go – this should be a playful transition rather than 'brakes on' and a startled horse. You don't want to scare a horse in extension because if you do, every time you hit the diagonal, he'll think 'Am I going to get another sock in the teeth?' and that's not really the reaction you want.

Moving on

Work on extension in different paces (*see* left). Once you are satisfied with your horse's extension in trot, on your next schooling session, move on to either walk or canter, depending on which pace you think your horse will find easiest.

With progress you can also repeat this exercise, doing a few metres of extension then collecting, a few metres of extension and then collecting, sometimes even throwing in a downward transition to walk or halt.

THE ELUSIVE AIDS TO EXTENSION

These are so difficult, as what you need varies with every horse and you have to judge what works for yours. You need to generate the energy for the extension, but your legs shouldn't be kick, kick, kick. Everything should be still, otherwise you will throw the horse off balance.

I often find with my horses, especially when they are highly strung, that if you put your legs on in extended walk, all they are going to do is jog on; so what you want to be doing, literally, is going with that rhythm with your seat. It's really important that you loosen your hips and swing – almost push – in the movement of the horse. Your hands should be doing the same thing – going with the neck movement. You do really want to ride extension in the rhythm of the horse. You don't want to overpace it. Often you see people sitting too far forward or too far back – you want to sit vertically.

WHAT IS A CORRECT WALK AND WHAT IS A TROT?

❑ **The walk:** must be four equal hoofbeats, meaning that the time that elapses between the footfalls of the left hind and the left front hooves should be the same as between the right front and the right hind ones. The horse should have a generous overstep, and he should accept the bridle and use his neck in a stretching arc, as this encourages suppleness through the back.

❑ **The trot:** in a correct trot, the horse's legs move in diagonal pairs, working in perfect synchronization with a period of suspension between. The hind legs should step well under the body, lifting the horse sufficiently clear of the ground to emphasize the period of suspension. As in the walk, he should be accepting the bridle and using his neck in a stretching arc, to encourage suppleness through the back.

JEANETTE BRAKEWELL

The British event rider Jeanette Brakewell, who comes from Uttoxeter in Staffordshire, has consistently been bringing home bronze, silver and gold medals since 1999.

At the age of eight Jeanette announced to her family her ambition to ride in the Olympics, and she has twice fulfilled that mission, on both occasions as part of the silver medal-winning UK team. In 2003 she was part of the gold medal team at the European Championships, and was individual silver medallist at the World Equestrian Games, Jerez, in 2002.

Her successes on her 17-year-old horse, Over to You, are testament to the power of a horse and rider partnership. At Badminton in 2003 the two finished on their dressage score, and at Jerez her fearless cross-country performance set her up for an individual silver medal. In 2006, at Burghley Horse Trials, Jeanette finished in seventh place.

Q: What aspect of your personal performance are you working on at present?
My dressage, and trying to stay relaxed at a three-day event. I don't get worked up, but it is quite difficult to get yourself 100 per cent mentally prepared for a big test. I have to make sure that I ride through the test in my mind so that when I get in there I really ride every bit of the test. It's easy to coast from movement to movement and not give it your all – you need to really concentrate for those seven minutes.

Q: Aspirational riders will watch you ride and learn from your techniques. Whose performance do you watch?
Mark Todd – he's so in balance with horses. And Ginny Leng (now Elliot).

Q: Everybody has days when the prospect of working in a school or arena isn't a happy one. How do you get over that?
Discipline. Sometimes I'll find I'm quite tired, I'll even have a lie-in if I have to catch up on sleep so I can give my horse 100 per cent. If I'm really tired and grumpy... well, I think it's no good at all if you lose the plot with your horse, so I will put it away and go inside and get a cup of tea, and then I'm off again.

Q: If I asked one of your pupils 'What's the thing Jeanette goes on about the most', what would it be?
Gripping knees – I hate that!

Q: Good training is based on communication with the horse. True or false?
True, but a horse will only do what you ask it to do, and it will only do it right if you ask it the right way.

Q: What would be the three pearls of wisdom you'd pass on to anyone with equine ambitions?
Get an education first. Set yourself goals and something to aim for, and stay focused. Plan where you want to be, and be realistic as well as ambitious.

Q: When you sit on a horse for the first time, what are you looking for?
The general picture has to look right. The attitude has to be very good, in fact I think attitude has to be the most important. But at the end of the day it has to have the conformation to stay sound.

Q: What would you identify as the keys to successful horsemanship?
Being relaxed around horses, and being very disciplined about handling from the ground. Also management, and knowing every horse inside out. I check their legs personally every day before I put their boots on.

Q: Do you have a formula for goal setting?
I use the programme of events the horses are going to do. I put them all down on an Excel spread sheet, names on top, events down the side. I fill in where all the horses are going to go. My personal goals are generally based around the horses. I always have something – recently I've been slack about drinking enough water, so I'm making sure that I take in enough.

Q: Whatever level of rider we are, we all have those magic moments when we feel really connected with our horses and the situation. Can you describe the last 'magic moment' that you had?
At Badminton this year – we went clear in the show jumping, and moved up from 12th or 13th place to 4th.

CONTENTS

Jumping narrow fences

'I use this exercise to give a horse or rider confidence over narrow objects.'

The exercise

❏ You'll need either a block, a bale of straw, or some similar safe, narrow object, and a couple of poles. Set up the block near the middle of the arena in a position where it can be approached off both reins. Place the poles in a chevron shape, one on each edge of the block, to help channel the horse into the narrow fence.

❏ Make sure that the horse has been properly warmed-up over simple, confidence-building fences first so that he is in jumping mode.

❏ Approach the fence in either trot or canter. Trotting sometimes gives the horse more time to work out what he is being asked to do.

❏ Once he has jumped the fence confidently a few times, put one of the guide poles on the ground, but in a similar position. Now try the jump again.

❏ When he is jumping the fence confidently, drop the other pole to the ground.

❏ Progress by taking the poles away one at a time.

What you should be looking for

Make sure that the horse has focused on the fence. Feel whether he needs straightening with the left leg, right leg, left hand or right hand so that he is channelled forwards and straight to the centre of the fence. This exercise teaches the horse to be obedient to a line, and to keep going forwards from your leg aid: in other words, straight and focused – this will help his confidence.

What can go wrong?

The most usual problem is that the horse runs out. Make sure that you set him up properly, that you keep the leg on and maintain the impulsion forwards to the fence, and that you keep your own focus on the middle of the fence all the way in to take-off! If the horse keeps running out, then you could use the guide poles once again so as to regain his confidence.

'When a second fence is set up following the narrow fence, this not only keeps the horse's reactions sharp, but the rider's, too.'

Moving on

A second narrow fence could be added to make a double, or the second fence could be put a few strides away on a curving line. This will teach the horse to look for the fence, and will help to keep his reactions sharp.

'If you find you hit a brick wall in your training, have your horse's teeth and back checked to make sure there is nothing hindering him; then seek professional advice.'

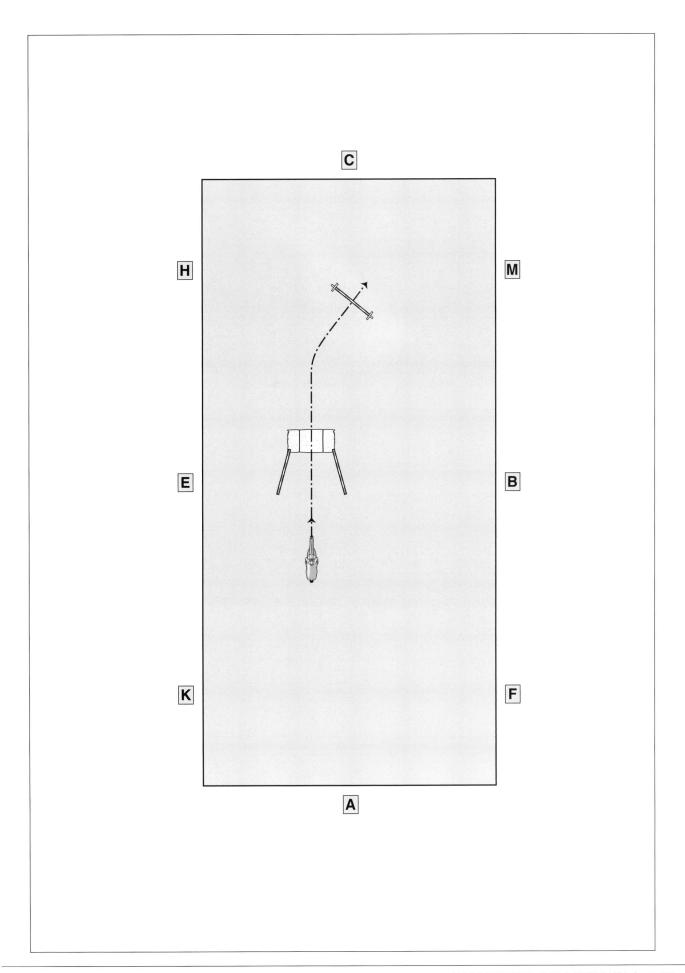

Working on achieving straightness

'This exercise involves working large around the arena and then riding 10m circles in each corner, and is to help improve the horse's rhythm, straightness and accuracy. It's best ridden in trot or canter – walking would take for ever!'

The exercise

❏ Begin working large, in working trot. Establish a good rhythm, and then as you come into the next corner, make a half-halt to sit the horse back slightly and put him in better balance in preparation for a 10m circle.

❏ Once on the circle, channel your horse between your leg and hand with a slight inside bend, making sure he doesn't lean on the hand or push against either leg, and at the same time channel his energy forwards, because this will help him to stay straight. Coming out of the circle, ride straight across the short side, and then ride another 10m circle in the next corner.

❏ Coming out of the circle, and before heading off down the straight, half-halt again as the circle may have generated energy that needs to be contained.

❏ Continue putting a 10m circle into each corner of the school.

❏ Ride your circles accurately, in balance and on two tracks (meaning that your horse's hind feet travel exactly the same line as his front feet). Then repeat the exercise on the other rein, trying to achieve the same result on both reins.

The first few circles may be a little unbalanced and not very smooth, but as you repeat the exercise in each corner the horse will start to understand, and will wait and anticipate the movement, allowing you to ride it more accurately.

What's being achieved?

In this exercise we are trying to achieve rhythm, straightness – and 'being straight' means both on a straight line and when following the line of a circle or curve – control and accuracy.

What you should be looking for

It is important that you follow the horse's shoulders around the corners with your own shoulders, and also that you stay straight in the upper body, making sure that your weight doesn't slip to the outside of the saddle and collapse through the inside hip.

What can go wrong?

Your horse loses his balance and therefore his straightness on the circle, and his shoulders or quarters fall either in or out. The rider should feel where the straightness is being lost, then correct it using whichever leg or hand aid keeps the horse upright and on two tracks, while at the same time maintaining the rhythm and balance.

Moving on

The next stage would be to ride the exercise in canter.

STRAIGHTNESS

At every level of training it is important and necessary to work on keeping your horse straight. Like humans that favour the left or right hand, most horses are also genetically crooked. This is further aggravated by the fact that the shoulders are narrower than the hindquarters, encouraging the horse to favour one rein or the other. Straightness is important for the following reasons:

❏ With his weight evenly distributed the horse avoids strengthening one side of his body more than the other.

❏ When a horse is straight it can achieve the optimum forward thrust.

❏ If a horse is not straight it cannot have an even contact on each rein.

❏ A horse must be straight to be collected.

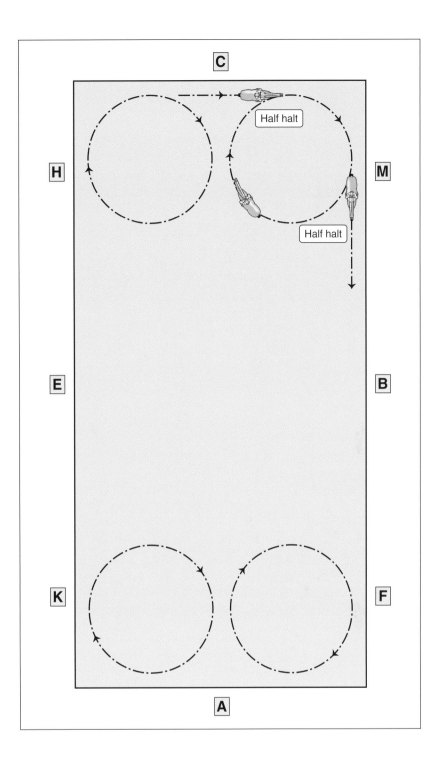

Concentrate on rhythm and straightness

'Your approach to the poles must be ridden straight, and the turn made on the correct line, so be careful not to overshoot or cut the corner. This exercise is to teach rhythm and straightness.'

The exercise

❏ Put down four to six trot poles approximately 1.2m (4ft) apart (adjust the length to suit your horse's natural length of stride); place them so they can be approached off both reins.

❏ Trot over the poles, rising softly in the saddle, and allowing your horse to take the contact forwards over the poles.

❏ Once he is established over the poles, add a cross-pole approximately 2.4m (8ft) after the last pole. Use the trot poles to create a bit of energy in order to produce a confident, round jump over the cross-pole.

❏ On landing make sure your departure line is straight, and that a correct turn is made at the end.

❏ Repeat the exercise off both reins.

What you should be looking for

Encourage straightness and an even rhythm to the poles. Feel for how the horse is reacting to the exercise. He may become complacent and catch a pole. If he does, do nothing different the next time, just make sure he is still responsive and in front of the leg – he should learn from his mistake and make a better effort.

Double check

Be conscious that your shoulders stay upright over the poles and that your upper body folds softly and straight over the fence. Also be aware that there is not too much seat pressure through the exercise. The lower leg should remain secure at all times – keep the lower leg around the horse with the weight down through the heel, and not gripping with the knees.

What can go wrong?

The horse rushes the poles. Ask yourself whether you are putting unnecessary pressure on him, be it from the leg, seat or hands, which could cause him to react by running away. If he still picks up speed, try making a shorter turn to the poles.

Moving on

Increase the height of the cross-pole, or add any other fence, either at a bounce distance or a stride away from the cross-pole, to make a grid exercise. This exercise can also be done using canter poles, rather than trot poles.

JUDGING THE DISTANCE

The correct natural distance for your horse between two poles will vary according to his height and stride and the pace you are working in. Getting it wrong can affect his confidence and willingness to try again. It is therefore useful to have a friend as 'eyes on the ground' to be ready to adjust your poles in the early days until you have measured out and become accustomed to the distance that suits your horse. Standard distances are:

❏ walking or trotting 1.2–1.5m (4–5ft)

❏ cantering 2.7–3.6m (9–12ft)

Varying the distance between the poles by either a little more or a little less can be used to encourage your horse to lengthen or shorten his stride; however, do not begin on this type of work until he is totally comfortable with a distance that fits his natural stride – and then you should never make any changes in more or less than 7.5cm (3in) increments.

'Gripping with the knees is my pet hate!'

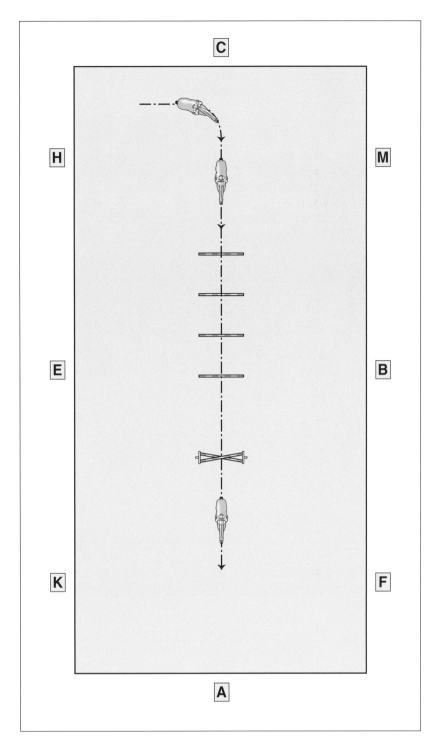

Learning your lines

'For this exercise, the idea is to stay on your line the whole way round and have your horse in balance!'

The exercise

❏ Set up two jumps on a 20m circle, one opposite the other. You should begin with two cross-poles.

❏ From canter, jump each fence individually, or jump one fence and then go inside or outside the other. Whatever route you choose, stay on your line the whole way round, and have your horse riding in balance.

❏ You can vary the jumps, building up to a cross-pole and an upright, two uprights, or a cross-pole or upright plus an oxer.

❏ Ride this exercise on both reins.

What's being achieved

Riding the jumps on a circle requires horse and rider to focus on straightness, from approach, through take-off, to landing and keeping your line, and helps the horse to develop an instinct for landing on the correct leg.

EXPERT TIP

Focus on the line you want to stay on. Draw a line in your mind's eye. If you feel the horse is cutting the corner, add a little inside bend and push him away from the inside leg; or if he's falling out, keep the outside contact and use the outside leg to keep his shoulders moving around the curve or circle.

IN BALANCE...

The definition of a horse being in balance is when he is maintaining a 'consistent rhythm with constant impulsion, neither falling left nor right from his rider's chosen line'.* To achieve this state of grace is one of every rider's earliest ambitions, as the horse's balance is affected and interfered with by the rider's weight and position. Here's an exercise to help, one that's deceptively simple...

1. Ride the exercise in trot.

2. Ride the 'corners' as part of a circle and be sure that work on the track and on the diagonals is straight. Repeat on both reins.

*Andrew Day, *101 Schooling Exercises*

What you should be looking for

Make sure that your horse's shoulders are coming around the circle and that you are not falling out (*see* Expert tip). The secret of success is to try and maintain a good rhythm and the horse in self-carriage as much as possible.

Moving on

Increase the height of the jumps to make the exercise more demanding; alternatively, add fairly wide oxers to help the horse stretch through his back and stay on the line.

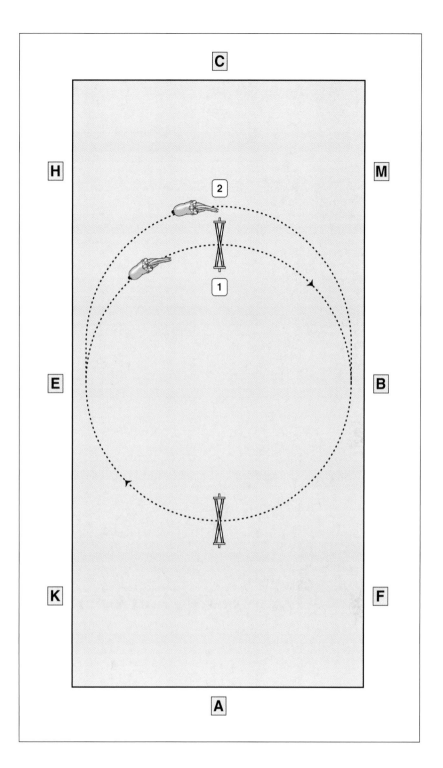

Finding the brakes

'The point of this exercise is that you will be able to say "whoa" to your horse when you want to.'

The exercise

❏ Set up a cross-pole in the school as shown – be sure you have enough space to jump it from both sides. Jump the fence in trot initially, and then in canter.

❏ After the fence, ride your horse forwards into a halt. It might take a few strides to get to the halt, because he's a bit keen.

❏ Once you have it, turn your horse around either with a turn on the forehand, or a pirouette, go straight into trot again, and jump back over the fence. Whether you use a turn on the forehand or a pirouette, be sure to get your horse moving away from the leg during the turn. This exercise keeps horses on the aids.

❏ When you have jumped the fence, take three or four strides and then decide when you want to walk the horse.

❏ Eventually when you've done the exercise a few times, and the horse starts to anticipate, it will begin to slow down for itself. The point is, you want to be able to say 'whoa' to your horse when you want to!

What's being achieved

This is a good obedience exercise for horses that do get a bit keen and strong.

What you should be looking for

Your turn should generate sufficient impulsion to put you straight back into your pace – a step of walk and then into canter, for instance.

Moving on

Once you feel your horse has mastered this exercise, you could try putting up a second jump along one long side of the school. Alternate between the original exercise, going over and back across the cross-pole, or going on to the second jump. If your horse is waiting for the next fence, rather than running into it, you are achieving the point of the exercise.

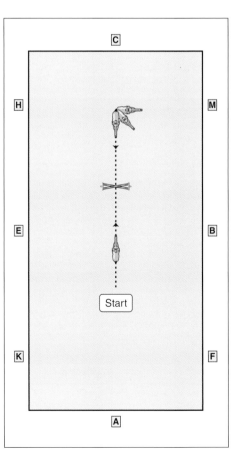

Keeping the rhythm

'This exercise deals with a horse that's keen.'

The exercise

❏ Put two fences a distance of four canter strides apart, placing them in the arena where you can jump them from both reins. (This will obviously depend on your horse's strides.) Begin with two uprights.

❏ Focus on having your horse in self-carriage, going forwards and relaxed, and jump both fences, maintaining the four strides. If your horse is nice and relaxed and in self-carriage, carry on around the arena and do this quite a few times.

❏ Every time you repeat this exercise, stick to that same distance.

What's being achieved

You're trying to discipline your horse to keep the same rhythm.

What you should be looking for

Concentrate mainly on the straightness of the turn to the fence, staying on your line, middle to middle of the poles, and keeping the horse straight throughout so that he jumps straight through his shoulders, not crooked.

'If your horse is still a little keen, ride the previous (brakes) exercise a few times, and hopefully he will slow down himself.'

What can go wrong?

If your horse is getting strong, bring him to a halt between the two fences. It can help to ride this exercise after the 'brakes' exercise, and hopefully if you do that exercise first, when you jump the first fence in this one you won't send him to the next.

Alternatively, you might find that after repeating the jump a few times, your horse gets a little bit flat. If he does that, then once again you can put your halt in and get him back on his hocks.

Moving on

Try the exercise with an upright and an oxer.

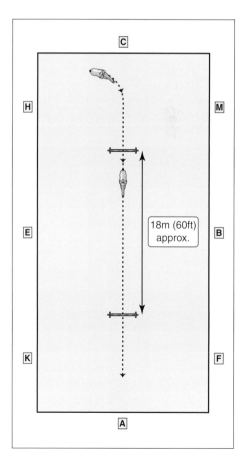

Jumping on alternate reins

'This is really a mini course, with just two jumps! This exercise will teach the horse to land on the correct leg, jump from a turn, and remain in rhythm.'

MORE COURSE IDEAS

Here are some more 'course' ideas using two jumps:

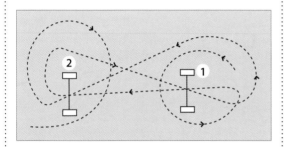

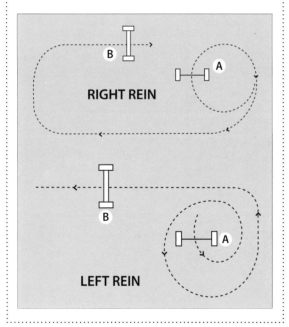

RIGHT REIN

LEFT REIN

The exercise

❏ Place two fences on a figure-of-eight, as shown in the diagram. Beginning at the C end of the school, in canter, jump one fence, continue across the diagonal on the figure-of-eight, jump the second fence, and so on.

❏ Carry on around the figure-of-eight, so you are constantly changing the rein.

❏ Once you are comfortable over the two jumps on the figure-of-eight, incorporate the outside track to extend your 'course'. For example, beginning at C on the left rein, jump fence A and then fence B on the figure-of-eight, rejoining the track at M; then go 'large' and jump fence A from the opposite direction on the FXH diagonal, rejoin the track and then jump fence B from the MXK diagonal.

What's being achieved

This very simple exercise will help your horse learn to land on the correct leg, jump from a turn, and remain in rhythm. It's good for horses of all levels: advanced horses will find it easy as, if they land on the wrong leg, they can do a flying change to correct it; but it will teach a younger horse lots about what it is meant to be doing.

What you should be looking for

You will land, hopefully, with your horse on the correct leg for the first turn. If not, correct it before you make the turn. You want your horse to be balanced around the corner and on a good rhythm on the straight to the next fence, where you are obviously going on to the other lead. There's no need to keep stopping and starting. If your horse keeps landing on the wrong leg, as you go into your first turn, have a pole on the floor and ride a flying change over the pole.

Moving on

After your fence, put in a 10m circle at A or C as a discipline for the rider or the horse.

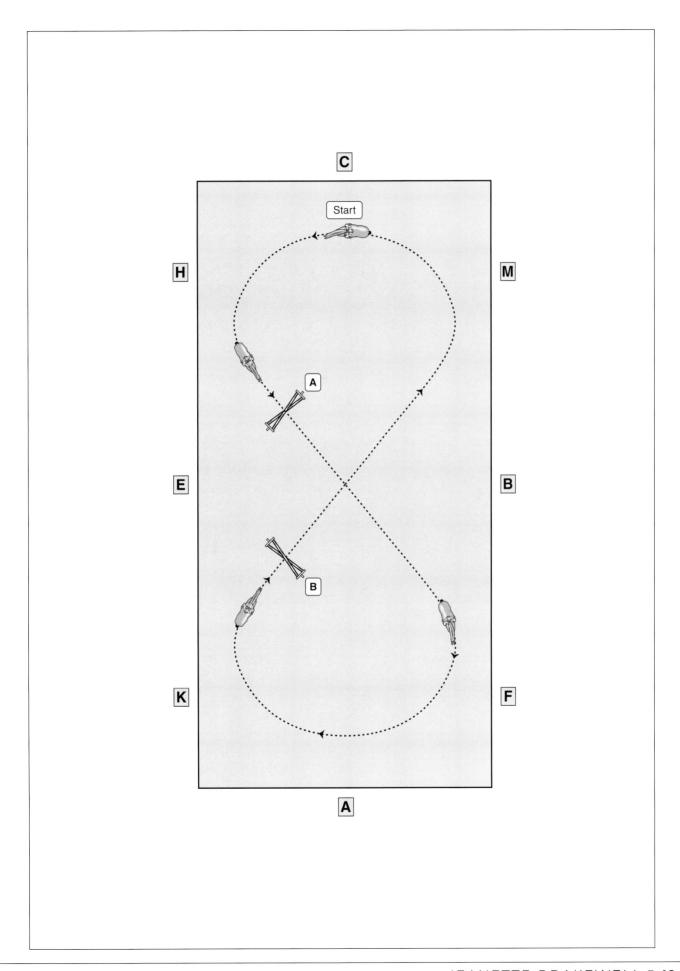

Balance and a double bounce

'This is quite a good exercise to video people doing because the horse has to react so quickly that the rider often doesn't manage to stay in balance.'

The exercise

❏ Set up three potential cross-poles on a straight line approximately 2.7–3.6m (9–12ft) apart, with the first and final poles on the floor and the middle one raised.

❏ On the right rein and in canter, ride through the combination until your horse has the gist of what he is being asked to do.

❏ Now put the last cross-pole up, and then once he is happy with that, put the first cross-pole up. You can vary the height and have the first and last a bit smaller and the middle a little bit bigger, according to your horse's capabilities. You also don't have to stick with cross-poles but can introduce an upright, too.

What's being achieved

As well as being a very good gymnastic exercise for a horse's brain and body, this exercise is also good for teaching riders to be in balance.

What you should be looking for

Make sure that your weight is down in the heel. Most riders either get in front of the movement, or fall behind it, and that affects the way the horse jumps the fence. If you're behind the movement, you'll end up on the back of the saddle, and if you are in front, you have to grip with your knees or use your hands to stop yourself going over the front end. Try to remain out of the saddle as much as you can be, so that your knee and ankle take all the shock away from the back of the horse.

'I always teach people not to grip with their knees as it covers up where their true balance is.'

Moving on

If your horse finds this easy, you can build up the exercise on a curve. If it is on a curve, you're better off using uprights. You can either make it easier for your horse by giving him a bit more room riding to the outside of the curve, or you can make it tighter and harder by being more towards the inside.

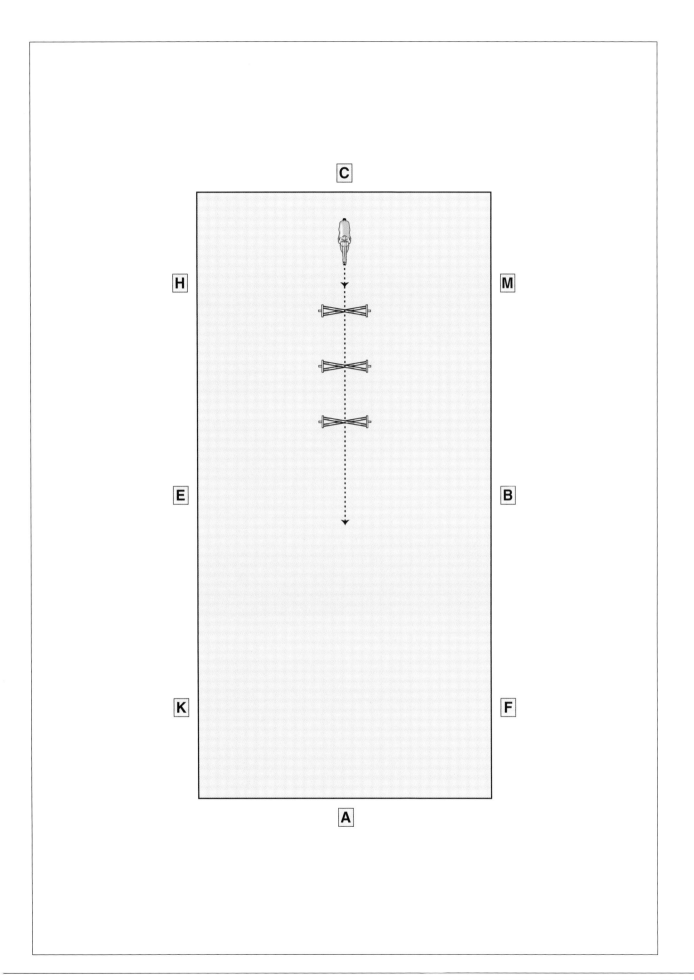

Half circles to help a horse that falls in

'Remember circles in corners? This is very similar, except rather than being on the outside track you are on the three-quarter line.'

The exercise

You will need more space than a 20 x 40m arena to ride this exercise.

❏ Ride on the three-quarter line, and when you reach the corner, turn outwards to ride a 10m circle.

❏ Come out of the circle and ride across the three-quarter line on the short side, turn outwards once again to do your 10m circle and then down the three-quarter line on the long side.

❏ Repeat at the next short side, and on both reins.

❏ This exercise can be done in trot or canter – it's quite a good one in canter because the horse almost thinks he can do counter canter, but in reality horse and rider stay in true canter but are actually on the 'wrong' lead for the direction of travel.

What's being achieved

This is a very good exercise for teaching horses not to fall in. Often, they come to a corner in an arena and they know they've got to turn so they turn before the rider asks them to do so – and they generally fall in. Because you are actually working backwards, in a way, it's a very good exercise to teach horses to stay out on a line. And it's also very good for their straightness, in that you are not relying on the fence to keep you straight, you're on the three-quarter line. It's good discipline for the rider and the horse.

What can go wrong?

In the trot the most common problem is loss of balance on the circle or rushing off as you come off of the circle. To avoid this, concentrate on maintaining your rhythm throughout.

In the canter, there are two situations in which your horse may become confused if your aids are not clear. Your horse may not be sure he is going to do the circle and may try to continue around the school. Or, if you are on the right rein, he may anticipate the left lead, try to change, and go unbalanced.

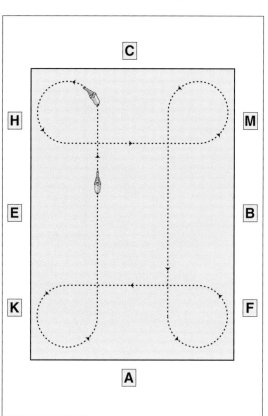

Leg-yielding: inside leg to outside hand

'This is good for a horse that's being a bit idle. Carry your stick in the hand that you want him to move away from.'

The exercise

❏ On the right rein, and in trot, turn up the centre line and leg-yield across to the long side changing the rein.

❏ Go around the arena, and then come down the centre line again from the top end of the school, and leg-yield across on the other leg.

❏ Once you have the hang of this exercise, you can either go down the centre line and ask your horse to move away from your left leg across to the right, or go the other way and ask him to move from your right leg across to the left.

❏ You can do it in canter, but it is more beneficial as a trot exercise.

What's being achieved

This exercise teaches the horse to move from the inside leg to the outside hand. However, if your horse has a problem moving away from one side or in one direction, you can stay working on the same side.

What you should be looking for

Keep your horse straight, with just a little indication of bend, but not over-bending. Keep his legs crossing over, and you want him to continue moving away from your leg. It's important that his body is parallel to the long sides, and it's probably best not to have too forward a trot as he may become rushed and confused.

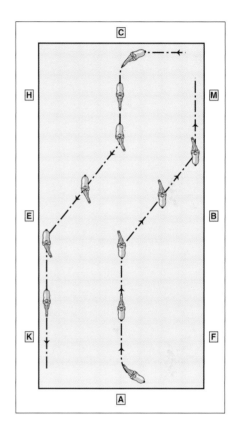

KAREN DIXON, MBE

Karen Dixon's name has been synonymous with eventing since, at the age of 18, she represented Britain in the 1982 Junior European Championships and came home with an individual and a team gold. She has since gone on to represent Great Britain in the Olympics on four occasions: at Seoul from where the team came home with a silver medal, Barcelona, Atlanta and Sydney. She has been twice national champion at the British Open (Gatcombe), and placed in the top three at Burghley CCI**** and Punchestown, and was part of the medal-winning British eventing teams at the World Equestrian Games in 1990, 1994 and 1998.

Based near Barnard Castle, Co Durham, she is married with two young children and continues to compete and to bring on young horses. Her non-confrontational and practical approach to training horses, which she passes on in these exercises, is an inspiration to all aspiring eventers.

Q: What's the best piece of advice you've ever been given in regard to training horses?

In training, build a secure and solid foundation so if you are going up the ladder and something goes wrong, you can go back to the horse's education. If you've dotted the i's and crossed the t's on everything so that there is no loss of confidence, you can go back to what the horse knows and you can start to build again.

Q: What do you do when you come up against a training brick wall?

I get off, lunge the horse and watch. Basically I take myself out of the equation. Then I'll have the horse's teeth, back and soundness checked to make sure it's not hurting anywhere. I might give it a week off. I don't like to challenge them head on until I know that everything's all right; only then would I think that they were maybe taking the mickey.

Q: Aspiring riders will watch you ride and learn from your techniques. Whose performance do you watch?

Mark Todd was always my hero. He's a fantastic horseman, as well as being brilliant at eventing, show jumping, dressage, and training race horses. He's an all-round star for me. I always admired him, and watched him, and tried to emulate the way he rides, in a soft and positive fashion.

Q: Who coaches you?

Jo Graham helps me with my dressage, and Mark Phillips has helped me enormously with my jumping over the years.

Q: Everybody has days when the prospect of working in a school or arena isn't a happy one. How do you get over that?
I usually lunge. If I'm in a bad mood I don't get on.

Q: If I asked one of your pupils 'What's the one thing that Karen goes on about the most', what would it be?
Being positive. Riding with your leg, not your hands.

Q: When you sit on a horse for the first time, what are you looking for?
Spirit. I like a naughty-but-nice horse with natural cadence, that jumps off the floor with a bit of purpose and is enthusiastic about its jumping.

Q: What would you identify as the keys to successful horsemanship?
Rhythm and balance, being positive and looking ahead. Have perseverance. When you're in a rut and things are going wrong, take yourself back to riding in a positive and confident way and the results will come back. Learn to train, train to compete, and compete to win.

Q: Whom do you admire most in the equestrian world?
William Fox-Pitt as a rider. Mark Phillips as a trainer and course-builder.

Q: Whatever level of rider we are, we all have those magic moments when we feel really connected with our horses and the situation. Can you describe the last 'magic moment' that you had?
I had a fantastic ride on Too Smart in Sydney when everything clicked and he made it feel easy. When it feels right, it's great and you feel invincible.

CONTENTS

EXERCISE 22

Pole position

'You know how horses tend to jump too big after the fence? This exercise is to make the horse jump the fence so the highest part of its jump is over the fence.'

EXPERT TIP

It is good to have somebody on the floor to make sure the poles stay where they are put and to adjust them if necessary.

The exercise

❑ Put a pole on each side of a fence, three strides out from take-off and landing. The height of the fence doesn't matter – you can start with a cross-pole.

❑ Canter over the fence, circle around or circle back, but keep on doing it until the horse is backing off, jumping the fence slowly and correctly with the highest part of its jump over the fence and not beyond. Jump from both reins as long as the ground poles are an equal distance from the fence.

❑ You can build the fence higher, add parallels and all sorts – as long as you keep moving the rail on the landing side a bit further away as you put the fence up and if you have a parallel.

What's being achieved

The point of this exercise is to make the horse back off the fence, and then jump it with the highest part of its jump over the fence and not beyond.

What you should be looking for

You will hopefully see your horse begin to slow down and back off, looking at the pole on landing and then jumping over the fence. As a rider you don't have to do anything – let him learn.

What can go wrong?

If the poles get knocked and move and you don't correct them, you'll start misjudging them. This is where you need your helper on the ground.

Moving on

This can be a very simple exercise, or you can make it very difficult by putting the fence up and leaving the distance from the poles to the fence quite tight – this draws your horse into the fence, and so it will have to back off and really jump it.

'This is a good exercise because it doesn't matter what level of horse you're riding, it will learn something. Whether it's a youngster that's learning to canter its fences, or whether it's an advanced horse that's got a bit bold and forward after the cross country and you're coming back to do your show jumping the next day – it's good to teach them this exercise.'

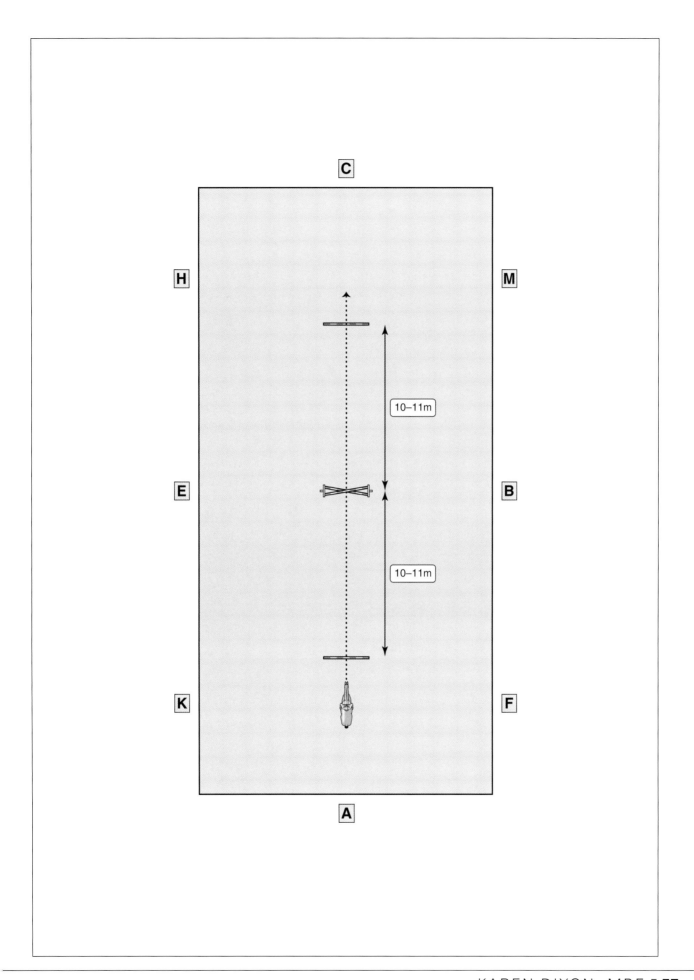

A treble plus poles

'This takes the first exercise a little bit further. I tend to incorporate it in a course that I am doing so the horse comes to a treble and it learns to wait and not to run through.'

The exercise
❑ Build a treble with one stride between each element. Have a pole on the floor in between the first and the second fence, and then a pole on the floor in between the second and third fence.
❑ With a youngster or a novice horse, you can start with three cross-poles. I tend to keep them all the same height so you can jump the treble from both directions.

What's being achieved
The point is to slow the horse down and get it to wait. The pole on the floor checks the speed and stops the horse from running at the fence. At home you should be training your horse to think wait, wait. The poles on the floor give the horse something to focus on without the rider going for his or her hand. This is far easier to ride than grabbing at the reins and saying 'slow down, slow down'. It's far easier for the horse to do it, too, because the pole on the floor is giving it a reason to slow down.

What you should be looking for
Sit very still and let the horse do the checking, don't try and ride him through the combination. If you sit very still, the poles do the work for you.

What can go wrong?
The rider starts to ride the horse through the treble like it's a normal treble rather than letting the horse use the poles to back off.

Moving on
Put the middle fence up, or put a parallel in the middle and let the horse stretch over that fence, and then back off over the last element, which could be an upright.

'I find with these eventers we all ride that they're bold and they run on a bit and the reason we have the show jumps down is that they have got a little bit too forward.'

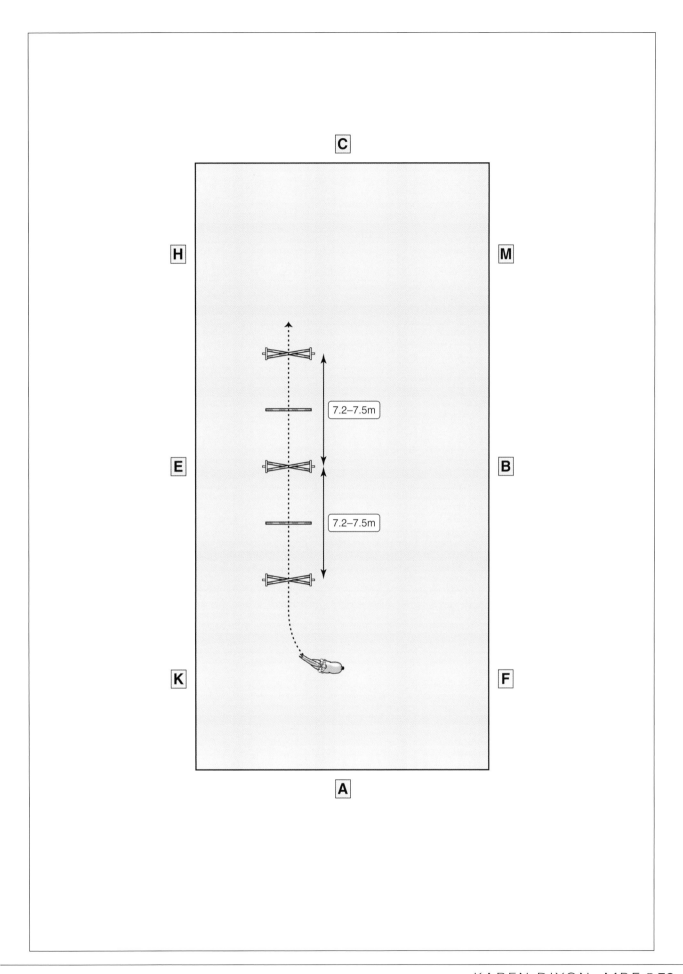

Two fences – lots of options

'For everyone who says they have too small an arena and in the winter they can't ride in the field, this is a good exercise to get lots of jumping without changing the fence.'

The exercise

❏ Set up two jumps, an upright and a parallel, with ground rails on both sides, in the arena as shown on the diagram, with a distance of two strides between.

❏ By jumping these two fences singly at an angle as an upright and a parallel, or as a double and from both directions, you get lots of jumping without having to change the fences. For example, I'll angle across over the upright, and then circle back across the parallel and then up through the middle of the both of them...

What's being achieved

These two jumps give you lots of variety, and the exercise also teaches you to ride with your legs, rather than your hands to steer the line to the fence. It exposes quite a lot of people who tend to ride with their hands because the horse has no idea they are angling to the fence and tends to run out, so it's a good exercise because it will be evident if you don't have your leg on.

'I wouldn't start angling fences with a young horse until you've got them so they are true and honest enough to jump a fence without worrying.'

What you should be looking for

You need to learn to wrap your leg on so you keep the horse straight off your leg and not your hand. This is a simple exercise, but you have to seriously think about rhythm and balance, and keeping both on the turns. You will also need to keep the horse in front of your leg to ride it properly.

What can go wrong?

If your horse consistently runs out as you approach at an angle, this shows you are not using your legs properly and you need to work on angled fences a bit before carrying on with this exercise.

You don't want to start angling fences with four-year-olds; this is an exercise to do when they are confident and jumping fences fluently and happily.

Moving on

Increase the height of the fences.

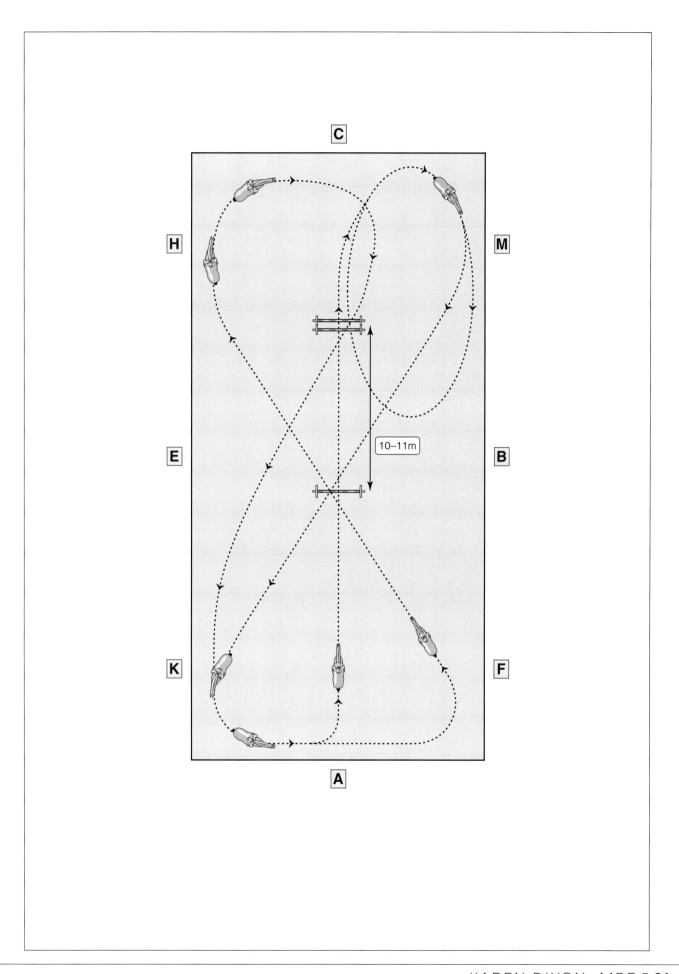

Introducing corners

'This is a very good exercise to teach young horses at an early age.'

The exercise

❏ Set up an upright with a barrel on its side underneath it, at a height your horse is confident about jumping.

❏ Once your horse is jumping this, build a little parallel with two wings on the left and the barrel on its side as the other wing. Jump over the parallel.

❏ Continue to jump the parallel, gradually getting nearer and nearer to the barrel. When your horse accepts this and is popping the fence confidently, then you can open the angle, but stay near the barrel.

What's being achieved

If your horse can hold a straight line to a fence, and jump narrow and angled fences, then corners should not be a problem. Practising these fences at home does as much for the rider's confidence as it does for the horse's.

What you should be looking for

The most important thing with this exercise is not to teach your horse to run out. You must be sure that you are riding and steering him from your leg and that he knows what you are asking from him.

What can go wrong?

If things do go wrong and your horse starts to run out, pop a pole up, resting on the top bar, straightaway. If this becomes a reccurring problem, try the following: if you are jumping a left-handed corner, where the horse could run out to the left, have your whip in your left hand and have a right lead canter. The horse has to change legs to run out, so it will have quite a lot to think about and do if that's its intention.

Moving on

Corners go from about 40 degrees on a novice course to about 90 degrees on an advanced course, so you want to try to make your angle wider. However, I have to say that making a big corner is mainly for the rider's confidence, so that you can say 'I jumped a big corner at home', or whatever. If the horse is straight and it is going to jump the corner, then actually you will be okay. If you watch people jumping corners when they are competing, unless the horse has got a problem – and then it will run out whatever – it's mainly the rider that screws it up, either by checking too much or actually firing the horse at the fence.

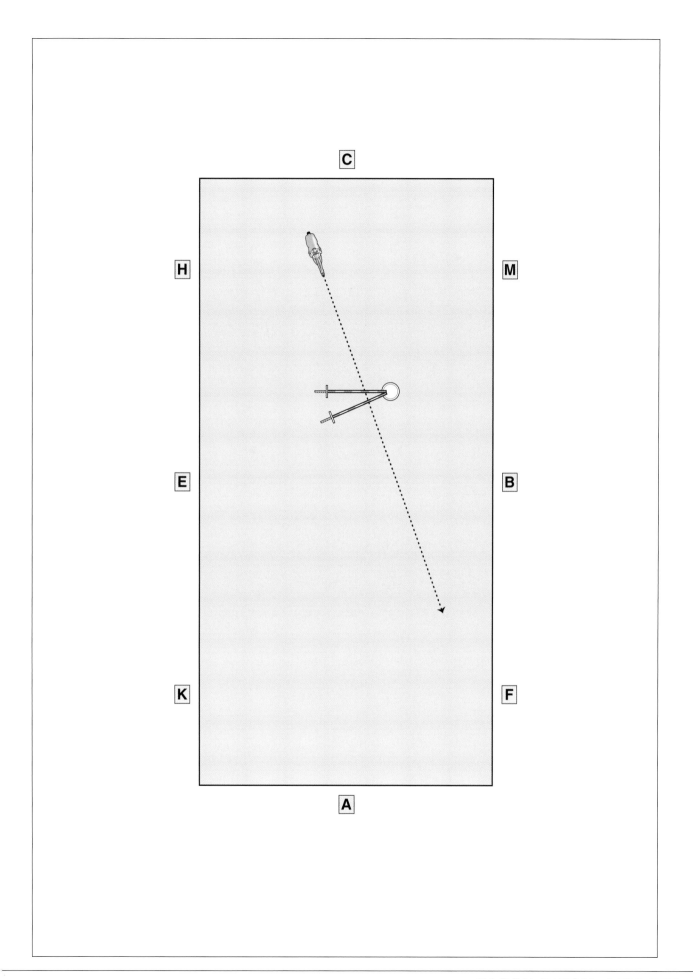

Improvising bullfinch and owl-hole type fences

'I teach my horse to jump a bullfinch at home; I don't have any cross-country fences so I do my own thing!'

EXPERT TIP

With any difficult fence such as a water tray or a bullfinch, I would start with a cross-pole, and then have one stride to the difficult fence so you are not responsible for putting the horse 'on the spot'.

The exercise

❏ Fix a few bits of brush or twigs into a filler. (Be sure to start small, and gradually build up the fence.)

❏ Place a small cross-pole one stride in front of the filler.

❏ Walk your horse past the filler several times until you are sure that it isn't spooked by the brush.

❏ Jump the cross-pole first. This will put you on a perfect stride to your bullfinch and give you one less thing to think about.

❏ Once your horse is happy with a few twigs, start to build the fence up.

What's being achieved

This exercise – like any exercise tackling scary fences – is all about building up the horse's confidence. I had a horse at Belton that wouldn't jump the last fence of the cross-country because it had a plant under it that kept whooshing in the wind. My horse completely rooted itself about seven strides out, and wouldn't take a step forwards. I came back and cut up bin liners, tied them under the fence and gradually got the horse used to them. Then I started jumping the fence and the bin liners, and kept adding things to make it worse and worse and worse. It turned into one hell of a fence, but because the horse was confident that the fence wasn't going to kill him, he was okay, and the exercise built up its confidence – and that's all it's about.

What you should be looking for

You need to sit up slightly behind the movement and ride positively, with a stick in hand saying 'Get on!'. You've got to be quite aggressive to get them over it, but once you have, you can play the nice guy.

'Always try and walk a horse past a scary fence to get it used to it. Don't try to scare it to death straightaway! Try and build on a simple beginning, making it scarier as you go along.'

What can go wrong?

The most common problems are run-outs and stops. We've already discussed run-outs, so if your horse keeps putting in stops you have to ask yourself why. If he really is genuinely absolutely terrified, then you have got to get another horse to go over the fence first. In this way you will gradually build up his confidence until he can tackle the jump on his own. But if he is being pretty dogmatic about it and rooting himself just for the sake of it, then what I tend to do is get off and lunge the horse over the fence. Like this it is tackling the fence 'on its own', although I will chase him if necessary, so he takes a bit of responsibility. By the end of it, horses like this are going around on their own trotting and popping, or cantering and popping, and then I get back on them and I play the nice guy – and then I haven't fallen out with them.

Moving on

Just keep on building up that brush!

JUMPING OWL-HOLE TYPE FENCES

These days there are fences on most cross-country courses where you are jumping under something. I improvise this by attaching a rope to a tree by the side of my arena. I cut some bushes and tie them on the rope, and then pull the rope out with a broomstick.

I will walk, then trot, then canter underneath it with these bushes above until my horse is not at all phased by them. Then I will have the rope with the brush lowered a bit, and will walk, trot and canter underneath it again.

Next I put up a cross-pole underneath it, and pop over that, and then an upright. I never do anything big initially. Once the horse is happy and confident, you can get more adventurous. I have put rugs over the rope and all sorts of spooky things.

Once horses have gone under it and have realized they are not going to bang their heads, and are not going to get hurt, then you've cracked this one.

When you ride this, make sure you go with the horse and don't sit up! This is the time to stay consistent in your riding and give the horse confidence that it's okay.

Jumping into water

'I would say the golden rule is loose rein, hands down, body back.'

EXPERT TIP

I tend to leave jumping out of the water to the day of competition as you could have a stupid accident in training. The key is not to hassle or chase the horse, and to wait for the jump or step up to come to you.

The exercise

When you begin to school your horse in the water don't say 'Right, I'm going to jump that great big log' and lurch into the water, because you will have a problem.

❏ Everything you do in training is about confidence building, so begin by trotting and cantering through the water first.

❏ Once your horse is comfortable and confident with the sensation of water around his feet and legs, find a step from which to jump off into the water.

❏ Do this with a loose rein, hands down, and body back.

❏ And then it's just a question of repetition. You do it and you do it and you do it – and once your horse is happy and he's hopping into the water on a loose rein, then you go and jump your log, or your table, or your bigger fence into the water.

❏ Once you're in the water, run one hand down both reins to recover them, and shorten them as quickly as you can, but keep your body back for the first stride.

What's being achieved

Like all exercises dealing with difficult or scary fences, this one is also about building up the horse's confidence.

What you should be looking for

Every time a horse jumps into the water he will put his head down. If you've got a tight rein you'll get tugged forwards, and then you are in the danger zone – so loose rein, hands down and body back, so you are not going to get jerked, and the horse isn't going to jump out through your hands.

What can go wrong?

Riders keep their reins too short and hang on. The horse starts jumping away from their hands, and massively big, and then it is just a vicious circle between the horse jumping too big, landing too far out, and the rider getting jerked forward: the whole thing is just a fall waiting to happen.

'If your horse is on a tight rein it will go boof into the water on a big jump and land, and you'll get tugged forwards.'

EXERCISE
28

Ditches and coffins

'You need to stay looking up, not come shuddering to the bottom, looking down and on a loose rein, because that way you won't go over.'

The exercise

❏ It is possible to recreate a ditch at home using black bin-liner bags secured over a board, or by painting one side of a filler black, with ground poles on each side, for example; or you can make a coffin with two rails and your 'ditch'.

❏ If you have a young horse, train it over ditches in company so you have somebody to give you a lead.

❏ Don't approach the ditch in gallop from halfway across the field: begin in trot. You must look up, not look down, and ride your horse just as if the ditch is a rail or a pole on the ground.

❏ Unlike the water jump, hold the contact, and ride the horse positively forwards from your leg. Let your horse work out its feet for itself. Look up, contact and leg on.

❏ If you are coming into a coffin, the same rule applies. When you come to that first rail you have to have slowed up enough to be able to ride forwards to the fence – that is the key – so you can attack it, with what I call controlled aggression.

What you should be looking for

Your horse has to learn to pop the ditch out of trot or even walk – so, trot and pop, walk and pop – so it is really comfortable with the fence.

When jumping coffins, your horse doesn't want to be flattening and hitting the fences. It has to be jumping the rail, jumping the ditch, jumping the rail. Controlling the speed is the secret to achieving this.

What can go wrong?

If your horse stops in front of a ditch, go back to giving him a lead. If he drops his head and stops at the ditch in the middle of the coffin, you need to hold on to the rein, sit up, and give him a slap with your schooling whip. You don't want to be hitting it at the first rail. However, if you've done your work at home that shouldn't be necessary.

'Don't gallop halfway across the field to the ditch, giving it raaa, and then, when you come to it, slamming all the anchors on.'

EXERCISE

29

Riding through a turning line

'This is good to practise at home to get right so the horse doesn't fall out through its shoulder in competition.'

The exercise

❏ Put two fences on a turning line about three or four strides apart. Your aim is for the length of your horse's strides to remain equal from the middle of one jump to the middle of the next.

❏ Canter into the fences, turning your horse off your legs and riding from the middle of one fence to the middle of the next. Keep your outside hand low and close to your horse's neck, and your outside leg on.

What's being achieved

This exercise is good for the rider because you learn to ride your horse off of your leg, and to see a line.

What you should be looking for

If the horse isn't listening, you need to give him a slap to make sure he gets in front of your leg. If he is waiting and waiting and not responding to your leg aids, you are better off giving him a sharp slap on the neck, shoulder or bottom. If you are forever trying to dig your spurs in, the horse is likely to go a bit numb to your aids, so you are better off making him a bit sharper to your leg.

What can go wrong?

If your horse keeps putting in an extra stride it is probably because you are resorting to your hands to make the turn. Concentrate on using your leg aids.

If you end up jumping the first fence in the middle and the second off to one side, you have to keep at it, focusing on keeping your outside hand low and your outside leg on until you get to the middle.

Moving on

Once you've established an even stride between the two fences, try to either increase or decrease the number (that is, if you began with three strides between the two fences, try to fit in four, or vice versa).

WORKING ON LEG AIDS

This is a simple exercise to help you work on your leg aids:

1. Ride down the centre line in trot, ask for a bend to the right, and ride a 10m circle to the right before X.

2. Rejoin the centre line, cross X, ask for a bend to the left and then ride a 10m circle to the left.

3. Rejoin the track, go large, and repeat the exercise trying to fit as many well balanced 10m circles on the centre line, to the left and the right, as possible.

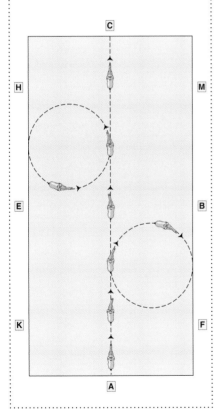

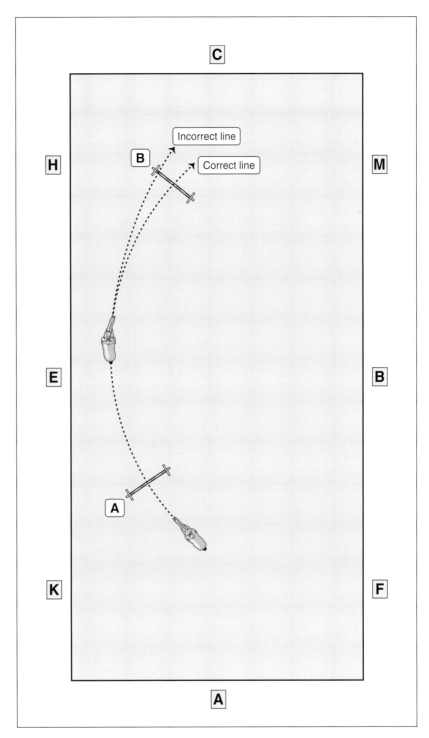

A grid for young and old

'This is a good all-round exercise.'

The exercise

❑ Set up the grid as shown in the diagram, with a cross-pole, one short stride to a bounce made of two small uprights, and then one stride to a parallel.

❑ For your youngsters, start with the poles on the floor, and then put them up to cross-poles and then to uprights.

❑ Make the bounce a bit bigger for the more advanced horse, and build a decent parallel on the end.

What's being achieved

This is a good exercise for youngsters because it teaches them about bounces. And it is a good exercise for the more advanced horses because the bounce before the parallel rounds them, and makes them back off. Also this grid slows them up a bit.

What you should be looking for

Sit very still and let your horse do the jumping for you. The more upright the position of the rider, the easier the horse finds it, as the more we move the more we unbalance our horse – so the stiller we can sit, particularly when the horse has got to do something quickly, the better off the horse is, and the rider, too.

What can go wrong?

This is a really constructive exercise, and fairly foolproof. With a young horse you just build up and build up the jumps and their confidence. With an older horse, the only thing it is likely to do is rush the bounce a bit and have it down, in which case go back a step and then gradually increase the height once more.

Moving on

Gradually increase the height of the jumps.

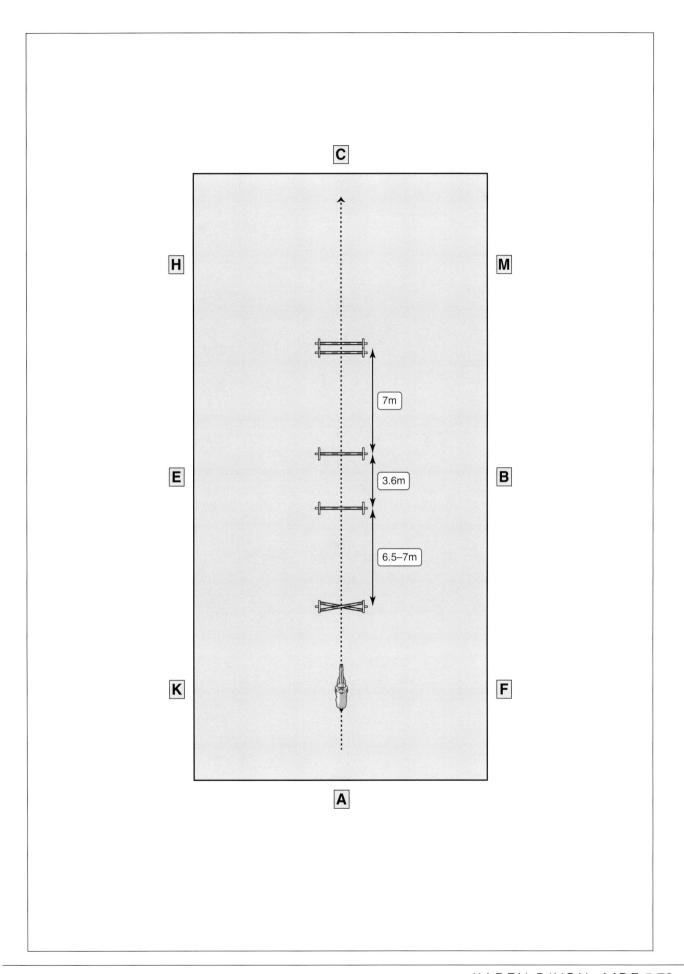

LUCINDA & CLAYTON FREDERICKS

Team Fredericks, Lucinda (née Murray) and Clayton, have consistently been in the ribbons for many years. Yet 2006, even by their standards, was quite a year. They took first (Clayton) and second (Lucinda) places at Chatsworth *** , won the British Open Championship (Clayton) at Gatcombe, and the team bronze and individual silver at the World Equestrian Games (Clayton) held in Aachen. Even so, all of these successes were somewhat overshadowed by Lucinda's disappointment at not qualifying for the Australian team at Aachen – until in September she won the Land Rover Burghley Horse Trials.

Both have been involved with horses from an early age, Clayton as a supporter of showing in his home continent of Australia, and Lucinda as a keen event rider here in the UK. Clayton took up eventing after 10 years of winning the State Show Rider of the Year, and once crowned National Young Rider Champion, decided he had to move to the UK to further his international career. Here he met Lucinda, and they settled in this country; they now live in Devizes, Wiltshire, with their daughter Ellie.

Both are renowned trainers world-wide, always enthusiastic and approachable, willing to pass on their knowledge and to help others. Their training techniques benefit from their partnership, and are living confirmation of the old adage that 'two minds are better than one'.

Q: What's the best piece of advice you've ever been given?
In show jumping: make a good job of jumping the first fence, it will help with the rest of the course.
In dressage: ride your horse inside the arena in the same way as you do outside, from day one.
Cross-country: keep your eye on the part of the fence you are going to jump from as far out as you can.

Q: Name three things you look for when you begin to train a horse.
Good temperament, the feeling it gives you off the ground, and the quality of its canter. You can usually manufacture a trot.

Q: Aspirational riders will watch you ride and learn from your techniques. Whose performance do you watch?
Andrew Nicholson: he turns a mutt into a four-star performer.

Q: If I asked one of your pupils 'what's the thing Lucinda and Clayton go on about the most', what would it be?
Sitting up, and not getting in front of the movement.

Q: What would be the three pearls of wisdom you'd like to pass on to anyone with equine ambitions?
Train your horse to a level above that at which you compete. Learn to ride the bad as well as the good. Don't go too fast, too soon.

Q: What do you do when you come up against a training brick wall?
Go find someone who can help, get some advice. Ask someone else to sit on your horse and see what they can do.

Q: What aspects of your personal performance are you working on at present?
Lucinda: I am trying not to try too hard, because sometimes you lose your natural feel. I did that a little bit last year.

Q: What's the best piece of training equipment you've ever used?
Lungee bungee, Myler bits, Southern Stars saddle.

Q: Who coaches you?
We help each other, or Jane Bredin helps with our dressage and Bina Ford with our show jumping.

Q: Do you have a training formula?
No, because every horse is different. With some you would never go into canter until you have established a trot. I had a horse that I would never canter before going into a test because I couldn't hold the trot. And then you get Headley Britannia that you have to canter huge amounts to get her bubbliness out, and this helps with her trot.

CONTENTS

EXERCISE 31

Pirouettes for turns with energy

'On cross-country courses these days you often get two fences close to each other on a corner – or even three, sometimes – and basically we use a pirouette in between.'

EXPERT TIP

With a greener horse, begin with travers on a circle rather than a quarter pirouette. Once you've got him balanced and turning on the hocks, then take the jump.

THE EXERCISE

❏ Set up two fences, four or five strides apart as shown in the diagram (1), and at a height your horse is comfortable with.

❏ Jump the first jump, beginning from canter. Think about the position of your upper body – on landing, sit back.

❏ Depending on both your abilities, either ride to a halt or continue in canter.

❏ Ride a quarter pirouette, getting your horse to really turn off the outside leg, keeping him in balance on his hocks.

❏ Be sure to bring his shoulders round – it's really vital that you do that, rather than just pulling on the inside rein.

❏ Now, in canter, jump the second fence – you should have a couple of strides distance to do so.

❏ Repeat the exercise the other way.

What's being achieved

Putting a horse into a pirouette should enable him to find his hocks and balance. Pausing to collect the pirouette will teach him to wait.

PIROUETTES NOT HAPPENING?

Here's a simple exercise to work on:

❏ Imagine a box in the centre of your arena from three-quarter line to three-quarter line and around X.

❏ Ride a collected walk along one side of the box and ask for a slight inside bend.

❏ At the first corner of your box, ride a quarter pirouette.

❏ Make a normal turn at the next corner.

❏ Before reaching the next corner, ensure you are still in collection, and then ride another quarter pirouette in that corner.

❏ Make a simple turn again at the fourth corner.

Repeat on the opposite rein.

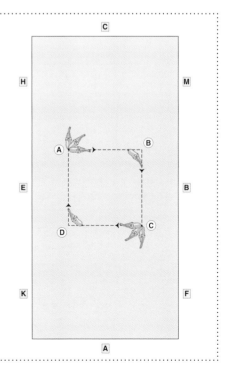

What you should be looking for

Don't try to do this at speed initially as it could all get in a bit of a muddle. Getting this right takes a lot of repetition and practice, but if you use your voice in training, your horse should go steady and turn from a voice command.

What can go wrong?

To start with, your horse might rush the fence and pop out the outside shoulder – they often don't even get the shoulders around. Slow things down a pace.

Moving on

Once your horse has really mastered the turn, ride the exercise in canter, or you could try popping another fence into the angle (2).

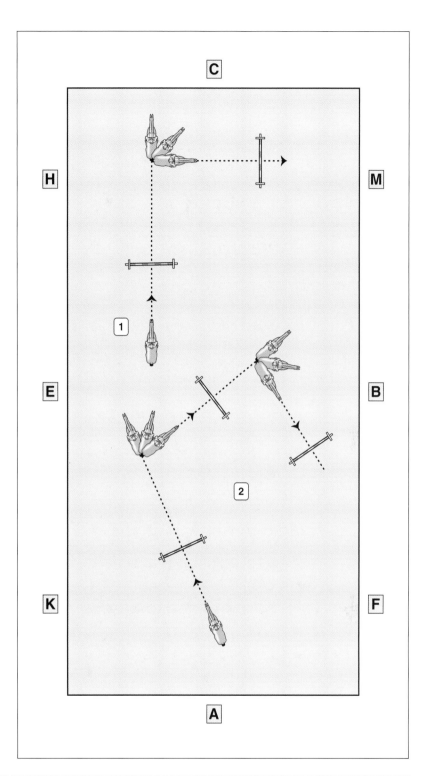

Shoulder-in and travers on a circle

'As a progression from flatwork I do a lot of jumping on a circle. This exercise is more for the exercise than the jump. The jump adds a bit because it distracts the horse a little. This makes it more difficult for the rider to balance, which means you have to work a little harder!'

The exercise

❏ Set up a big circle, at least 20m, with a fence somewhere on the circumference. The fence should be small, its size in accordance with your horse's abilities, and could even be a cross-pole.

❏ Beginning in trot, put your horse into shoulder-in on the circle. Either use the long sides to establish your shoulder-in or, on the circle, pass to the inside or the outside of the fence for a couple of circuits, if necessary, to settle him into the exercise.

❏ On the approach to the fence, straighten up for the last couple of strides and insist that the horse goes right to the base. Really be focused on the fence and watch your upper body doesn't come forward. Develop your position so this is less and less about contact and you're encouraging the horse to become lighter and softer.

❏ Reduce the stride rather than accelerating and galloping forwards, and increasing the length of the stride. It's preferable for the horse to be collected and engaged in the hindquarters upon the approach, as opposed to pushing away.

❏ Change the rein and do this exercise from the opposite direction.

What's being achieved

This exercise engages the hindquarters, helping the horse to balance in front of the fence, teaching him to sit on his hocks, come up in front and wait in front of the fence, not to be rushing in.

What can go wrong?

'Don't go for longies, get right into the base.'

With a greener horse it might be worth adding two poles in front of the jump to help the rider in. Straighten up before you go over the poles, which will also help your horse to keep his rhythm. If you find he still rushes, get rid of the jump and work on canter poles on a circle.

Moving on

Once your horse is happy with this exercise, try putting him in travers and repeating the exercise. You can then make the jump higher, and could add a placing pole in front and behind.

SHOULDER-IN AND TRAVERS ON A CIRCLE

In **shoulder-in**, your horse should have his hind feet on the circle and his shoulders in a little to the inside (on three or four tracks). He should be evenly bent through his body.

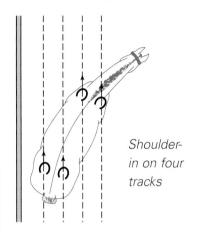

Shoulder-in on four tracks

In **travers** your horse should have his front feet on the circle and his haunches a little to the inside (on four tracks). He should be evenly bent through his body and his outside cheek should be parallel with the arc of the circle.

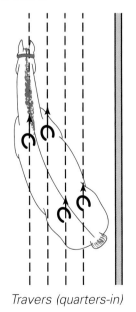

Travers (quarters-in)

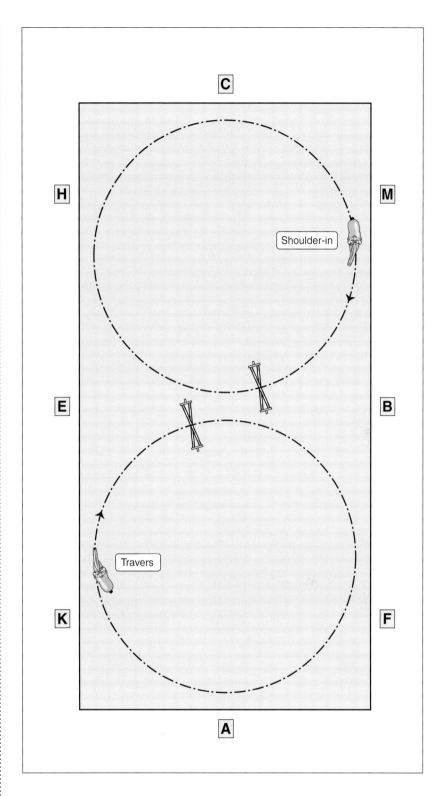

Training young horses to jump out of trot

'You never know on a cross-country when your horse might slip or slide on an approach, so he has to be able to trot up to a fence. This gives him time to jump off his hind legs without a lot of speed.'

The exercise

❏ Set up four or five quite tall cross-poles on the centre line, but going across the school so you can ride them as you would on a serpentine.

❏ Ride square turns off the long side, in trot, but make sure that you wait until the horse's front feet get to the base of the cross-pole before you jump over it. It's very obvious when they don't do that. If they take off a stride early, they only really push off from one hind leg rather than both hind legs – rather an uncomfortable feeling.

❏ When you land, go straight, half-halt and collect, and then make a square turn.

❏ Ride along the long side, then make another square turn back across the school to the next cross-pole, and repeat.

❏ Do this exercise on both reins.

'This is not an easy, comfortable exercise.'

EXPERT TIP

Riding the exercise in trot is important. You trot into the base, you don't need speed but you do need to sit up, and not go sooner. All you have to do is stand up in your stirrups when you get there.

What you should be looking for

This has to be ridden with discipline – you're not allowed to cut the corners, not allowed to land and forget to turn the way you are planning to turn. Make sure that you trot to the base of the fence. At first your horse will expect to be allowed to cut the corner or run out on his forehand, but the more you practise, the better you will be at landing, sitting up, half-halting, performing a square turn and looking early enough to focus on the next fence.

'This is brilliant for any horse that lands and runs out on to his forehand.'

What can go wrong?

Your horse will either try to take off too early or break into canter before the fence, but you must stay in balance with him – and hold the mane if necessary!

Moving on

You can ride this exercise in canter, too. Build up from the trot, and then go into canter. You can make the fences upright and go up to 1.35m (4ft 6in) uprights in this way. Canter keeps the horse going forwards. This exercise will help to teach the horse flying changes as they'll change legs as they land, or they'll land, wait, then change the lead and turn. So this also teaches them to be polite!

EXPERT TIP

Don't forget, no matter what, keep both legs closed against your horse to give him security and keep him straight, so he jumps off of both hind legs together.

BONUS

Sometimes, if your horse is really on the forehand, you can go to the edge of the school, halt and do a pirouette or turn on the haunches and get yourself on line, and then trot back.

EXPERT TIP

You can do this exercise with more emphasis on one rein if you have a horse that is particularly difficult on one rein.

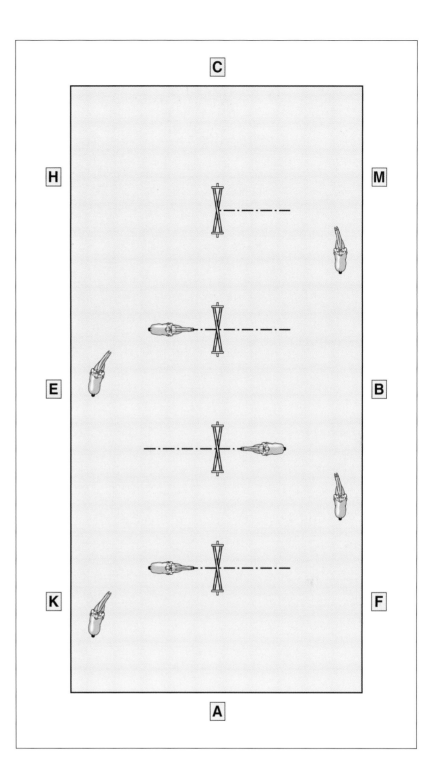

Canter poles

'Until they can do this, our horses don't leave the floor.'

The exercise

❏ Begin with one pole, then two, then three, and build up in a straight line to, at the most, ten. Adjust the distance between the poles to suit your horse, around 3.6m (12ft). You will need a 60m x 20m arena – or bigger! – to do this safely.

❏ Establish a collected canter and ride over the poles. Ride into the first pole with your horse's feet just in front of it. Ensure that the back feet wait until the front feet are over, and the pole is not between the horse's front legs – this is a common mistake.

❏ Canter down the poles, halt, turn around, and canter back. Then halt, turn around and canter back again.

❏ When you and your horse are comfortable with the rhythm and with crossing the poles correctly, add a jump at one end. Canter down the ten poles and pop over the jump.

❏ You can gradually build the jump up.

What's being achieved

This is a great exercise for increasing the height of a jump with confidence and helping the rider stay in a rhythm, stay straight, and see a stride. It encourages horses to take level strides, whether shorter or longer, to a jump, and teaches the horse not to change his stride.

'We have had a very green rider and a green horse jumping a great big jump in this way and they feel marvellous after it.'

What you should be looking for

The aim is for the rider to place the horse's front feet just in front of the first canter pole. They are not allowed to canter astride the pole. The front legs go over, and the back legs wait, just like a jump. The rider will have to be half-halting all the way down the line of poles – half-halt on landing and half-halt before the next pole and go on down the ten poles, half- halting over every single one of them.

What can go wrong?

If you're having trouble getting your horse over the poles with both feet in pairs, practise doing travers coming into the jump (*see* Exercise 32).

Moving on

This exercise is really quite hard, but if you do feel the need for a challenge, raise the poles or increase the height of the jump – just slightly.

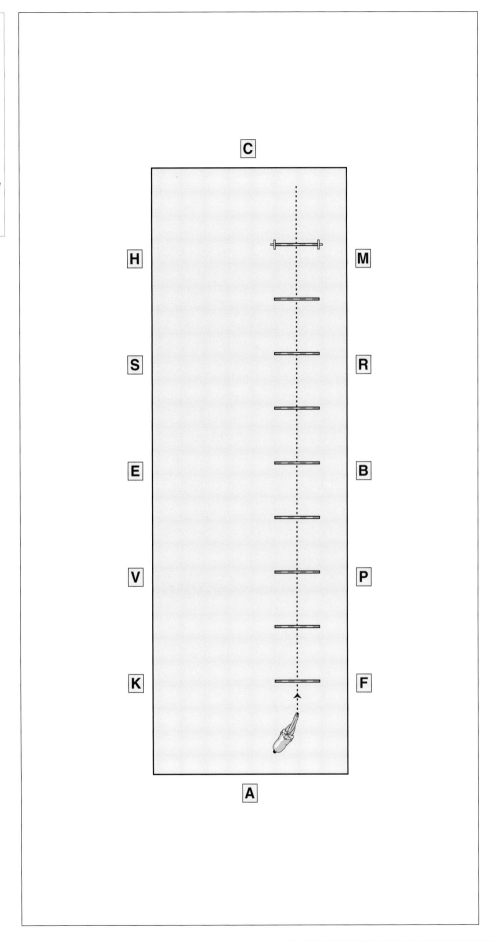

Seeing a stride

'Don't just count the last three strides into a jump – that is completely wrong.'

The exercise

❏ Place a single pole in the middle of the school, in a position where you will have enough space to ride up to ten strides into the pole. Now focus on the pole as much as you would focus on a jump, and focus on it from as far back as possible – try about eight to ten strides.

❏ Come into the pole at canter, and count the horse's inside front leg hitting the ground. So you are counting one, two, three, four, and looking at, and focusing on the pole. Make sure you are counting the footfalls in the rhythm, not willy-nilly.

❏ Don't leave it until the last three strides before you start counting: it's too late, you can't adjust the stride, and you can't adjust the horse. The adjustments need to be done in the strides from ten to three. The last three strides need to be fairly level, and depending on the type of jump, will need either more of a push from the rider or more of a wait.

What's being achieved

You are counting to maintain rhythm, and learning to see a stride without the stress of worrying about a jump. It doesn't matter where you start counting, it's all about keeping an even rhythm. This exercise also helps you learn to focus and jump at an exact point on a pole so that you repeat this at fences.

What can go wrong?

Your horse may straddle or break into trot over the pole. You have to keep your leg on to keep your horse engaged and really focused on the pole. If he does straddle the pole, try to remember that the front feet go in front of the pole. As they go over the pole, do a small half-halt and keep your legs on: this will cause the back feet to effectively jump the pole.

Moving on

Practise moving further and further away from the pole and riding to it in a dead straight line.

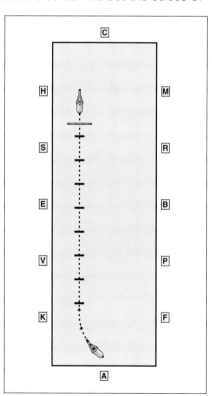

Changes of stride on a diamond

'This will train your horse to shorten and lengthen his stride in a controlled fashion.'

The exercise

❏ Set up a diamond in the middle of your school with one pole on the centre line at G, one on the centre line at X, and one on each of the three-quarter lines at either side.

❏ Cross the poles in canter, and count the number of strides between each. It should be around four.

❏ Now by changing the shape you make between each of these poles and lengthening and shortening your horse's stride, you should be able to decrease the number of strides to three, or increase it to as many as eight.

What's being achieved

The rider learns how to control a stride, to open it up or compress it. A well-designed course of jumps will test this ability.

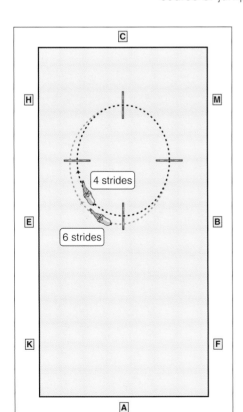

What can go wrong?

Some horses will get a bit 'buzzy' doing this exercise, but they usually settle to it once they get the idea. If your horse continues to be excited or can't maintain a certain length of stride for too long, take him out of the exercise, give him a breather in walk on a long rein, and then start from the beginning again.

Moving on

Performing this exercise on a circle is easier than riding it in a straight line as you can make your circle bigger or smaller to meet the pole correctly and keep going, even if your rhythm is a little awry! The next step would therefore be to try this on a straight line.

RHYTHM VERSUS LENGTHENING

It is important that you know your horse's comfort stride, in which you and he are in balance. Once you have this pace consistently, work on asking for lengthened and shortened strides, but be sure not to lose the rhythm. A simple exercise to work on lengthening and shortening strides is to place poles on the ground at a distance of four and a half times your horse's normal canter stride (try 4.5 x 3.6m – about 16m – to begin with). Now work on riding four or five strides between these two poles.

Lengthening and shortening strides between fences

'You get two fences on a related distance and the rider panics in between.'

TIP

Some horses will need opening out, others will need shortening, and so the distance between the pole and fence depends on the horse and rider's strengths and weaknesses. Increase and decrease the distance between placing pole and oxer by small increments of 15cm (6in).

The exercise

You'll need a helper on the ground for this one.

❏ Begin with a placing pole, four regular strides away from an oxer, set at a comfortable height for horse and rider. Canter over the pole and fence as many times as it takes to establish a feeling for the horse's regular stride.

❏ Once you can feel a regular four strides, then adjust the distance between pole and oxer so that it becomes a shorter four strides. Try to feel the stride with your body, without doing too much, just maintaining the shorter canter coming in and maintaining the shorter canter through the related distance.

❏ Once you're satisfied with that, have the pole moved back to a standard stride, and then open it up to a forward stride.

What's being achieved

This is an important training aid for horses and riders, so they learn to remain relaxed between fences, because if a horse approaches a fence in a relaxed fashion, he's less likely to 'cramp' over the rail and have a fault or a stop.

What can go wrong?

Most riders find it very difficult to sit and do nothing in the early stages: they feel like they have got to be driving at the fence or taking a half-halt. It is important as a rider to learn to just jump the fence and stay in balance with the horse and not interfere.

Moving on

Replace the placing pole with a small cross and increase the height of the fence, but remember to adjust the distances as you build the fence up.

EXPERT TIP

Some riders find this very difficult, in which case put placing poles in the middle, between the jumps; however, don't try to do this on your own – for safety's sake you will need someone watching from the ground. And remember, if the fence is getting bigger, you will need more distance between the two elements.

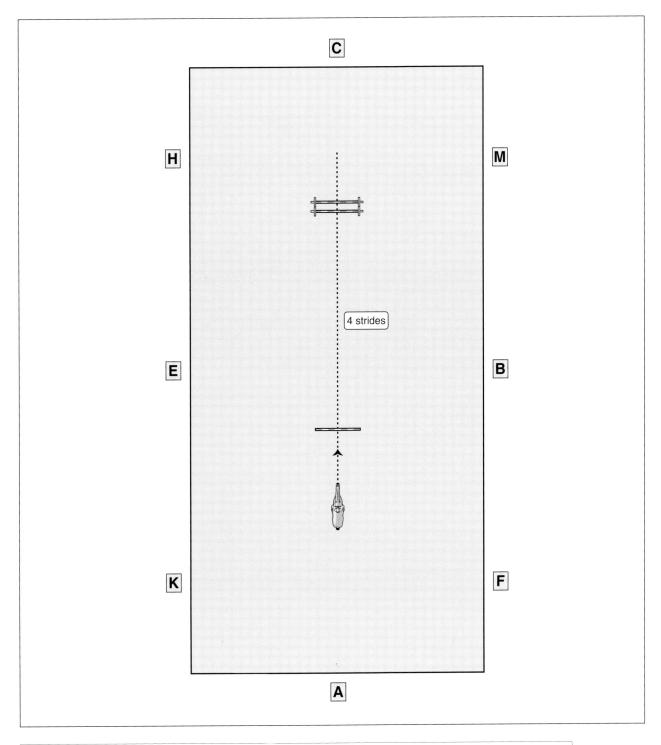

EXPERT TIPS

Here are some tips for lengthening strides between fences:

❏ *Lengthen your horse's stride after the jump. This is when he has the most natural forward impulsion.*

❏ *Make sure that you don't get ahead of your horse as you take off for the next jump.*

❏ *Your horse should remain relaxed through his back as he extends his stride. Excessive chivvying may lead to unwanted tension.*

Changing bend and angles

'We use this to get a horse off the inside leg and also to create a consistent feeling in both reins. All the time you are changing the bend and the angles.'

The exercise

❏ Begin on the track and, in trot, ride travers and renvers along one long side, shoulder-in across the short side, renvers and travers down the opposite long side, and shoulder-in to A or C.

❏ At A or C, come off the track and on to a 20m circle, ride shoulder-in, renvers, travers, shoulder-in, renvers, travers all the way around the circle, finishing in shoulder-in.

❏ Come off the circle in shoulder-in at A or C, back on to the track, and ride a half-pass just after the next corner to change the rein.

What you should be looking for

The important thing is, that when you change the bend through the neck you do it quite gradually so it is not a whip-around to the other side; that's why I think this particular exercise helps get the horse channelled over the back and into the contact, equally.

What can go wrong?

Sometimes horses find it hard to maintain the rhythm as you change through the bend. This is something you have to concentrate on. You have to be conscious that you may not need to exaggerate your leg position too much. This exercise can help you to establish the horse's responses without needing so much of an exaggerated aid.

Moving on

Ride this exercise on the centre line. Use a mirror and you'll see just how difficult it is!

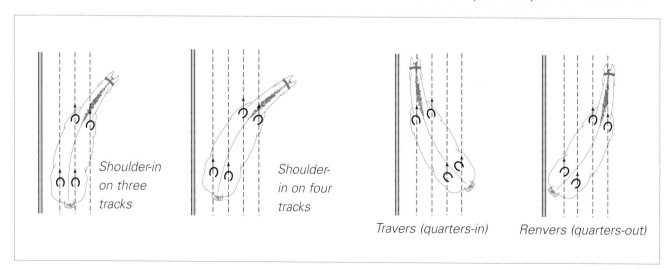

Shoulder-in on three tracks

Shoulder-in on four tracks

Travers (quarters-in)

Renvers (quarters-out)

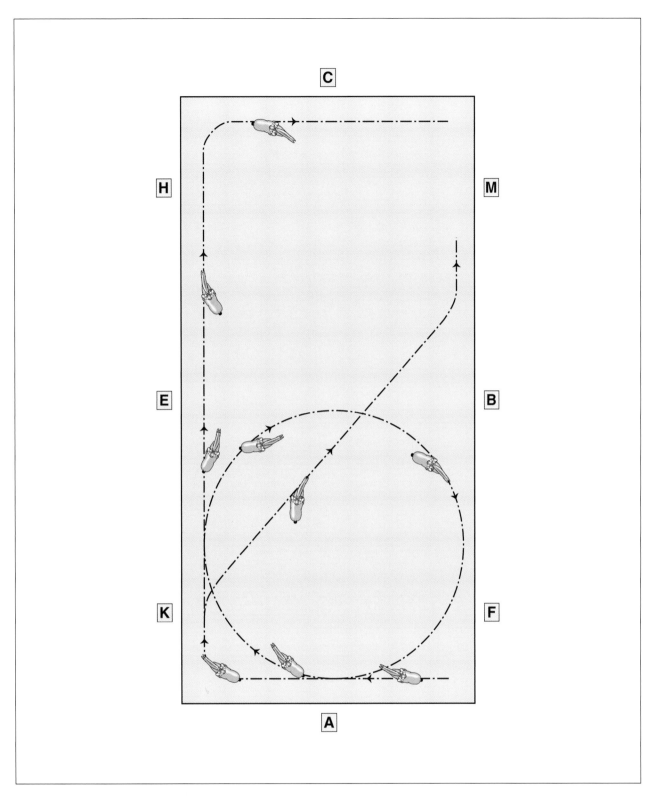

'One common mistake is that riders get confused and then they have their legs all in a pickle, usually exaggerating the leg aids. All it is, is changing the inside leg.'

Lucinda's exercises for medium trot

'In medium trot, straightness is big. A lot of horses will go off and do a really big medium trot, but they've gone wide behind – spreading their back legs and feet – but the pirouette will prevent them from going wide.'

The exercise

❏ Establish a good, active and collected walk. As soon as possible, on a long diagonal, ride a working pirouette (*see* page 149).

❏ Come out of the pirouette and allow the horse to trot slowly but powerfully forwards.

❏ Now build up the trot, but as soon as your horse starts running, take it down again and then come back to walk, and straight into a pirouette.

❏ Rejoin the track and repeat on the opposite rein.

What you should be looking for

You have to make sure that your horse is straight: make sure his ears are in line with his shoulders, and his shoulders are in line with his hips.

What can go wrong?

❏ If your horse is falling on to one shoulder, carry your stick down that shoulder to encourage him to lift it up, and use the stick if you need to.

❏ If you have a horse that goes on to the forehand, carry your lower legs further forwards. Some horses do need to have the rider's leg further back in medium trot, but not many.

❏ If you can't slow your horse down, half-halt every time you sit in the saddle. In fact, it's always a good idea to train a horse to do medium trot in rising trot.

Moving on

You can do exactly the same in canter to get more expression in a medium canter. And it doesn't half make them jump up!

> ### MEDIUM TROT UP A HILL
>
> Lucinda's preferred way to develop a medium trot is to work the horse up a hill. It has to be the right type of slope – not so steep that he just can't free up and go, but steep enough that he can't run. She starts off with him very, very deep and slow, and he builds up. As soon as he rushes when pressed forwards, she slows him down. She then lets him go on again and, once again, he runs and she slows him down – so he learns never to run. This is how she taught her Punchestown CCI*** winner of 2002, Bally Leck Boy. 'I only ever taught him a medium trot up a hill. It's all to do with them lifting their back and pushing from behind, in a balance. They have to push levelly, and you have to make sure that you do as much on one diagonal as you do on the other.'

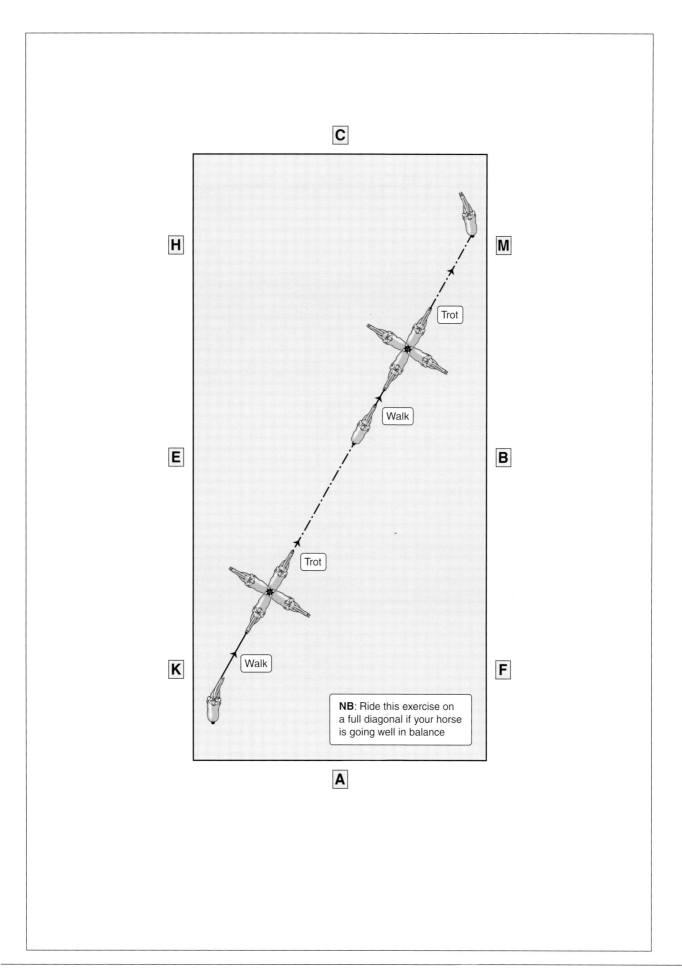

NB: Ride this exercise on a full diagonal if your horse is going well in balance

WILLIAM MICKLEM

A leading equestrian coach, trainer and author, William Micklem is behind the success of some of the top names in the equestrian world today. From a very young age he was immersed in the world of horses, running a yard with his father and three brothers – a yard with which several horses famous in equestrian history were associated.

Twice listed for national junior teams in eventing and show jumping, fate dealt William a hand that prevented him from following that particular dream. However, at the age of 20 he fulfilled another dream by qualifying as a BHSI, and went to work with the renowned trainer Robert Hall at Fulmer. He then worked in the United States, where he taught leading American riders including Karen O'Connor.

After the US he went to Ireland, and from 1977 until 1983 he was a national coach for the Irish Horse Board (Bord na gCapall). In 1984 he became national coach for the Irish Junior and Young Rider event teams, which enjoyed great success.

In 1987 he was appointed Training Director for Gleneagles, where he remained until 1993. During this time William also wrote manuals and presented equestrian videos for the Pony Club, amongst others.

Since 1994 he has worked as coach, author and consultant to a wide variety of organizations including the American Association of Riding Instructors, the British Riding Clubs Association, The Equestrian Federation of Ireland, Equitana USA, the World Breeding Federation, and the Irish Horse Board, promoting equestrianism. His book *The Complete Horse Riding Manual* has been a huge success worldwide. He is also responsible for discovering Karen and David O'Connor's Olympic medal horses Biko, Custom Made and Gilt Edge, and bred both Karen O'Connor's Mandiba, and Zara Phillips' young horse prospect, High King.

In 2003 he conceived and produced Ride On, the acclaimed celebration of the Irish horse world, which was performed at Punchestown racecourse.

Q: What's the best piece of advice you've ever been given in regard to training horses?
Training has to be a blend of effort and delight...

Q: What do you do when you come up against a training brick wall?
You should ask why this has happened:
❏ Is it because I am asking too much for the horse to do mentally or physically?
❏ Is it because the horse is uncomfortable or in pain?

❏ Is it because there is something missing in the progressive training
which should be put in place?
❏ Shall I try moving back to something easier?
Only if the answer to all these questions is 'No'
would I move on to some lateral thinking and
imaginative solutions...

**Q: Name three things that you look for when you
begin to train a horse.**
Calmness, forwardness and straightness ... they are at
the heart of training at any level.

Q: What's your training formula?
Simplicity and love ... laced with buckets of energy.

**Q: How do you identify problems in your own
performance, and how do you work on them?**
I try to avoid thinking of training problems, which
is a negative approach: I prefer to look at needs,
challenges and goals.
　　　Everyone can benefit from a good coach,
and everyone can benefit from regular objective
assessment. In tennis, golf, swimming, gymnastics,
athletics, football and all key sports, good coaches
are an integral part of participating in that sport. We
need to do more in order to make this the norm in
equestrian sports.

**Q: Aspiring riders will watch you and learn from your
techniques. Whose performance do you watch?**
We all have our own personal heroes or role models
whom we watch, or just think about, for different
reasons, and see them in our own different ways.
Mine would include Herbert Rehbein, Bert de Nemethy,
Mark Todd, Nuno Oliveira, Michel Robert, Nelson
Pessoa, William Fox-Pitt, Reiner Klimke and Jack le
Goff. I would also have other role models from other
sports and non-sporting activities, which I think is an
important dimension for all performers.

CONTENTS

EXERCISE

40

The key: riding off the inside line of a circle

'The circle is the mother of all exercises, and everything in dressage is built on the horse's ability to circle well. However, circles are continually ridden badly with the horse's forehand being held to the markers and boards on the outside because of the one thing we use – a dressage arena – which is supposed to enable us to ride circles well.'

EXPERT TIP

The surprising thing is that people who ride in open fields without arenas tend to ride circles better, keeping the forehand in front of the quarters, because they just concentrate on where they want to go, looking to the inside and riding off the inside line automatically. Riding in an open field for a period is a good way to break the damaging habit of riding off the outside line using the markers and boards.

The exercise

❑ The aim of this exercise is to learn to ride the circle off an inside line (C in the diagram), rather than an outside line which makes the horse croooked.

❑ Like all new ideas, it takes time for it to become second nature, but it is beautifully simple and has huge benefits.

What's being achieved

Crookedness is the enemy, and there is a constant demand in all equestrian activities, at all levels to develop and maintain straightness. This requires the ability to position the forehand in front of the quarters, and the horse cannot work efficiently unless this happens. By riding off the inside line on a circle this is achieved in most cases.

What you should be looking for

The diagram shows three different ways of riding a circle. What most riders do is hold line A, which just encourages the horse's natural tendency to move with the forehand to the outside. Line B is a step better, imagining the horse's spine following the circle line – but the best way by far is line C, where you imagine the circle line on the *inside* of your horse.

The key is simply to look for the inside line at all times – then most riders automatically make the right actions: the hands move slightly to the inside, and the weight remains centrally placed, thus achieving the desired positioning of the forehand.

This is made clearer by contrasting it with what happens when riding inefficiently off the outside line. In this situation riders tend to move their hands and weight to the outside, which encourages the horse's natural tendency to go with the shoulders to the outside. It also tends to create too much bend in the neck, encouraging further movement of the forehand to the outside.

What can go wrong?

There are two common faults. Firstly, a non-allowing 'backward' rein contact that restricts the forwardness of the horse; and secondly, a stronger or more backward feel in the outside rein than the inside, caused by inward pressure of the rein on the neck, which creates a loss of bend to the inside or, at worst, the wrong bend. The rein contact in both reins should remain allowing and equal.

Moving on

Riding on the inside line is vital in all movements, but in the next exercise, the lightbulb serpentine, it is clear how the progression is to do it on both left and right circles and maintain the control of the shoulder through a change of rein.

It will also become apparent that, having achieved this riding on the inside line, moving into 'shoulder-fore' is only a small step away.

'It is often said that a rider should "think" shoulder-in all the time when riding in an arena. It has stood the test of time and counteracts the magnetic attraction of the boards of the arena. Habitually riding the inside line for all circles and parts of circles achieves the same thing in a more simple and practical way.'

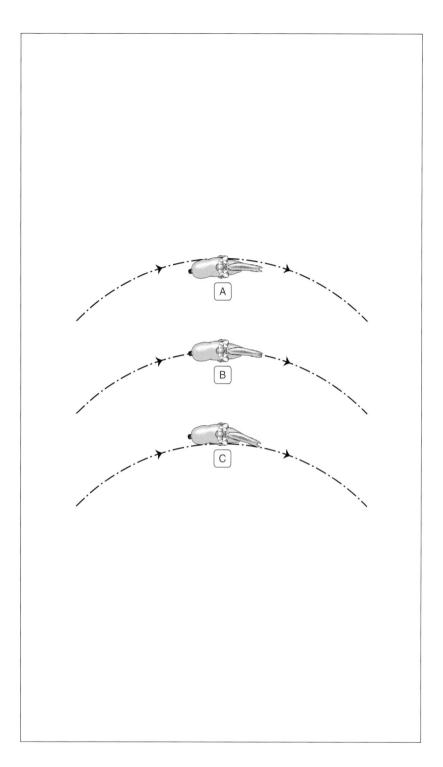

Changing the rein and the light-bulb serpentine

'We would all agree that to ride a straight line is the most difficult thing to do, so why do we so often choose to change the rein in a way that involves quite long periods on a straight line? One of the best ways to change the rein is with one light-bulb serpentine loop and then gradually progress to a full light-bulb serpentine.'

'This man is infuriating,' you might say, 'I know how to change the rein. Across the diagonal or down the centre or half way line.' But the fact is that so many riders miss out on one of the best ways to change the rein.

The exercise

❑ Once your horse is between the aids in trot and you can do a good circle shape on both reins, then how you change the rein becomes very important.

❑ Beginning at the A or C marker, ride a 20m circle line through the corner. Having left the track just past the quarter marker, gradually reduce the bend until at X you have no bend. At this moment you should begin to introduce the new bend.

❑ Ride towards the quarter marker on a line that gradually develops the curve of a 20m circle and you touch the track again, 10m from the corner, reflecting the shape you began with (see diagram A).

❑ Repeat the same shape and process for the alternative change of rein (diagram B), which actually makes it easier to get back to the track, or with a full light-bulb serpentine (see diagrams C and D) with the change of bend taking place over a reduced number of strides.

What's being achieved

This method allows a more gradual change of rein with virtually no straight line to ride. Looking at the diagrams you will see that it is possible with this shape to *gradually* reduce the existing bend and *gradually* add the new bend, which means no straight line to ride except for the briefest moment. This makes it so much easier to change the rein, to control the bend, to control the shoulders and to keep your horse connected. It is also better muscularly for the horse. Looking at the shape of the traditional changes of rein, shown by the dotted lines in diagrams A and B, it is obvious that these are also less flowing.

What you should be looking for

As the change of bend happens you need to ride off the new inside line so that the forehand stays in the right place. Because the change of bend is gradual, rather than the instant bend change of a figure of eight for example, this is not difficult. In addition look for the steps staying regular on both reins and the horse growing in confidence and suppleness.

What can go wrong?

This movement is a classic example of a win win situation, because the main thing that can go wrong is losing control of the shoulders to the outside, but in this situation the shoulders are actually pretty much in the right place for the new direction. It is then just a matter of holding them in this position rather than having to correct their position, which is easier on both horse and rider.

Moving on

❏ Now progress to the full serpentine, which is initially best done in an arena with a little extra width.

❏ You can also add circles, as shown in diagrams C and D, to confirm the bend if the change of rein has not gone well, and then continue with the serpentine. It is also easy to incorporate leg-yielding.

This shape is used so often in the future. It is a great exercise to use for warming-up and suppling at all levels, for use immediately before a dressage test, for teaching flying changes on the flat and over fences, and in difficult times for just making the horse go 'Aah, I know this, I like this.'

'The typical serpentine asked for in standard dressage tests includes straight lines, parallel to the short sides, before each half circle. This makes it more difficult than a light-bulb serpentine, especially because the horse tends to try and anticipate the turn, falling to the inside and going with the wrong bend.'

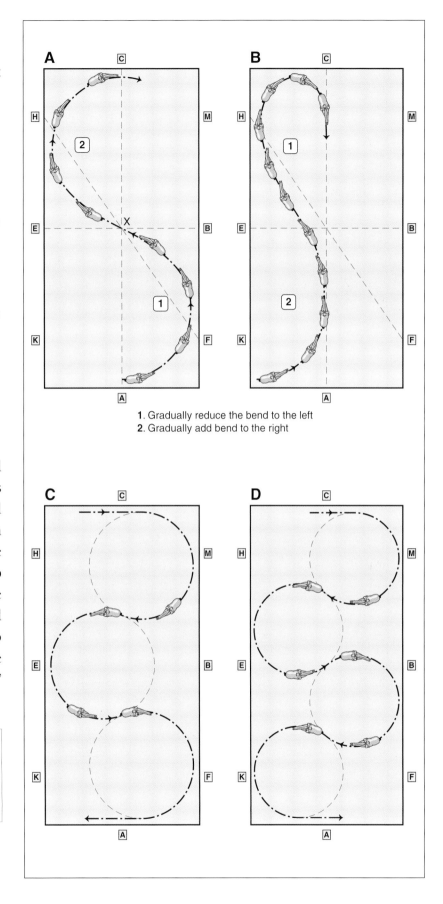

1. Gradually reduce the bend to the left
2. Gradually add bend to the right

EXPERT TIP

When you use this shape for doing flying changes do some loops in counter canter so your horse does not anticipate the change.

Building 'backwards' – an extraordinary difference

'The normal way to build a jumping grid is to keep adding fences after the first fence in the grid, but for more novice horses and riders, and for horses that have lost their confidence, building a grid "backwards" makes an extraordinary difference for the better.'

The exercise

❏ Start by planning what type of grid you want, and where the last fence will be positioned.

❏ Now build that fence in that position. For example, if your last fence is going to be an oxer, work out where it will be in your arena and jump that fence first, beginning as low as you feel confident.

❏ Add the second fence in front of it when you are ready to progress, and then carry on building 'backwards', before raising all fences as appropriate.

What's being achieved

So often you see a grid being used and a horse hesitating at the first or second fence when a third fence is introduced, causing the earlier fence to be hit and a loss of confidence in the horse. The same thing happens when a new element, such as a different filler, is added to the final fence, or if the horse is worried about the size of the final fence. Building backwards largely avoids this type of problem, and means that the horse has a much greater chance of remaining confident. It is worth remembering that what a horse learns first stays with him strongly, and therefore a bad experience with a grid as a youngster can stay with him and create problems long into the future.

'I am recognized as a specialist in the use of grids to improve a horse's performance, but it is important to remember that the wrong grid can ruin the confidence of a horse, and small changes can make a grid almost unjumpable.'
Bert de Nemethy

What you should be looking for

The primary objective is that the horse jumps out of the grid with confidence and enthusiasm, having entered the grid calmly. He should remain as straight as possible, so 'V'-poles on the ground can create a 'funnel' to ensure this. However, these 'V'-poles should be introduced at the start so they do not surprise the horse as the exercise progresses (*see* diagram).

What can go wrong?

The most typical mistake is to forget to lengthen the distance between fences when coming out of canter, and not trot. For example, having trotted to a fence, landed in canter, and jumped the final fence successfully, it is then possible to add a new fence. But the distance between the two original fences must then be lengthened by between 60–75cm (24–30in) because you will be coming to the second fence out of canter now, not trot.

Moving on

When starting in this way a horse should enter a grid with the positive thought that he can always get out of the grid successfully; and he should enjoy grids – this is hugely important for the future. At this stage you can progress to improving the jump more by using Exercise 43 among others – job done!

BONUS

It is important to get added value from all exercises if possible, because this makes training more efficient. Therefore I use this set-up to introduce a different filler each time, using fillers that come in a number of separate sections. I introduce the filler at the start in the fence that will be the last fence in the grid. This is done by leaving a clear space in the middle of the fence and gradually bringing the filler inwards, according to each horse's progress, until it fills the whole fence. In this way a horse is never frightened nor does he learn to stop, and he gets used to all types of filler at an early stage.

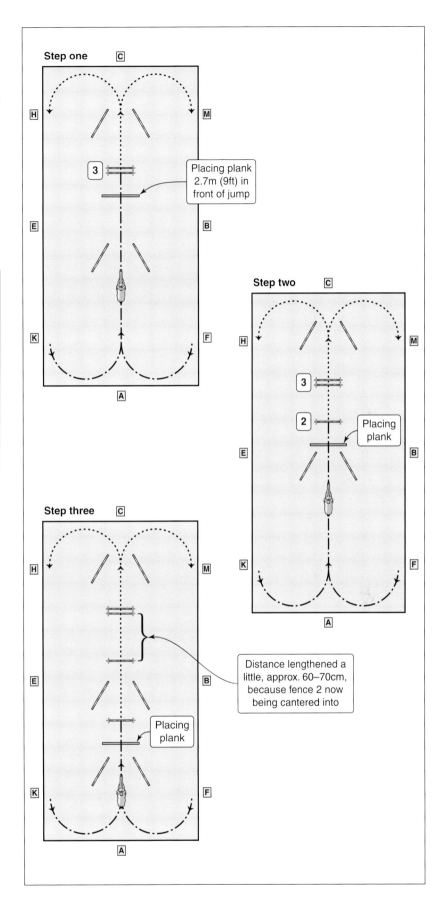

Step one

Placing plank 2.7m (9ft) in front of jump

Step two

Placing plank

Step three

Placing plank

Distance lengthened a little, approx. 60–70cm, because fence 2 now being cantered into

Two oxers to excellence

'Some riders just accept how a horse jumps, but huge improvements can be made with the right grids. One of the most effective is to use a placing fence out of trot followed by two square oxers.'

'With any work, always finish with the horse willing and able to do more. All the knowledge about different exercises is useless if the trainer asks too much and breaks the spirit of the horse.'

The exercise

❏ Set up a grid of fences as shown in diagram A.
❏ Initially the distances, height and width of the fences can be organized to exactly suit each horse and give them confidence.
❏ It is very important that your approach is exactly the same each time. The exercise illustrated is designed to be approached out of trot, so the same trot with the same speed must be repeated.
❏ Do not attempt to progress unless your horse is jumping calmly and willingly and is going straight. Then the distances and fence sizes can gradually be changed to improve the jumping technique, usually by making the inside distances a little shorter and the oxers a little wider, which means that the mid-point of each fence remains in the same position. The type of distances and widths that you will use are shown in diagrams A and B.

What's being achieved

The oxer is the best type of fence to encourage a round, athletic jump with the highest point over the middle of the fence. Many horses need this exercise because they have learnt to do a long flat jump, taking off too far from the fence and making the highest point quite close to the back rail. This is the type of jump encouraged by an ascending oxer, which has the back rail higher than the front rail.

What you should be looking for

A good jump has to have a good take-off. The two hind legs need to be together as a pair and well forward under the body, rather than apart like a normal canter stride. The canter has to be first improved on the flat if this is not happening consistently, but then this exercise will encourage the horse to habitually put the hind legs together. The width of the fence will encourage both sufficient height in the jump, and the shoulders and elbows to come forward. As the angle of ascent becomes a little steeper, achieved by getting the take-off point a little closer to the front pole, the horse will be encouraged to stretch his head and neck more over the fence, which will then help to release the hind legs over the second half of the fence. Horses with bad technique will tend to cramp behind, holding the hind legs tight, and thus making it difficult for them to jump width, in particular.

What can go wrong?

Some horses begin to anticipate and canter early, which is not acceptable. Equally holding the horse back and creeping slowly to the fence and suddenly going faster at the last minute will probably mean the horse is too tense. The best thing to do in this situation is a figure-of-eight in front of the fence, out of trot, varying how many circles you do in each direction. Keep circling until the horse settles and you can go down the grid.

Moving on

The real test is over a course of fences in a competition. However, patience is essential: one swallow doesn't make a summer, and it takes time and repetition to make a good jumping technique a habit. And even then, some horses never jump in a classical way, although this is not a disaster. If a horse learns to be confident, and becomes stronger and more athletic, then they will jump better. So treat each horse as an individual – and remember that the one thing you can always do to help improve your horse is to improve your own balance and harmony.

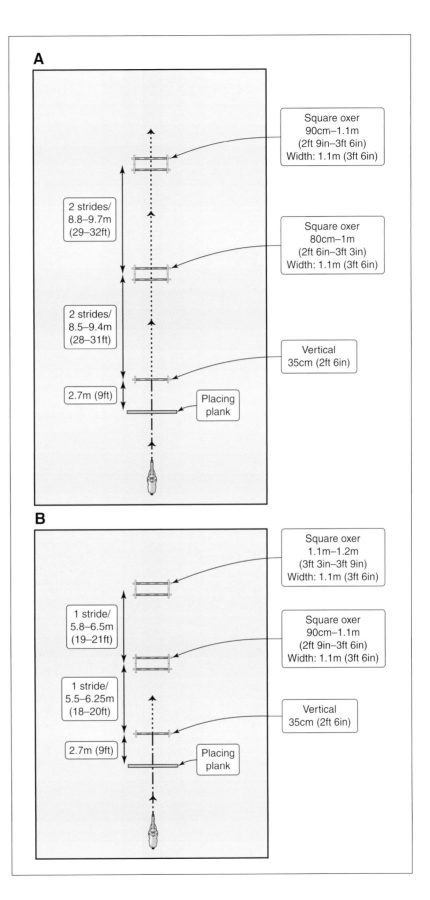

A

Square oxer 90cm–1.1m (2ft 9in–3ft 6in) Width: 1.1m (3ft 6in)

2 strides/ 8.8–9.7m (29–32ft)

Square oxer 80cm–1m (2ft 6in–3ft 3in) Width: 1.1m (3ft 6in)

2 strides/ 8.5–9.4m (28–31ft)

Vertical 35cm (2ft 6in)

2.7m (9ft)

Placing plank

B

Square oxer 1.1m–1.2m (3ft 3in–3ft 9in) Width: 1.1m (3ft 6in)

1 stride/ 5.8–6.5m (19–21ft)

Square oxer 90cm–1.1m (2ft 9in–3ft 6in) Width: 1.1m (3ft 6in)

1 stride/ 5.5–6.25m (18–20ft)

Vertical 35cm (2ft 6in)

2.7m (9ft)

Placing plank

Against the clock from the beginning

'It isn't sensible to wait until the day of a competition to go against the clock for the first time. Not only will you be unlikely to be competitive, but you also run the risk of blowing the horse's mind.'

The exercise

Thinking ahead towards future challenges will help direct the training. A good example of this is preparation for jumping against the clock, which is an essential skill for both show-jumping and event riders.

❑ Set up a course of poles on the ground, as shown in the diagram.

❑ Jump the line or track of the jump-off course, in canter, without going any faster than normal.

❑ When this is being done with quality, fences can be added at a height with which your horse is confident, and as the flatwork improves, the speed can be increased.

❑ This does not mean that you gallop over the fences at home – far from it. Practise jumping at an angle, doing turn-backs to a fence, leaving out a stride, going faster and slower, and quietly practising all the techniques required when you need to go faster than normal.

'The faster a rider goes on a horse, the more important it is to maintain a consistent balance. A still load is a light load, and a light load will not disturb either the horse's concentration or the jump.'
Yogi Breisner

What's being achieved

In this way you can learn what lines are possible, what your horse is capable of, and what it feels like to go against the clock. It also becomes possible to evaluate what combination of shorter lines and faster speeds are possible with each horse.

What you should be looking for

As ever, the first priority is the direction, the line you wish to take, and a key part of this is the ability to control the forehand and keep it in front of the quarters even on tight turns. If the forehand is lost to the outside, precise control is impossible and the jump will be less efficient.

As the speed is increased and the number of strides reduced, it is vital that control and calmness are not lost. Some horses can only go against the clock occasionally because they cannot cope with it mentally, but the same horse may be able to do well by taking very tight lines and going just a little faster. This can be practised.

What can go wrong?

Slipping and sliding is always a risk, and the horse should be well studded up, but the risk will remain – as is the chance that the horse will put his eyes on the wrong fence as he makes a tight turn in an arena crowded with fences. A rider has to be aware of the potential for this sort of problem, and must learn how to stay cool, calm and collected. More classes are lost by the *rider* becoming over-excited than are lost by over-excited horses.

Moving on

A winning round against the clock at the highest level is something of enormous skill, not only on the day but also in the preparation of the horse and rider. By being ambitious enough to 'have a go' and to think about what is necessary to win, riders will improve both their flatwork and their jumping ability, and therefore be better overall for it.

FIFTH LEG TRAINING

A key quality of a successful speed horse is that they are very clean, and that they try hard for the rider. Therefore training for going against the clock has to include exercises such as the previous one with two oxers, jumped without a rein contact. It is what I call 'fifth leg' training, referring to the ability of the horse to find an extra leg during difficulties and to look after the rider. Too many riders restrict their horses and/or dictate every move so that this vital ability is not cultivated. Jumping without a rein contact ensures that the horse has to take a greater responsibility for his own balance. Most horses tend to jump better like this, and the riders learn that they can trust their horse to support themselves and jump clean. Riders learn that a strong rein contact restricts rather than supports. If you were sitting on top of a garden shed that started to fall, no amount of pulling on an edge would stop the shed falling. Similarly, pulling on the reins to try and support the horse is futile.

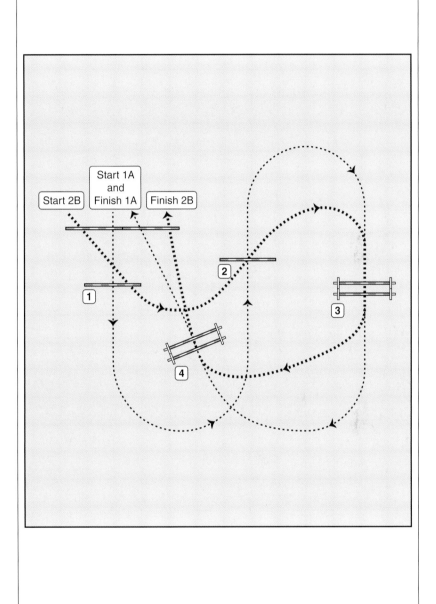

The merry-go-round

'This is a classic shortening and lengthening exercise, and one of the most simple but versatile you will ever come across. It is probably my favourite.'

EXPERT TIP

To begin with I would put up wings on the narrow middle fence so there is no running out. It is important that you reward the horse at the very moment he jumps the narrow fence without deviation. A key element of training is to reward behaviour you want repeated. In this way it is possible to train a horse to always try and jump even the narrowest of fences.

The exercise

❏ Place a set of planks on the ground as shown in the diagram – with just seven planks you will find enough challenges there for many days of work. Line B is set up for three 12ft (3.66m) canter strides, while the two diagonals require either a slight shortening of 1ft (30cm) per stride or lengthening of 1ft (30cm) per stride. However, it is possible to use different distances to suit the needs of each horse.

❏ Begin with line B, the middle line. The key element in this exercise is to keep a regular three-stride pattern between the planks. Then tackle lines A and C, which will require you to come at slightly different speeds in order to shorten or lengthen the stride to suit each line.

❏ When the exercise is being done well by horse and rider, proper fences can be introduced.

What's being achieved

'It is possible to find something to benefit virtually every horse in this exercise. The important thing with this, and all exercises, is not to work mechanically, but to tailor each exercise to suit the individual needs of each horse. These needs are always both mental as well as physical.'

This exercise teaches the rider about the difference in speed required to change the length of a stride to suit each line, and is a wonderful exercise to teach the horse to jump fences in a regular way and stay obedient to the rider's aids. By starting with just planks on the ground it is possible to establish the way of going without worrying about jumping.

With fences introduced, you will get the added value of jumping a narrow fence, and also a narrow fence at an angle, as the middle fence is only half the normal width.

What you should be looking for

Initially this is all about flatwork, and specifically the confirmation of a horse and the rider's ability to maintain a quality canter while making small changes of speed. This in itself will help develop a horse athletically, and build the relationship between horse and rider. Then when fences are added it helps develop a calm and regular approach. Having chosen a line, the canter should remain the same, whether there is just a plank on the ground or three proper fences. The fences should be designed to suit the needs of each horse and rider combination – though I often make the first fence small and the last fence an oxer, so the entry fence is like a placing fence, and the oxer will also improve the jump and build confidence.

What can go wrong?

Once you know all the various tests incorporated in this set-up, the big danger is trying to do too much, too quickly. Always revise the basic exercises before progressing, and don't progress unless each exercise is done well. There is no reason why there should be 'failure', and every possibility of building from good quality work.

Moving on

The variety of possible exercises within this set-up is huge. It is very useful to take any of the first two fences and then go to one of the two final fences not in the direct line. It is possible to link any two fences or series of fences, and produce different challenges. This is great preparation for both going against the clock, and for cross-country riding. The rider learns that they can find a speed and stride length to suit any distance, and how important it is to ride with controlled precision. What a truly great exercise.

EXPERT TIP

It's important to allow the horse to do the jumping without the rider's weight changing all the time. In between fences the rider's seat should only 'kiss' the saddle or be slightly out of it, with most of their weight going through the legs, so that on take-off and landing the horse will not be aware of any change in the rider's weight or position. This is a major help in developing a consistent approach and departure when jumping.

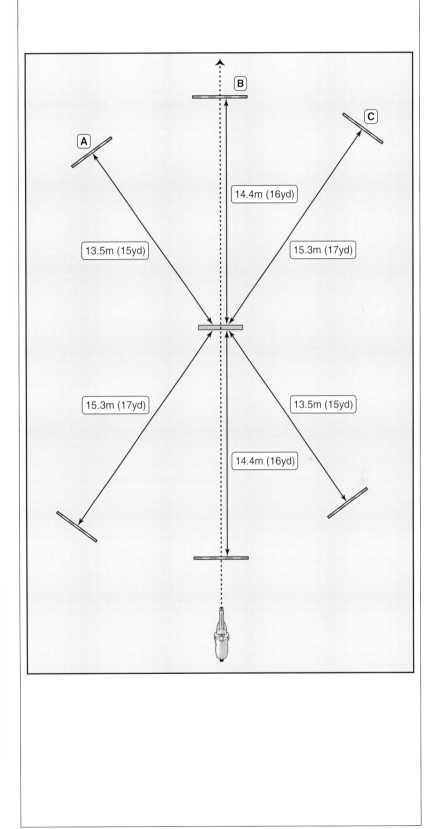

Angled fences

'As soon as regular jumping is begun, some fences should be jumped on an angle, starting with just a few degrees off being straight, and building to 45 degrees to be ready for a one-star three-day event.'

The exercise

❏ Begin by arranging three barrels and a ground line as shown in diagram 1, and jump the middle barrel at an angle as indicated. Comparing the diagrams will show that jumping the line of three barrels at an angle is very similar to jumping a corner. So to establish a horse in jumping this fence at an angle, and staying on a line before and after it, is an ideal preparation for a corner.

❏ Now arrange six small barrels to form a corner, as shown in diagram 2. Plastic barrels are good to use, as you may hit your leg on a standard wing, and sawn off wings are not safe. It is also possible to get barrels of three main sizes suitable for any level. Ideally I would also use flags, even when schooling.

❏ Jump the corner, using exactly the same line and angle as with the original three barrels (line A in diagram 2).

❏ Control of the direction is your first priority, so the fence should be small to make it easy, and should not be made bigger until the line is held precisely.

What's being achieved

Corners and combinations of corners are now possibly the most influential test in modern cross-country courses, so jumping fences at an angle at an early stage is hugely important as essential preparation for jumping corners. The other element of this preparation for corners is jumping narrow fences, which generally speaking we are good at practising; but few people introduce fences on an angle early enough, or jump narrow fences on an angle.

What you should be looking for

The basis for holding a line is good flatwork, and this exercise should not be started until the horse is good on both reins and the shoulders can be controlled sufficiently to enable a straight line to be ridden. You also feel your horse wanting to jump 'between the flags' and this can be taught with well-timed praise. Of course, the quality of the jump also has to be good, so work will have to be done with different grids and exercises alongside this work to ensure that this happens.

What can go wrong?

Good practice is vital. It should become a habit for the horse to jump *without* running out, therefore wings could be used, or extra outside barrels at each narrow fence or corner to ensure this is the case. In addition, planks (not poles) placed on the ground at an early stage can help guide the horse on the straight line, both before and after the fence.

'The good cross-country horse has to be brave and a good jumper, but this is not enough. The need for accuracy and control are an inescapable part of modern cross-country courses, and the schooling programme must include creative work in these areas from the start.'
Mark Phillips

Moving on

More advanced courses will have corners with bigger angles, but all this requires is the ability to jump closer to the apex of the corner. Line B in diagram 2 shows the more advanced jumping line required for a wider corner. In addition, course builders will design narrow fences and corners requiring an approach on a curved line. This demands greater honesty from the horse and the ability to ride the inside line of a circle (*see* Exercise 40).

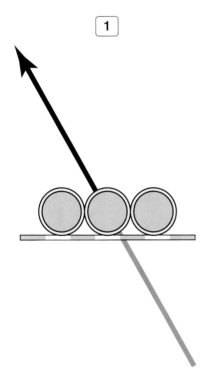

1

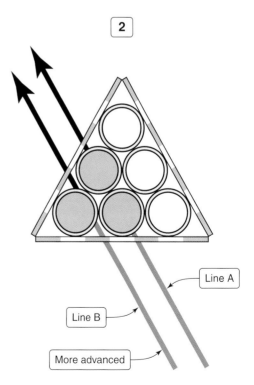

2

Line A

Line B

More advanced

Cross-country safety – the safety position

'I would like to see all riders show their proficiency in the safety position before being allowed to compete. Similarly all horses should be put through a fifth leg training and assessment programme before going across country. These are the safety factors that can make a real difference.'

The exercise

❏ There is a simple way to establish a 'safety' position that is seldom used: it is simply to ride to a bank in a slow trot and jump down.

❏ This allows a rider to concentrate on the second half of the jump, which is where all the difficulties are, and because the speed is slow it gives more time to make the required moves.

❏ The rider's position off the bank will be the same as that required for all drop fences, and indeed for all cross-country fences where one has to expect the unexpected.

What's being achieved

What is required as a priority is a secure position of the lower leg, with the weight going down through the leg, and the line from the middle of the knee down to the ball of the foot remaining perpendicular. Therefore as the horse descends, the rider's feet move in front of the girth. This can be seen in diagram 1.

Unfortunately riders are often not served well by their coaches in the area of drop fences: 'Sit back!' these coaches cry, and their students end up leaning back with their seat in the saddle, and their lower legs moving back, trying to balance themselves. Then the direct contact with the saddle, combined with no leg support, means they are kicked forward by the horse's back, or the force of landing, and end up either on the horse's neck, or on the ground, or, worst of all, in the water (*see* diagram 2). This is why this exercise is needed and why you have to ride with shorter leathers across country.

'It is not necessarily the water fence that is so influential in high level competitions, but the drop down into the water. Many riders lose their balance and are not in a position to steer their horse to the next fence, which is usually only a few strides away.'

What you should be looking for

What riders should do is not think 'back', but instead 'up'. They need to open up the knee and hip joints going down a drop until they are in a sort of dressage position with the weight through the legs and the seat clear of the saddle (*see* diagram 1). As this is done the reins have to be slipped, but not lost, and the rider's suppleness maintained. In this position it is possible to put the foot a little more forward in emergencies for extra security. This is, in fact, just a greater degree of what should happen over the second half of a normal fence. So if the right movement can be established off a bank, it will really help the balance for all types of fence.

What can go wrong?

To begin with riders often feel a little unnatural and stiff with this position, and sometimes fall backwards. But it will quickly feel normal, and then safer. It needs to be done often off a bank at a slow speed, because everything happens so quickly over a normal fence that the right movement is difficult to achieve initially.

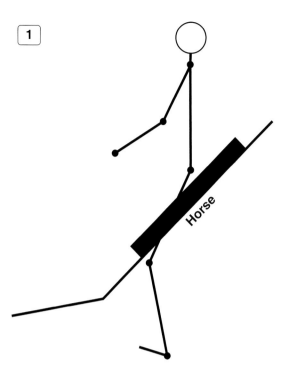

Diagram 1 – A safe position for drop fences. Opening up the angles at the knee and the hip joints and moving into a dressage position without the seat in the saddle. Always keep some angle in the knee joint and remain supple.

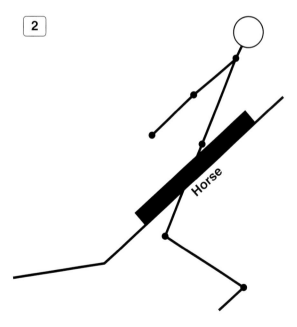

Diagram 2 – An unsafe position for drop fences. Leaning back, ending up siting on the saddle and losing the weight through the lower leg and the position of the lower leg. The rider is invariably pitched forwards from this position.

Role playing: being Tiger Woods for a day

'The use of role playing and modelling is a powerful tool I use to overcome certain problems and to develop the right attitude of mind. It is much easier to use, and more natural to humans than many realize, because role playing and modelling is already used by everyone to some degree in our daily lives.'

Some see themselves as they are and say 'Why?' Others see themselves as they might be and say 'Why not?'

The exercise

The importance of mental preparation for sports is universally recognized, and the need is obvious at all levels in all equestrian activities. For example, many riders fail to produce their best work in competition because of a loss of concentration, the paralyzing effect of tension, or a lack of confidence. An even greater number probably fail to fulfil their potential because of a lack of discipline and motivation on a day-to-day basis at home.

❏ It is almost impossible to go through life without learning, copying and being influenced by those around you, either consciously or unconsciously. My special twist to this basic truth is that you can make this more effective by first identifying what is missing in your mental armoury, and then finding the right role models to improve your performance in these specific areas.

❏ Having identified the mental attributes required, select a role model that you like and know well – often not a famous person. However, because this exercise has to relate to many people, I have chosen Tiger Woods as our role model. Our task is to be Tiger Woods for a day, with the aim of becoming more 'cool, calm and collected'.

❏ The image that most people have of Tiger Woods is of a disciplined, rock solid and unhurried personality, who gets out of bed each day at the same time and does the job with inexorable consistency and persistence, whether in practice or competition. Just by focusing regularly on these qualities the wonderful bonus is that our behaviour will automatically move towards this image. This is a huge achievement for little investment.

❏ To accelerate this process we need to study Tiger further, including his body language, so we can gradually act as though we were him for brief periods when in a situation that calls for his qualities. You might find one mannerism that will trigger all of Tiger's mental qualities, or it may be his walk or the way he holds his head. It will also be helpful to select some key words, such as 'discipline', 'double check', and 'breathe'; and some phrases, such as 'winners succeed by effort not accident', 'measure it twice and cut it once', and 'many strokes fell the tallest oaks'. By putting key words and phrases and pictures of Tiger Woods on cards, in places where you will regularly see them, you will be helped to maintain and practise the Tiger Woods role play.

❏ Like all exercises, regular practice is required if the exercise is to be effective – but you can begin with bite-size sessions. For example, have a 15-minute Tiger Woods session at the start of each day to list your action steps, and decide on your key word and focus for the day. As ever, this will have added value if done with the support and encouragement of a coach.

❏ Tiger is also a very positive person with a 'can do' spirit. A 'can do' spirit also protects us from the paralyzing pessimism that is all too characteristic of

EXPERT TIP

The most powerful determinant of how much we accomplish in life is the level of confidence we have to take on a new challenge, and as a result of our actions, to succeed in it. This is because having this confidence is so self-motivating. What's more, we'll be versatile and tenacious in the face of problems and setbacks, all because we believe in ourselves. It just so happens, of course, that such dynamism, ingenuity and perseverance are key ingredients for progress, and it's largely thanks to them that our confidence then becomes a self-fulfilling prophecy.

anxiety and depression. To establish this attitude of mind use key words such as 'Yes!' 'Forwards!' and 'Courage'. Useful key phrases would be 'winners know they are able', 'play from strength', and 'focus on ability'. The boxer Muhammed Ali was doing a similar thing when he used to say, 'I am the greatest!'

What you should be looking for

You can use your image of Tiger Woods to ensure you carry this positive attitude with you habitually, without cluttering your mind. This is the aim. With regular use of role playing you will find that one image can trigger a wide range of desired qualities. The greatest value of role playing is that gradually you will no longer be role playing, because these attitudes will become an established part of who you are on a daily basis.

After a period of almost uninterrupted success in international competition at Junior and Young Rider level, Pippa Funnell had a difficult beginning to her senior career. Following a long period of disappointment Pippa used a sports psychologist, who emphasized the importance of working from her strengths. As Pippa said: 'It made a huge difference, not only to me but in particular to my horses. I worked from their strengths as well, from the things they could do, rather than what they couldn't do. This has made all the difference.'

Moving on

So how can we cultivate our own self-confidence? By far the most potent method is to set ourselves simple tasks that can be relied upon to give us a taste of success. When we witness ourselves succeed, our confidence takes a turn for the better, and little by little this enables us to reach our goals. This 'small action steps' strategy may not seem like rocket science, but just think what we often do instead: right from the start we either decide we don't have sufficient talent or intelligence, and stay firmly on the couch; or we bite off more than we can chew, drafting overlong 'to do' lists without a plan, and the result is invariably failure. Thus we deny ourselves the satisfaction and self-confidence of knowing that we're in control and can habitually complete tasks successfully.

However, using readily achievable action steps does not mean being without ambition or being aimless. The secret is to first set your long-term aims and plan backwards. Then execute these bite-size steps directed specifically towards achieving your medium-term goals. This stacks the odds in your favour and produces the opposite of a vicious circle. Being confident that we have the internal resources and method to take on a new challenge, we accomplish more, and in turn become more confident.

Good mental preparation should be an integral and long-term part of any training programme. Here we have mentioned just one technique, role playing, with regard to two main areas: being cool, calm and collected; and being confident. But this is just a beginning: the brain has huge untapped potential and powers, and those that harness more of it will achieve more.

What can go wrong?

In any sport, the focus needs to be on both the performer and the performance. Unfortunately, the development of the performer as a well-balanced human being often takes second place. If this happens, the performance will eventually suffer. Whatever the competition level, all performers need to keep their sport in context. There is a time to be a success in your life, and a time for your life to be a success, and the balance between these two aims is of the greatest importance.

If a life is entirely dependent on competitive success, then disappointment is almost inevitable. A performer needs to achieve happily, rather than achieve to be happy. If there is one outstanding characteristic of those who participate successfully in sport, it is that they enjoy themselves. Others, who are even more fortunate, actually love what they do, and it is true to say that if you love what you are doing, nothing is tedious or hard work. The only surprising thing is that enjoyment and the development of an appropriate lifestyle is so often missed in mental preparation programmes. Working out how to look after yourself as a human being is a vital part of your mental preparation programme.

DAVID O'CONNOR

Currently based in The Plains, Virginia, David O'Connor retired from international competition in 2004. He had competed internationally for the United States equestrian team since the 1980s, and some of his major successes occurred in the last four years of his career.

In 2000 he hit the headlines, bringing home from Sydney the first eventing gold medal for the Unites States in more than 25 years. On his horse Custom Made he recorded the best individual eventing score in Olympic history. In 2001 he won his third Rolex Kentucky three-day event on Gilt Edge, when he also came third on Custom Made. Success continued in 2002 when he led the US eventing team to a gold medal in the World Equestrian Games in Spain, and was named Rider of the Year by *USA Equestrian* later that same year. He is also one of only two Americans ever to have won Badminton CCI****, in 1997.

Always involved in the administrative side of the sport, David was re-elected president of the United States Equestrian Federation (USEF) in 2005, and this involves him working closely with the Fédération Équestre International (FEI). He continues to train the Canadian event team as well as his pupils at the O'Connor Event Team (OCET), and has become a cross-country course designer in the US.

Q: What's the best piece of advice you've ever been given in regard to training horses?
The horse doesn't have a goal. He doesn't know what you are working for, he only knows you are working.

Q: What do you do when you come up against a training brick wall?
Put the horse away and think about it on your own – violence starts where knowledge stops. When you don't know where to go, that's when people start to get strong with their horses.

Q: Name three things that you look for when you begin to train a horse.
Co-operation, intelligence, natural athleticism.

Q: What's your training formula?
Trying to understand what the horses think, always looking at it from their point of view.

Q: How do you identify problems in your own performance, and what do you do about them?
When I was competing I found that problems would come up in

competition, and competition will show you where your faults are. Then you have to go home and be very honest about those faults, and go back and work on them.

Q: Aspiring riders once watched you ride and learnt from your techniques. Whose performance do you like to watch?
I like to watch different people for different reasons. Philip Dutton for his cool head and individual technique, William Fox-Pitt for his smoothness, and Toddy (Mark Todd) before that. I enjoyed watching Ian Stark for his great balance and athleticism.

Q: If I were to ask one of your pupils 'What's the thing that David goes on about the most?', what would it be?
Attention to detail and understanding the horse's view.

Q: William Fox-Pitt once said that he was passionate about training young horses. What's your training passion?
Young, or any horses come to that – I try to show the horses what they can do, and not prove to them what they can't do.

Q: Whom do you admire most in the equestrian world?
My mentor, Jack Le Goff, US coach in the 1970s and 1980s, who won a ton of medals, and understood horses from a lot of different angles and was extremely competitive. I admired him for creating a programme in the US from scratch and really creating a whole sport, and for having a huge influence that is still felt today.

Q: And whom do you have to thank for being where you are today?
Jack and Lars Sederholm – they bet on me at a time when I really hadn't proved myself, and gave me a huge base of education.

CONTENTS

End to end

'This is a version of the four corners (Exercise 50) that works on collection and extension for a young horse or more novice rider. It also underlines the first of our four rider responsibilities – direction.'

The exercise

❏ Ride a 20m circle in trot at one end of the school. As you come to the track on the long side, use half-halts to collect your horse.
❏ Come off the circle and down the long side, lengthening the horse's stride.
❏ At the opposite end, using half-halts, collect the horse and ride another 20m circle.
❏ Extend down the next long side and then ride a 20m circle at the far end again.
❏ Repeat on both reins.

What's being achieved

This is an easy first exercise working on collection and extension, but it also helps with direction, and by direction we're talking about exactive riding on a perfect line – the rider has to decide exactly where that line is. The more you ride that way, picking exactly where the horse goes to the inch, the more the ability to do so will be transferred into all of your work – cross-country, show-jumping, everything.

What you should be looking for

The quality of the transitions forwards and backwards is important to this exercise.

What can go wrong?

The most common fault is letting the horse wander. This is your opportunity to work on your direction.

Moving on

Ride the circles in canter, and then progress to the Four Corners, Exercise 50.

THE RIDER RESPONSIBILITIES

A rider has four responsibilities to the horse he or she is riding: direction, speed, rhythm and balance, and seeing a distance, and these form the basis of all the exercises and training that we do.

1. Direction

Can you ride straight down a line that you have picked? We define straightness as thinking about where the hind feet are first, then where the front feet are, and then the head. Most people just think about the head, and the hindquarters swing all over the place.

2. Speed

You have to pick the speed the horse goes at, and not *him*, no matter what you are doing.

3(a) Rhythm

Rhythm is obviously not just the evenness of the tempo but also the quality of the gait, which must stay pure: the trot stays truly two-beat and the canter stays truly three-beat.

3(b) Balance

The horse should always be balanced, but he should also be able to stay in balance at different speeds. His balance will change and improve as he gets trained and becomes better connected.

4. Seeing a distance

You need to learn to see a distance into a fence when jumping; this will build the horse's confidence and help his rhythm and balance.

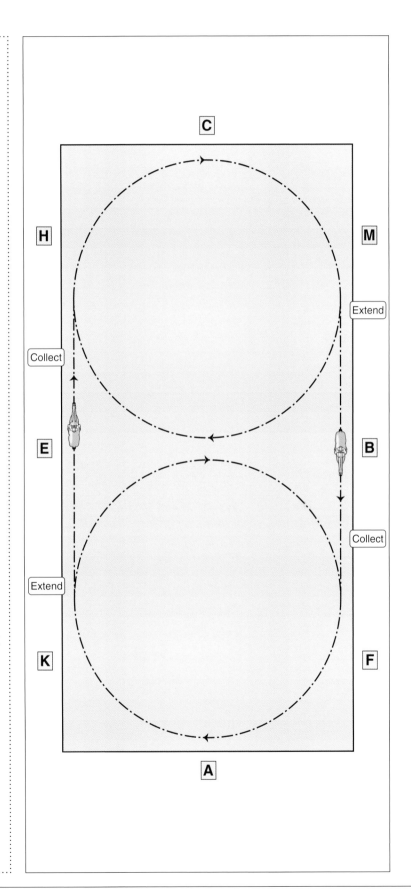

Four corners

'When you're in the ring you want your horse to wait for you, and when you're on the cross-country course it's all about lengthening and shortening – this exercise plays into both.'

The exercise

❏ In each corner of the arena, ride a 10m circle. This can be ridden in either trot or canter, depending on the level of your horse.

❏ During the circles, use half-halts to collect your horse as much as possible – in trot you are almost trying for a passage half step.

❏ As you come out of the circle, lengthen, in either trot or canter, every time you are on a straight side, whether it's the short side or the long side.

What's being achieved

Apart from working on collection and extension, we're getting the horses awake, here, in the corner, building up the impulsion using half-halts. Every time you go in the ring you want your horse to wait for you in the corners, so you're reinforcing that, too.

What you should be looking for

This is a more advanced exercise so you should be looking for the quality of the transition from collection to extension. You also want to get your horse to let go of himself when you are on the long side.

What can go wrong?

Riders don't go forwards enough going down the long side, and end up being a little too 'backwards'.

> **ESTABLISH FORWARDNESS**
>
> Is your horse going forwards enough?
>
> **1.** Check that you are not holding him back with the reins.
>
> **2.** Ensure your seat is sufficiently secure that you can go forwards in balance with your horse.
>
> **3**. Use your legs, voice, spurs and a tap of the whip if necessary to encourage your horse to go forwards.
>
> **4.** Have you warmed-up sufficiently?

Moving on

This exercise can be ridden at any level: if you begin in trot, then progress to canter. The circles can be made smaller, and the collecting in the corners can go all the way to passage (if you are in trot) or cantering on the spot (canter pirouette).

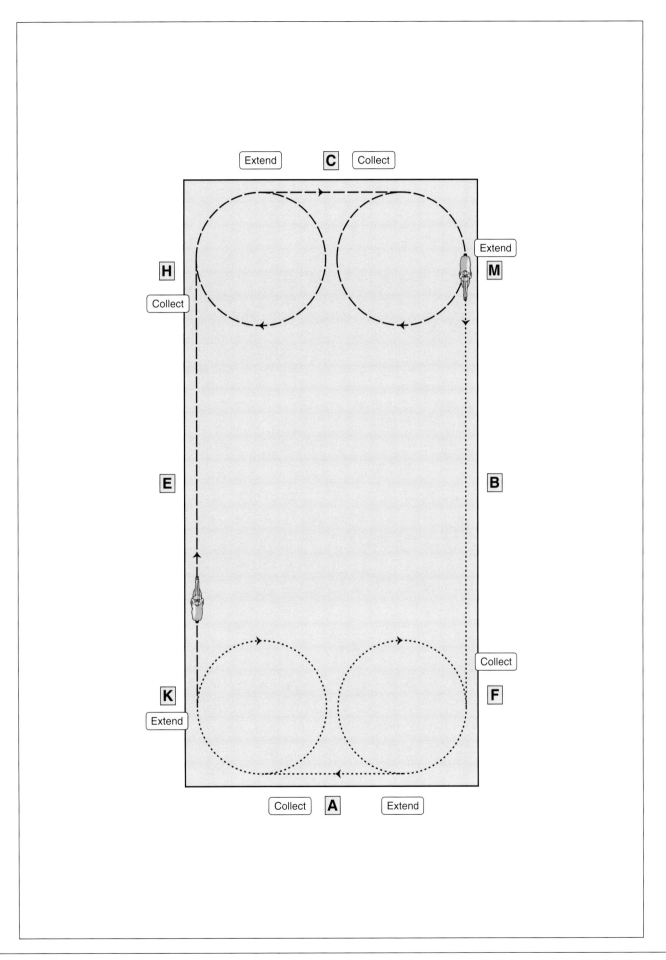

The castle exercise

'We do so much work on the centre line that our horses can get nervous at that turn at A or C. This is a "comfort" exercise.'

'For me, the horse should go forwards and increase its speed on the centre line.'

The exercise

❏ In trot, from just before the final quarter marker on a long side, ride a half 10m circle on to the centre line and then ask your horse to lengthen.

❏ At the opposite end of the school, half-halt to collect your horse, turn right and ride three-quarters of a 10m circle in one corner, across the short side, and three-quarters of a 10m circle in the opposite corner (*see* diagram).

❏ Then lengthen down the centre line in the opposite direction.

What's being achieved

This exercise works on direction and speed, and helps to accustom the horse to working on the centre line without pressure. Your objectives for Exercise 49, End to end, and Exercise 50, Four corners, apply to this exercise.

What you should be looking for

Concentrate on keeping your horse straight, using your legs rather than your hands. To check whether this is happening, give one rein away for a few strides and then take it back, and then do the same with the other rein.

What can go wrong?

Be prepared for your horse to drift off the centre line and correct him, using your legs, before it happens.

Moving on

Try the exercise in canter. Introduce changes of pace within the gait.

ARE YOU SITTING STRAIGHT?

Most problems with straightness of the horse originate from straightness – or lack of it – in the rider. Try this simple test to see whether you are crooked: ride a 20m circle on both reins in trot. Quit your stirrups and take your knees and thighs away from the sides of the horse and the saddle. If you don't fall either way, then you are sitting straight!

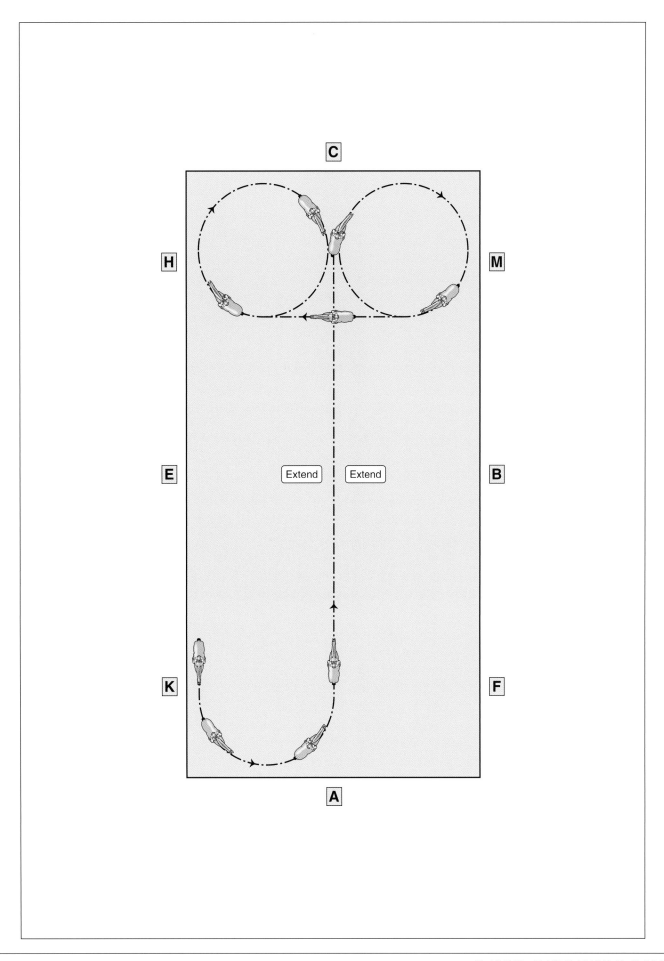

In and out

'In your dressage test, if you have a horse that runs through its corners you spend a couple of strides recovering before you begin the next movement. This exercise will help that tendency.'

EXPERT TIP

Make sure you ride your second transition as your horse comes out of the second corner, before you hit that second board.

The exercise

This exercise is based on Exercise 50, Four corners, in that you collect before, and ride a 10m circle in each corner of the arena.

❏ Establish a good working canter around the arena. As you come into your first corner from the long side, make a downward transition to trot.

❏ Ride a 10m circle in trot. As you come out of the circle, make a transition up into canter once again.

❏ Just before the second corner, make the transition down into trot once again, ride a 10m circle in trot.

❏ Make an upward transition and canter, lengthening, down the long side to repeat the exercise in the remaining corners.

❏ Remember to repeat this on both reins.

What's being achieved

This exercise teaches a horse to wait for your instruction coming out of a corner, and gives you something to push off from for your shoulder-in or your half-pass, or whatever you have to do as you leave the corner.

What you should be looking for

Accuracy in your transitions. You want to make the transition up into canter before your horse comes out of the corner, and into trot as you ride into the next corner.

What can go wrong?

Your horse runs out at the corner – keep practising.

Moving on

Once you've mastered from canter to trot, try canter to walk or even canter to halt.

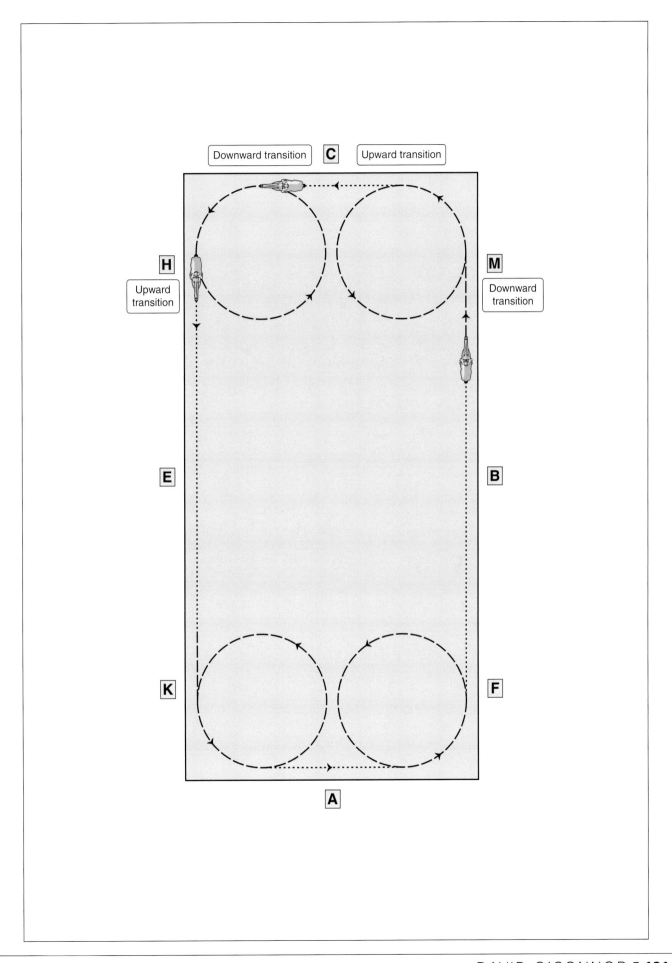

Shape and attention

'So much of our riding in eventing is about jumping a fence with something lower on the other side, like a ditch or water – this exercise is about getting horses to remember there's something on the ground, and keeping their jump in the air.'

The exercise

❏ Set up three oxers, 9.7m (32ft) apart. Start off with them quite low, at a height and width that you know your horse will be confident with, and certainly not wider than 60cm (2ft).

❏ Jump these three oxers in canter to establish that your horse is comfortable and confident with them.

❏ Once your horse is finding the oxers easy, place a take-off rail 2.7m (9ft) in front of each oxer and repeat the exercise.

❏ When he can deal with oxer and take-off rail with ease, the next step is to add a landing rail, 3m (10ft) behind each oxer (*see* diagram).

What's being achieved

This exercise is about the shape of the bascule in the air, and also about making a horse quick and clever with his feet. Ridden well, it is also very good for the confidence of horse and rider.

What you should be looking for

Always begin with the oxer, then add the take-off rail, and after that the landing rail, and make sure you do it in that progression.

What can go wrong?

Make sure your horse has enough footwork – impulsion and flexion – to be able to get his job done.

'Build this exercise up slowly to maintain and improve your horse's confidence.'

Moving on

You can increase the height of the oxers up to 1.13m–1.22m (3ft 9in–4ft), but you must be careful not to overface your horse. You could also raise the take-off and then the landing poles on risers so as to get your horse to pick his feet up a little more, but not more than 15cm (6in).

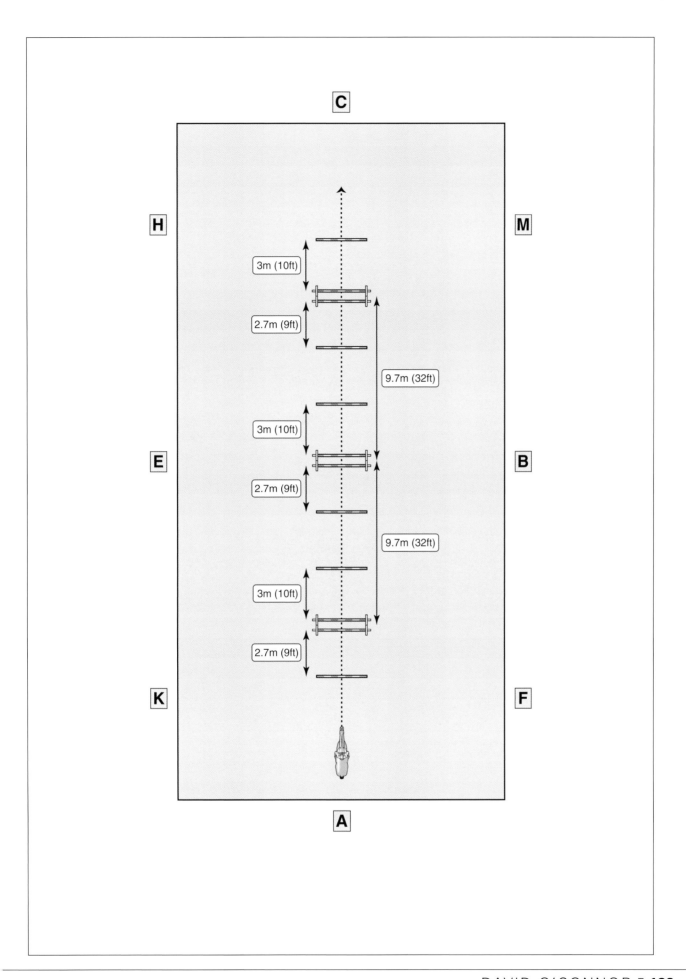

Collecting the strides

'The more collected your horse is in his dressage work, the more he is going to be able to collect between these fences.'

The exercise

❏ Set up a vertical fence and an oxer about 25.6m (84ft) (six canter strides) apart and at a height your horse is confident with.

❏ Establish canter, and jump both fences several times, beginning with six or seven strides in between.

❏ As your horse becomes more confident you should be able to put six, seven, eight, nine, all the way up to twelve strides between the two fences. Novice horses should start at six and seven, and the more advanced horses ought to be able to go to the higher numbers.

What's being achieved

This exercise also teaches your horse to land and be waiting for you, not just land and run off.

What you should be looking for

You should be able to follow the same collected canter that you have in your flatwork.

What can go wrong?

People either push their horses on a bit too far, or when they take back the rein they take back too much and the horse breaks into a trot. When you check back, you should use your legs and keep the horse's feet going.

'The rules are, the slower you go, the faster the feet have to go. The slower the pace the horse is travelling at, the faster his feet have to go – more energy and collection than going forward.'

COLLECTION IN CANTER

❏ Whilst continuing to ride your horse forwards, use half-halts to gradually shorten your horse's stride. This will cause the hind legs to engage and to take the weight being transferred back to them.

❏ Remember to do your half-halts in time with the canter stride.

❏ The more advanced your horse is, the less you should need to use your hands to collect your horse.

❏ If you shorten your horse by use of the reins alone the result will be a tense, shuffling, four-time canter.

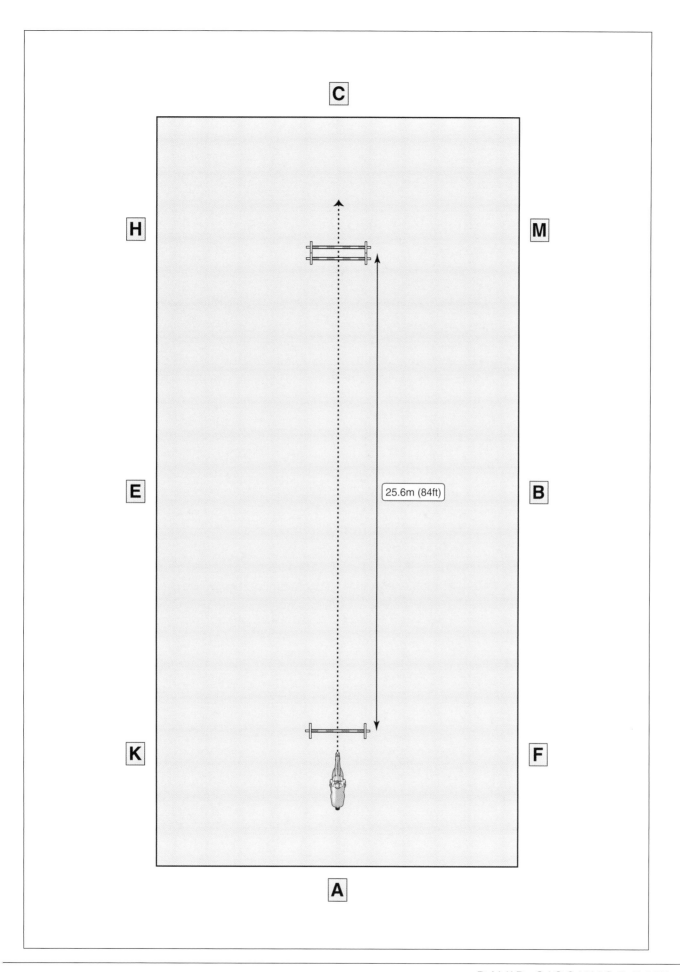

25.6m (84ft)

Counter bending

'In this exercise, the younger horses would go from shoulder-out to straight, and the more advanced horses would go from shoulder-out to shoulder-in.'

The exercise

❏ This exercise is based on Exercise 50, Four corners, collecting and riding a 10m circle in a corner, and lengthening down the long sides.

❏ Establish trot, and begin with a 10m circle in your first corner, before a long side.

❏ As you come out of your corner ask for a counter bend (shoulder-out) and then lengthen down the long side.

❏ As you collect for the corner, if you are riding a young or novice horse, straighten up, but if your horse is more advanced, ask for shoulder-in as you collect.

❏ Ride straight across the short side of the school and then repeat the exercise in the next corner.

❏ Repeat on the opposite long side and on both reins.

What's being achieved

This exercise achieves flexibility and flexion. It opens up the horse's inside hind leg, and lets it travel a little further. The shoulder-in work encourages the hind leg to move in a more circular motion.

What you should be looking for

You are also looking for your horse to be able to change speed, change flexion and stay on the line – that takes quite a lot!

What can go wrong?

Make sure that you are moving the shoulders one way or another, but that the haunches don't swing – you are not pushing the haunches around.

Moving on

Ride the exercise in canter. We usually do this exercise in canter, because in trot shoulder-out and shoulder-in actually do the same thing physically, working the horse symmetrically, one side and then the other. In the canter, however, it's different because of the lead.

'This exercise has great benefits for the eventer – it improves flexibility behind which is a big deal, and the control necessary makes people very, very aware of where the hindquarters are.'

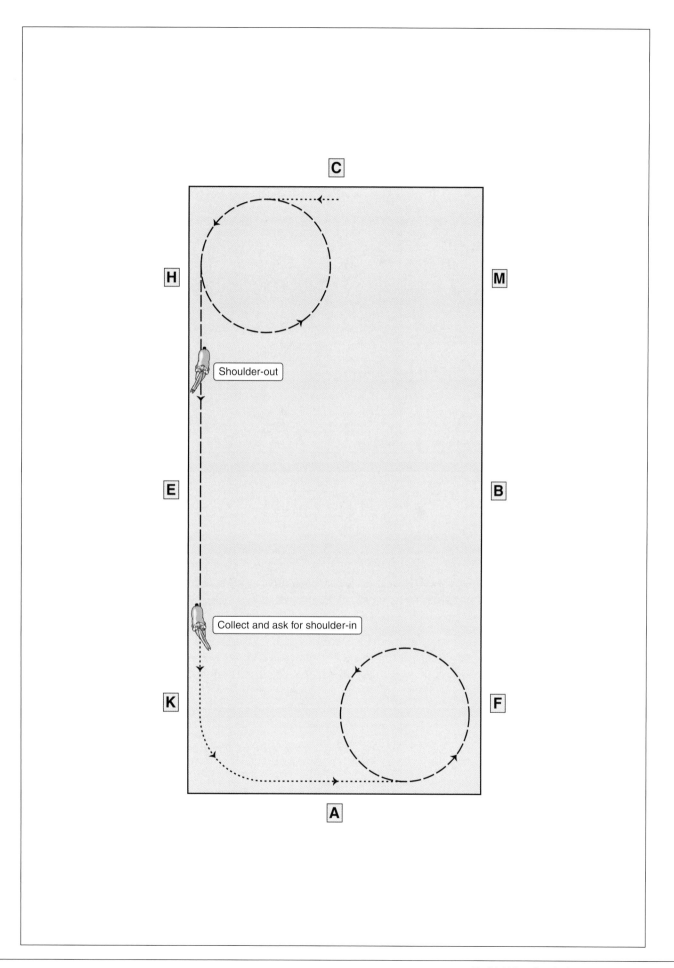

C

H

M

Shoulder-out

E

B

Collect and ask for shoulder-in

K

F

A

SANDY PHILLIPS

Sandy Phillips' training 'passion' is in teaching riders: 'I had such a hard time getting where I am myself that I try to make it easier for others.' This philosophy comes through in her exercises that cut to the quick of a problem or situation, and present a solution that makes everything sound possible. Her mantra is 'a rider must learn to ride from behind, forward into the contact', and is repeated time and again as the crux of what goes wrong – but behind the apparent simplicity of her training ideas, is a deep understanding of the mechanics of the horse in dressage.

Sandy has been with horses all her life. In 1968, aged four, she learned to ride Western style on her grandparent's cattle ranch; later, when she was at boarding school in Connecticut, she began competing in horse trials. In 1981 she finished second at Badminton. The following year she was selected to ride for the USA dressage team, and when the team went to Germany to train, Sandy worked with the legendary Georg Theodorescu, and remained training with him in Germany for five years. She competed internationally for the United States at two World Equestrian Games, and at the Olympics in 1984.

She continued to event, and didn't give up riding in horse trials until 1994 – at this point in her career she had been competing in two disciplines at international level for 14 years. She married Captain Mark Phillips, and took British citizenship in 1996; at the time of writing they live in Cherington, Gloucestershire. She represented Britain in the 1998 World Equestrian Games, and the 1999 European Championships.

Sandy was a senior selector for British Dressage, but relinquished this role in early 2006 so that she could compete herself – and in the same year she was selected to represent Britain for the second time at a World Equestrian Games, riding her 12-year-old, 17hh, German-bred mare Lara 106; the team came sixth. In September 2006 Sandy became British National Dressage Champion.

Q: What's the best piece of advice you've ever been given?
Georg Theodorescu told me that the horse's shoulder should always be in front of the quarters.

Q: What do you do when you hit a training 'brick wall'?
I don't come up against these because I think they are the result of lack of understanding either on the rider's or the horse's part. You get to the point where you are not in communication, and you have to go back to basics – start at walk again.

Q: How do you identify your training problems?
I learn a lot from the horse. Our horses tend to go in the same way because we make the same mistakes. Then I have my 'eyes on the ground' and video.

Q: What are you working on at present?
Something I always have to work on is straightness, my straightness and my horse's straightness.

Q: Whose performance do you watch?
Hubertus Schmidt and Anky (van Grunsven).

Q: And whom do you most admire in the equine world?
Hubertus Schmidt – he can ride any horse and doesn't have a coach.

Q: What sort of horses do you like?
Hot horses!

Q: What's the thing you go on about the most to your pupils?
Get your horse working forward into the contact.

Q: What do you look for when you begin to train a horse?
A willingness to go forward, a willingness to work with the rider, and athleticism.

Q: Can you recall your last equine 'magic moment'?
Every time I ride passage on my horse, Lara.

CONTENTS

Learning to regulate speed

'My overall premise is that the rider must learn to ride from behind, forward into the contact, and that's what this exercise establishes.'

The exercise

You will need a helper on the ground for this one.

❏ On a 20m circle establish a working rising trot. Ride a couple of circuits concentrating on, and feeling, the connection between your calf and seat and your horse's gaits.

❏ Now, take your horse with you and rise in a slower rhythm; this will improve your horse's rhythm, which will become more defined. Then rise quicker and 'bigger' and your horse will improve his cadence with a more ground-covering stride. You will discover you are able to shorten and lengthen your horse's strides by how you rise in the saddle. It's quite a revelation!

❏ Next ask your helper on the ground to tell you when the left and right hind legs hit the ground, and try to feel this movement. See if you can call out the steps yourself through all three phases of the trot.

❏ Practise changing speed for half and quarter circles – and don't forget to try this on both reins.

'Most riders don't feel, they think.'

What's being achieved

We begin this exercise in rising trot because in this gait, as the horse goes forward, it's easy to feel what's going on behind the saddle. When they sit, most riders tense against the movement, and so by feeling they learn to go with the movement rather than against it.

What you should be looking for

In this case, speed really means tempo, rhythm and cadence according to the gait. The bigger trot should not be accompanied by, on the rider's part, flapping legs or loss of balance, and the smaller trot should not be a poor attempt at sitting trot. It is important to be sure that the horse works from behind forward into the contact, rather than from the mouth backwards.

Moving on

This exercise can be ridden in canter or walk.

'You can regulate the speed at which the horse trots by how you, the rider, ride. What I often find when I teach is that riders follow what their horse does instead of dictating what the horse should do themselves.'

Riding spiralling circles – properly

'This works in all gaits from Novice to Grand Prix – I do it with my Grand Prix horse, Lara.'

The exercise

This sounds really simple, but it is actually so hard.

❑ Begin in trot on a 20m circle, and develop a 10m circle from that.

❑ Spiral out using the inside leg, going 10m, 12m, 14m, 16m, 18m and 20m, and controlling the tempo step by step.

❑ Now spiral in, using the outside leg, from 20m to 18m, 16m, 14m, 12m and 10m. If ridden correctly this is extremely difficult. Most people will make the circle smaller too quickly, going from 20m to 12m.

❑ Look at the centre of the circle and feel what is happening behind the saddle.

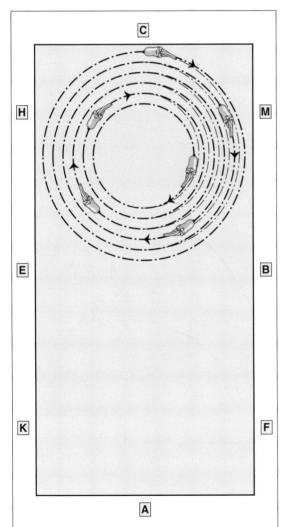

What you should be looking for

Your horse should maintain a uniform bend through his spine, without twisting or tilting his head; his hind feet should step into the imprint of the front feet. He should accept the aids from your inside and outside leg throughout

What can go wrong?

The rider has to be in control of the tempo, rhythm and engagement. This can only happen if the horse is ridden forwards from behind, otherwise the horse will quicken his step, lose engagement and stiffen against the bend.

Moving on

You can make this exercise as hard or as easy as you want. You could try riding it in canter, or working on smaller circles and towards pirouettes.

Quick transitions

'You can ride these transitions in any variation you want.'

TIP

Use this exercise to identify whether your horse's weakness is with downward or upward transitions, and then focus more intently on your aids for that transition.

The exercise

❏ Ride a square or rectangle either 20m x 20m for a novice horse, or about 18m x 20m, in the long arena, using the VP markers and the track if you are beginning at the A end, and the SR markers if you are starting at the C end (*see* diagram below).

❏ At each corner, ride a downward transition as you come into the corner and before you make the turn, and then an upward transition after the turn and as you ride out of the corner.

❏ You can now vary your transitions, doing them in walk/halt, walk/canter, trot/canter, or any variation you want.

❏ Try riding different transitions at opposite corners of your square, and repeat the exercise on both reins.

What's being achieved

This exercise teaches riders to make their aids quicker and more effective, with the horse becoming much more responsive. The transitions will improve your horse's suppleness and engagement.

DRESSAGE ARENAS

There are two sizes of dressage arena in use for competition, the 20m x 40m and the 20m x 60m. The former tends to be used up to Novice level and the latter for higher levels (although there are now Preliminary and Novice tests designed for the long arena). The quarter markers are always 6m in from the corner, the distance between the other markers being 14m on the smaller arena and 12m on the larger.

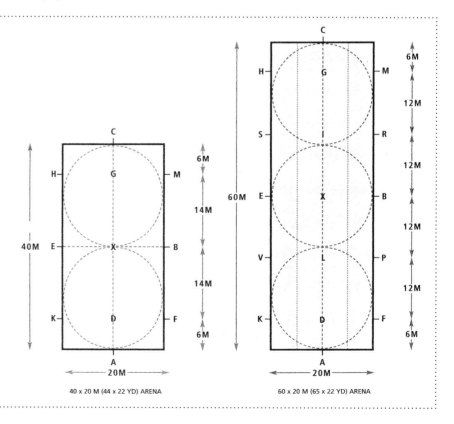

40 x 20 M (44 x 22 YD) ARENA

60 x 20 M (65 x 22 YD) ARENA

What can go wrong?

Be careful not to stiffen against the movement as you go into the downward transition, as this can prevent your horse from working properly through the back (that is, his hind legs will not remain active).

Moving on

Reduce the size of your square or rectangle using the corner and the half way markers (for example, if you are working at the A end of the school, ride the VLDA line as one half of your rectangle) and using jump poles to create an edge. The transitions will now come up very fast.

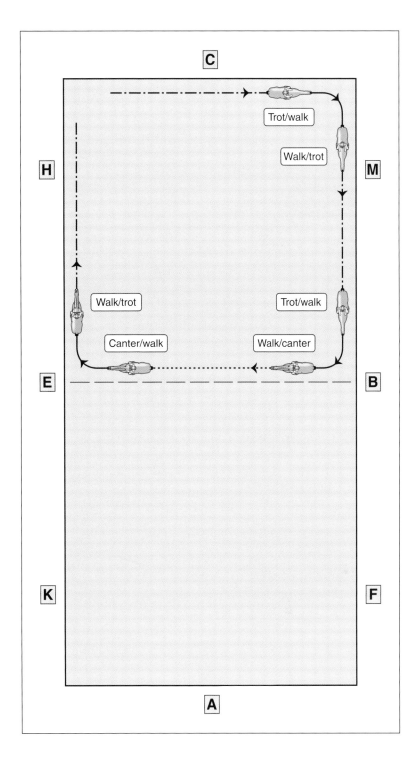

Rein-back and pirouettes

'This exercise is all about riding forward and connecting into the rein.'

EXPERT TIP

It is common to see riders coming against the movement when doing half pirouette: you must produce a balance that enables you to ride forward into the movement.

The exercise

❏ Establish a good walk. At a selected point on the track, ride into halt, then walk forward a step, and ride a half pirouette in walk.

❏ Come out of the pirouette, walk forward a stride, and then rein-back, and from the rein-back walk forward a stride, and then pirouette and so on.

❏ Introduce pirouettes and rein-backs at various points around the school, depending on what your horse needs. You can introduce trot or canter out of the rein-back, and always ride your pirouette from an upward transition.

❏ Repeat this several times and on both reins.

What's being achieved

This exercise teaches the horse to really shift its weight back and collect, but to stay forwards into the rein. You begin in halt, because the rider and horse are balanced. The pirouette engages the horse, and the rein-back engages it more.

What you should be looking for

Make sure that your horse maintains his rhythm throughout. He should transfer his weight from the forehand to his hindquarters in order to make the turn through the pirouette, enabling him to free his shoulders and feel more uphill, which will give him more 'air time' with the front legs.

What can go wrong?

If your horse gets 'stuck behind' – that is, he loses the walk sequence – ride the pirouette a little bigger so that you both have the feeling that you can go forward.

'Remember you are riding forward, going from leg to hand and not back from the hand.'

Moving on

Now take the exercise into canter and do canter pirouettes. For example, ride a walk pirouette, rein back, canter, rein back, canter and canter pirouette.

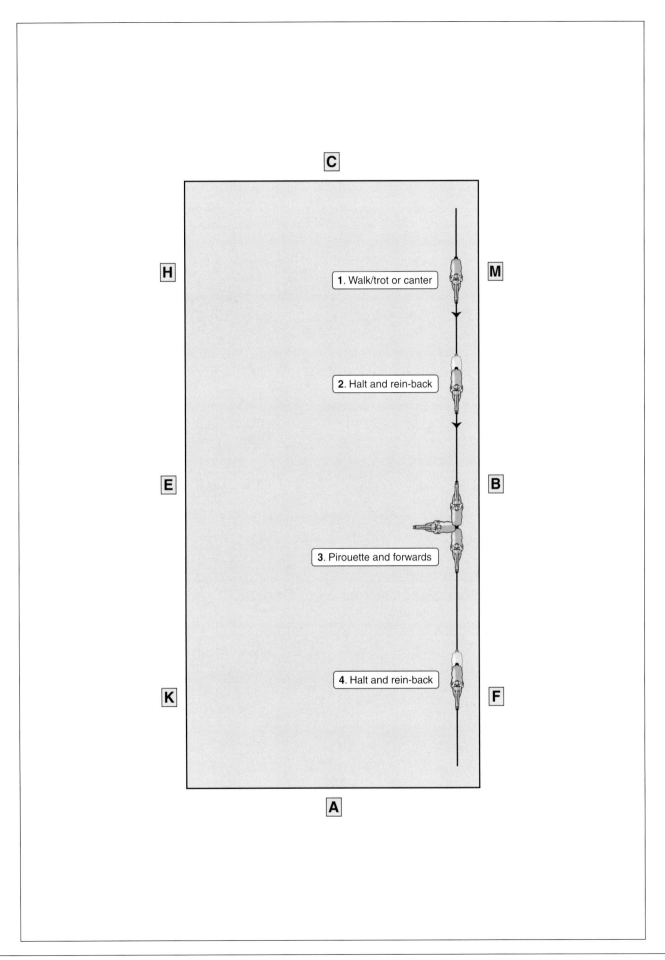

Riding half-pass

'Remember to keep riding your horse through from behind throughout this exercise and you won't have to worry about bend and impulsion – they'll come automatically.'

The exercise

❑ In trot, and from the quarter marker at the beginning of one long side of the school, ride a half-pass towards X.

❑ At X, leg-yield back to the final quarter marker on the original side of the school.

❑ Ride shoulder-in through the corner and the short side, and then …

❑ … repeat on the opposite side of the school and on the other rein.

What's being achieved

Any movement that asks the horse to move sideways and forwards will improve his agility and suppleness, and his response to your leg aids.

What you should be looking for

Remember in half-pass:

❑ the forward movement should always take priority over the sideways movement;

❑ half-pass is easier in a collected trot or canter as you have the necessary impulsion and engagement suited to this exercise;

❑ keep your horse bent around your inside leg.

What can go wrong?

If you don't get the bend you want, you don't get the compliance you want. At the end of the leg-yield you will rejoin the track and it is easy to establish a shoulder-in position. Riding shoulder-in through the corner and the short side makes the horse engage and bend even more, and so you then ride the exercise again from the opposite side of the school. If you have trouble with this exercise, go back to Exercise 56, working on controlling your horse's tempo.

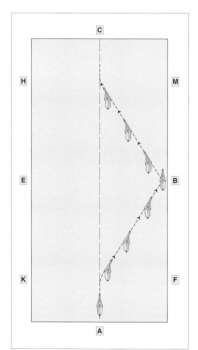

Moving on

Now try this exercise, making the change from half-pass right to half-pass left:

❑ On the right rein, come up the centre line in trot.

❑ Ride half-pass right, joining the track at the half-way mark, and then…

❑ …ask for half-pass left back to the centre line.

When training, whatever horse I have, I try to let it reach its full potential by the development of strength, suppleness, energy and relaxation.'

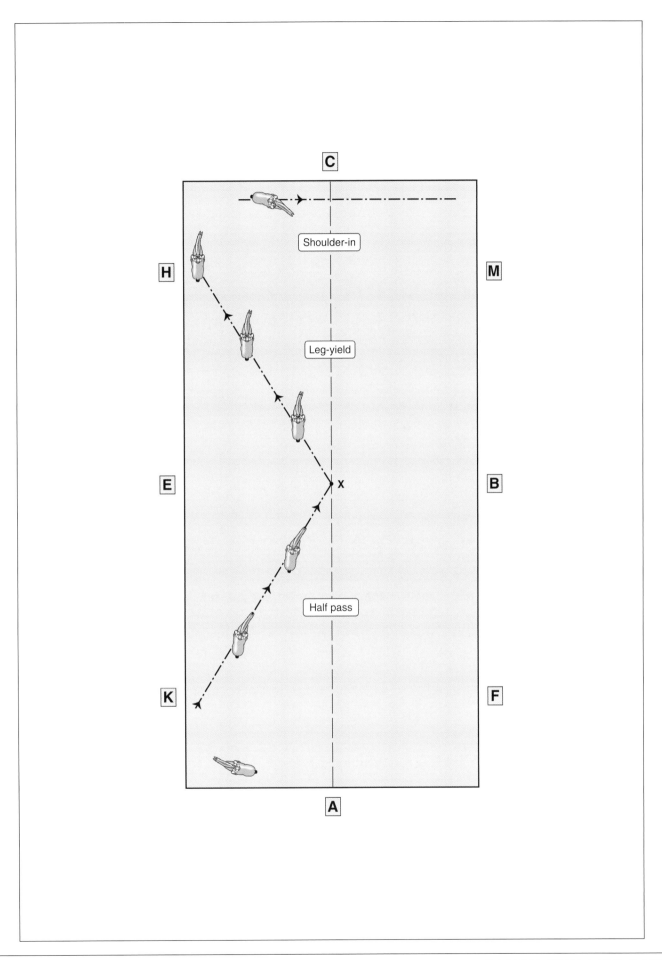

C

Shoulder-in

H

M

Leg-yield

E

X

B

Half pass

K

F

A

61

Changes in pace at the markers

'This exercise is all about the quality of the trot and canter.'

The exercise

This works best in a 20m x 60m arena where the markers come at 12m intervals and you have the possibility of five changes down the long side. However, it can also work in a 20m x 40m arena. Avoid going into a lengthened stride as you come into a corner.

❏ Establish a good working trot and come out of the corner on to the long side in working trot/collection, depending on the horse's level. Then, at every marker change the pace, alternating between a collected, working and lengthening pace.

❏ If you start in collection, lengthen the stride at the first marker, collect again at the next, lengthen the stride at the following one, collect again, and so on.

❏ Repeat on both reins.

What's being achieved

Changes of pace within a gait will make your horse really listen to your aids, therefore becoming more responsive and helping to increase his engagement. The periods of collection between each change really help the horse to gather his hind legs up beneath him ready for the next transition.

What you should be looking for

Be sure that you have your horse in front of your leg so that the transitions are made from behind with rhythm and engagement, not just running.

What can go wrong?

❏ Your horse may try to hollow: be sure to keep him working through from behind and not from the mouth backwards.

❏ A forward-going horse may be a bit reluctant to come back to collection after lengthening. You can position him in shoulder-fore to help him engage.

Moving on

Once you have established this exercise in trot, you could try working in canter, too.

WORKING, COLLECTED AND LENGTHENED PACES

Within walk, trot and canter the basic paces are known as medium walk, working trot and working canter. From this it is possible in each gait to collect or lengthen the stride. The important thing is to maintain the quality of the pace, and not to collect from the front end backwards or to attempt to rush the horse forwards into a lengthened stride. Extension, or extended strides, is introduced beyond Novice level.

To go to lengthened strides from a working or medium pace, your horse will need to first shorten the length of his strides. This can be taught via small circles and shoulder-in exercises that help transfer his balance from the forehand to the hindquarters. Once this transference of balance has begun (and via his training the horse shifts his balance back from the natural position – which is on his forehand – through the saddle to his hindquarters), then a horse is ready to work on lengthening. If your horse is on his forehand there is no point in trying to do lengthened strides.

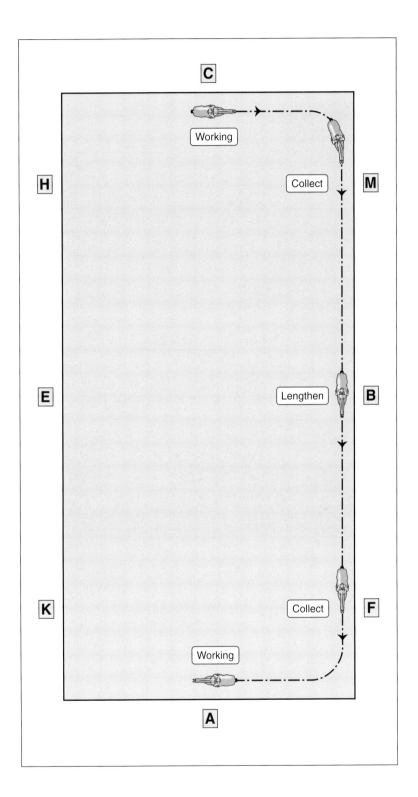

62

Simple changes on alternate leads

'Flying changes are easy to do if you have a canter that is really good.'

'It is very easy to take the front back, but the front needs to be where the front is, and you ride the back end forwards.'

The exercise

- ❏ To ride this exercise, establish a good collected canter on the right rein.
- ❏ When your horse is accepting your half-halts and feels balanced, make a transition to walk for two steps, then canter left three strides, make a transition to walk for two steps, canter right three strides and so on.
- ❏ I do this down the long side of the arena until my horse finds the transitions easy. Then (if I am on right rein) when I am in the last canter left, I ask for a flying change instead of a transition to walk.

EXPERT TIP

So as to ride a smooth transition, whatever transition it may be, make sure that, when you look down, your hands are in front of you, and when you make the half-halt, your hands do not move backwards. Ride forward into your hands and you make the transition easier.

What's being achieved

This exercise helps to affirm the aids in the horse's mind, and develops an active balanced canter. Because they are sure about the aids, they are engaged and in balance so the change should be effortless.

What you should be looking for

As you did in Exercise 56, feel and call out, if necessary, the three strides of canter, the two strides of walk, the three strides of canter. This is all about developing an active canter.

What can go wrong?

- ❏ If your horse breaks into trot when you ask for the transition from canter to walk, work on collecting him in canter and then riding on again without the walk transition until he understands what you are asking of him.
- ❏ If your horse anticipates the flying change and increases his speed, the change will be late behind. Transitions on a circle from counter canter to true canter via simple changes will slow him down.

WHAT DOES 'DISUNITED' MEAN?

This expression is used when your horse changes his lead only in front or behind. You have two courses of action if this happens:

- ❏ Halt and strike off in canter again on the original leg. Then ask for the change.
- ❏ If your horse is particularly stubborn, or not responding to your aids, try asking for a change back to the original lead and then for the flying change one more time. Don't forget to make much of him if he achieves this.

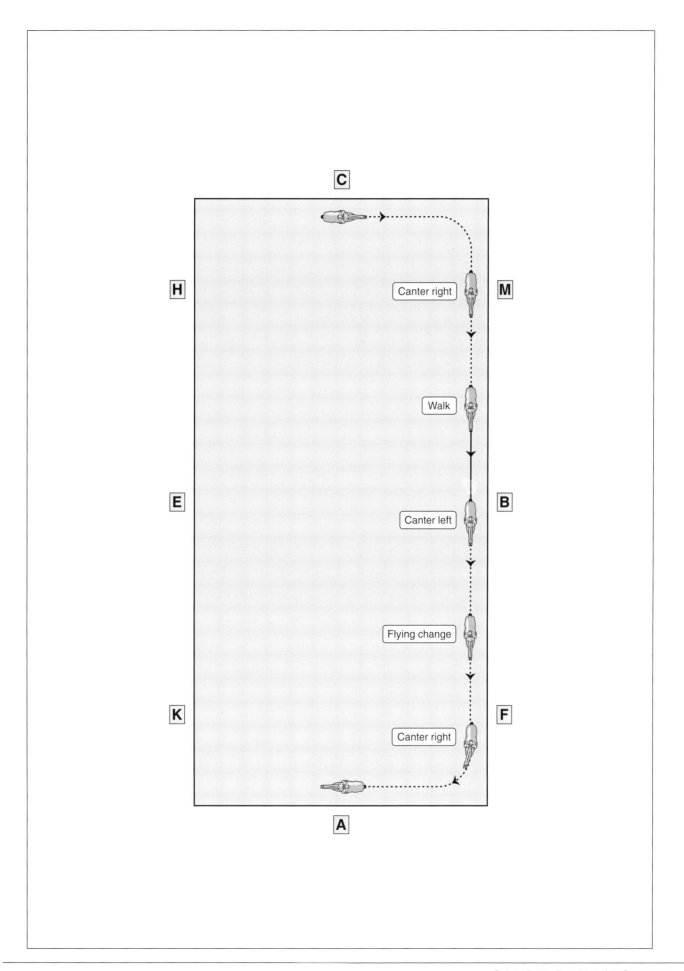

Counter canter to straighten a horse up

'Straightness is a big problem with every horse. Try this exercise to help – you can really feel the straightness.'

The exercise

❏ If your horse tends to fall out through the right shoulder when cantering on the left lead in counter canter, try this exercise on the left rein, and vice versa.

❏ Along the long side of the school, proceed in counter canter and concentrate on the front of the horse (nose and shoulders) going forward to the wall, so that the shoulders of the horse are in line with the haunches – then the horse is straight.

❏ Ride this exercise on both reins as a general exercise for improving straightness.

'I use a lot of counter canter. To me this is a tremendous tool.'

What's being achieved

Your horse will eventually have to bring his inside hind leg forward under the weight to make himself straight.

What you should be looking for

Your horse's forehand should be in line with the hindquarters.

EXPERT TIP

The problem with most counter canter is when cantering left, your horse falls on the right shoulder, so you need to put your right leg back and use your seat to move him to the left, to make him straight.

Moving on

Continue down the straight side in this exercise, but when you get to the corner collect into a very collected canter, as you would do for a pirouette. Then move on along the short side, and then collect again in the next corner, and then move on along the long side and then collect again in the far corner.

STRAIGHTNESS

Most horses tend to be bent to one side or the other. Like humans, this is partially due to a natural disposition, aided by the fact that because the front end is narrower than the hindquarters this naturally encourages crookedness one way or another.

So why do we need our horses to be straight?

❏ If the horse is straight, his weight is evenly distributed, and this ensures that wear and tear does not happen particularly on one side, and that, during training, muscles develop evenly.

❏ The horse is then able to push forward equally efficiently with both hind legs.

❏ The rider can use the aids properly.

❏ The horse can have an even contact on both reins.

❏ The horse is able to collect, as it has to be straight to transfer weight from the forehand to the hindquarters.

GUENTER SEIDEL

Guenter Seidel's passion for the ability and flair of the horse as it is expressed through dressage movement, and his compassion for the difficulties rider and horse encounter, is apparent as he talks about training. Trained himself as a classical rider, Guenter is three times an Olympic medallist, riding for the United States; in his own riding he is renowned for his inimitably quiet style in leg and hand.

At the time of writing, Guenter lives in Cardiff-by-the-sea, California, although he is a native German. He didn't begin to compete on the international stage until 1995. Whilst holidaying in southern California in 1985, Guenter was impressed with the area's commitment to equestrian sport, and decided to relocate. He spent many years training dressage riders and horses before beginning his own competitive career at the Pan Am Games in Buenos Aires, achieving an individual fourth place. Nominated for his third World Equestrian Games, in 2006 in Aachen, at the age of 46, Guenter rode his then 14-year-old Bavarian gelding, Aragon, on which he came individual 14th at the 2004 Olympics held in Athens. In Aachen he won team bronze and came 13th in the Grand Prix Kur.

Q: What's the best piece of advice you've ever been given?
Be fair and patient.

Q: What do you do when you hit a training 'brick wall'?
Rethink how I got there and try to fix the problem.

Q: Do you have a training 'formula'?
Yes: listen to the horse, and be patient.

Q: How do you identify your training problems?
I use video tape to see the problems, people on the ground and teachers.

Q: And what are you working on at present?
I am always working on trying to be a better rider.

Q: Whose performance do you watch?
You can learn from every rider, especially from their mistakes; I like to watch Klaus Balkenhol, Anky van Grunsven and Kyra Krykland, but I can watch anyone and learn from their mistakes and successes.

Q: And whom do you most admire in the equine world?
Conrad Schumacher and Klaus Balkenhol.

Q: What sort of horses do you like?
Horses that have a lot of go by themselves – even a little too much.

Q: And what do you look for when you get on a horse for the first time?
Balance and the desire to move forwards.

Q: What is your training passion?
To make each horse as good as it can be that day. To get on a horse and help it have a good experience that day, so that we're both happy – we're both satisfied with the lesson at the end.

CONTENTS

Leg-yielding on to a circle

'This is a great exercise for loosening up young or older horses.'

TIP

Try to keep the same balance and tempo throughout the whole of this exercise.

The exercise
❏ First work your horse in.
❏ Beginning at the long side of the school, and in trot, leg-yield across the school towards the centre line.
❏ From the centre line, turn on to a 15m circle, allowing the horse to stretch a little bit. (If your arena is only 20m wide, you will have to leg-yield to the three-quarter line.) Now pick him up again and go straight ahead to change the rein.
❏ Do the same from each side of your schooling area. This could be done as easily in large arenas or on grass.

What's being achieved?
This is a very good suppling and loosening up exercise. After the leg-yield, when the horse goes on the circle and stretches, it shows you that he is still thinking forward, that he is round and relaxed, and that you have kept your overall 'throughness'.

What you should be looking for
Make sure that your horse is off the leg, moving sideways, and that he stays working through the back and reaching forwards.

What can go wrong?
Your horse will probably have one side on which it is easier for him to keep rhythm than on the other, or one side on which he tends to lead with, or trail the haunches. It is normal for a horse to have one side that is easier than the other. What you want to work on is that they are even.

Moving on
1. Make your circle smaller and ride this exercise on a 10m circle.
2. From the leg-yield, stay on the circle and in collection. When you and your horse are ready – that is, progressing in an even balance and tempo – ride out of the circle in shoulder-in, initially, progressing to haunches-in and also to half-pass.

Diagram labels: C, H, M, E, B, K, F, A, 10m, 10m, 15m, 15m circle, 14m

Trot-to-walk transitions

'I like to start off these exercises on a bending line on a circle.'

The exercise

❑ Once your horse is warmed up and working in collection, go on to a 20m circle in trot and ask for the transition from trot to walk. Begin with two or three transitions evenly spaced around the circle, and as your horse becomes more responsive to your aids, increase the number of transitions and vary the number of strides between them.

❑ Your horse must stay elastic, working through his back, and be even in the rein and in the contact.

❑ Your aim is for the transition to become very easy and effortless, and there has to be praise after a good response.

❑ Remember to work on both reins.

What's being achieved?

These transitions are the simplest way to develop an awareness of response to your aids, and it's impossible to go wrong with them.

What you should be looking for

Make sure that your horse stays in the frame you want him to be in, depending on the level you are working at and what kind of collection you are working on. It is important that the horse comes back easily and goes back into trot easily. If that doesn't happen you need to sharpen up your horse's response to your aids.

> **SHARPENING UP YOUR AIDS**
>
> When the horse is not responding, don't get stronger on your aids, get quicker. Often, if you use a stronger aid, the horse actually gets duller. This doesn't mean that once in a while a horse doesn't need a stronger half-halt or a stronger kick, but it has to be sharp and quick. It is very important that you praise your horse after it responds correctly and let it know that that was a good reaction. The next time, try to do it with a lot less effort on your part.

Moving on

At the beginning, I think it is easier to do this with the horse in trot/walk, as it is easier for a younger horse to understand the quickness of the response required. Later there is piaffe and passage to get them quicker.

Playing with walk pirouettes

'I like to play around with walk pirouettes, introducing working pirouettes and working walking pirouettes. You can use this exercise to sharpen the horse that is lazy, and also to relax the horse that gets too eager.'

'Sometimes, to ride very, very good walk pirouettes shows the true colours of a horse.'

The exercise

❏ Established a good collected walk, and introduce walk pirouettes somewhere around the centre line of the school.

❏ Work with walk pirouettes until you are satisfied that your horse is loose and responsive in and out of the pirouette.

❏ Now canter on into a working pirouette and then back down a pace to a working walk pirouette.

❏ Ride out of the pirouette in collected walk.

❏ Play with walk pirouettes, working pirouettes, and working walk pirouettes around the arena at different points.

❏ These transitions will help a horse that constantly comes back at you and wants to make the pirouette too small, or one that wants to be too big, goes out, and will not come back to you.

What you should be looking for

You don't want to see any change in the balance from the collected walk going into the walk pirouette. Keep a perfect rhythm. Keep it active from the hind leg and with the correct bend – no tilt in the head.

In walk and canter pirouettes, it is important to get that quick response that helps to keep the pirouette active.

What can go wrong?

If your horse starts getting behind your leg when you do the canter, it is anticipating the walk and then, of course, you need to be in the canter stage a little longer. Also, make sure you are not making the pirouette too small.

If your horse anticipates the walk and gets lazy, then you're approaching the exercise in the wrong way. You need to make sure you're keeping the pirouette big enough. Keep the whole exercise less collected and more in front of you – just keep the idea of what you are trying to achieve in your mind. However, you make some horses active and they get a little hectic. For these horses, putting in the transition to the walk and doing a walk pirouette again will help to calm them down without losing impulsion. This works for horses that are lazy as well as horses that are too hyper and maybe get a little tense.

TO GET YOU STARTED

1. Establish a collected walk.
2. Down the centre line introduce walk pirouettes at varying points until you are satisfied that your horse is 'loose and responsive both in and out of the pirouette'.
3. When you are ready, ride out of the walk pirouette, make a transition to canter and introduce a working pirouette at an appropriate part of the school or arena.
4. On the working pirouette, introduce a transition back to walk and continue on a working walk pirouette.
5. Reduce this to a walk pirouette. Continue to ride walk pirouettes as long as it takes to get your horse in an even rhythm and 'loose and responsive in and out of the pirouette' once again.

EXPLANATION OF THE WORKING PIROUETTE

❏ A working pirouette is a canter pirouette with the hind legs describing a larger circle than for the regular canter pirouette.

❏ To ride canter pirouettes, your horse must be comfortable with a high degree of collection in canter and be able to ride half-pass in canter on both reins.

❏ To establish a working pirouette, canter your horse in travers on a small circle. (If he begins to lose impulsion, increase the size of the circle again.)

❏ From this he can progress into a working pirouette with the size of the circle decreased as he takes additional weight on to his quarters.

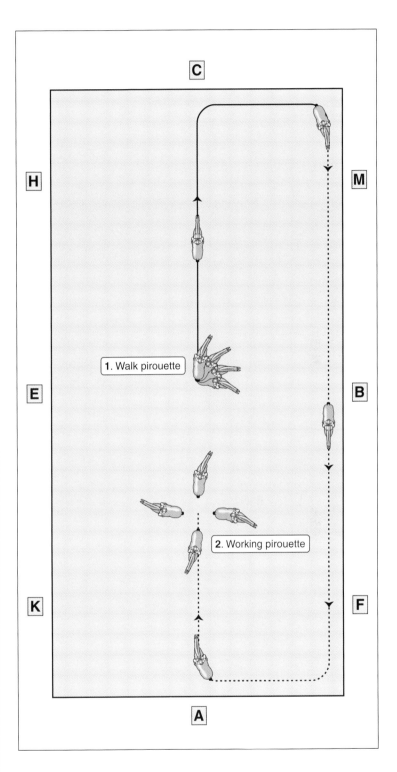

1. Walk pirouette

2. Working pirouette

Canter/walk transitions to teach counter canter

'For some horses, this is easy and no big deal at all – they do it effortlessly from the beginning, but for the others this exercise is very, very helpful.'

The exercise

❏ Begin by working on canter/walk transitions on the inner track.

❏ When you have a fairly good working canter and a good transition, and your horse knows the transition to walk and back to canter, and when you are coming from the short side of the school to the long side, make a simple change to counter canter just past the C marker (as in the diagram). Make sure that your horse is very straight along the rail; think almost of a little shoulder-fore.

❏ Towards the end of the arena make a simple change to true canter for the short end.

❏ If your horse is truly on your aids you can do a simple change to counter canter down the quarter line.

❏ The more advanced your horse is, the more changes he can do – aim for two or three changes along the long side, and resume the canter through the short side.

What's being achieved

This is a good developing exercise for the counter canter without getting the horse too stressed about it. It will also help the rider who over-rides the counter canter.

What you should be looking for

The important thing in this exercise is the straightness of the horse.

What can go wrong?

You over-ride the counter canter and you put the outside leg back to make sure the horse doesn't change and you throw the haunches in a little bit.

Double check

In a simple change the horse in canter is brought back to walk and after three or four strides, is asked to resume canter on the opposite leg.

COUNTER CANTER TIPS

1. Don't ride so deeply into corners in counter canter.

2. Both the forehand and the hindquarters should be on the same track.

3. The horse should be flexed to the side of the leading leg.

'You see so many horses in counter canter that throw their haunches in – let's say they're crooked and they don't go straight.'

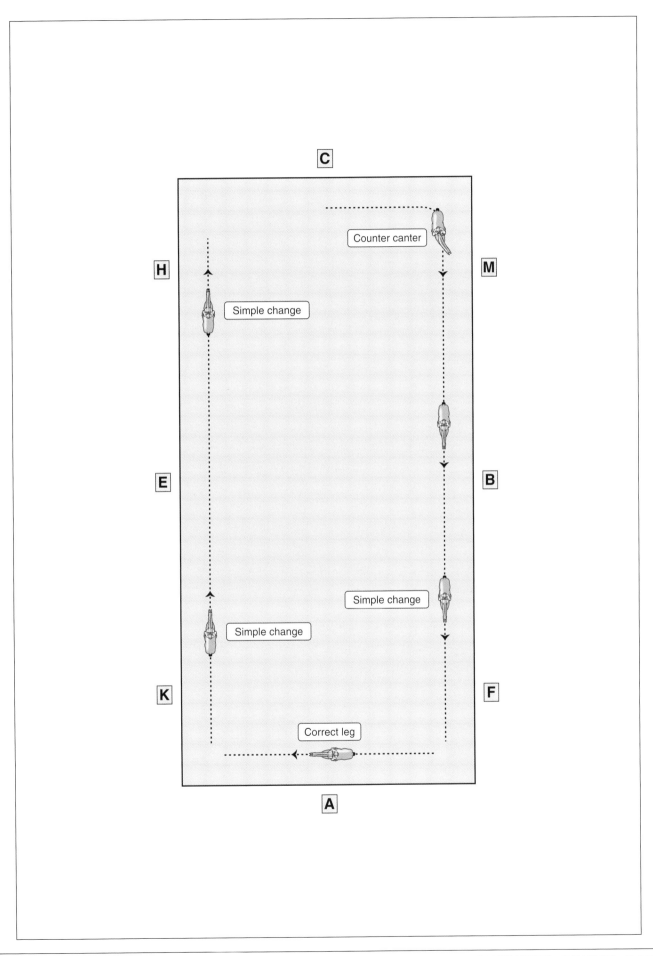

EXERCISE 68

To improve the half-pass

'This is a great exercise if you have lost the quality of your half-pass and to keep the flow going.'

A WARM-UP EXERCISE IN HAUNCHES-IN

Begin in walk and then progress to trot:

1. Ride a 10m circle in one corner of the arena at the beginning of a long side.

2. Half-halt, and just before rejoining the track, apply the outside leg behind the girth to push the hindquarters over so they travel up the inside of the long side in travers right.

3. Straighten before the corner.

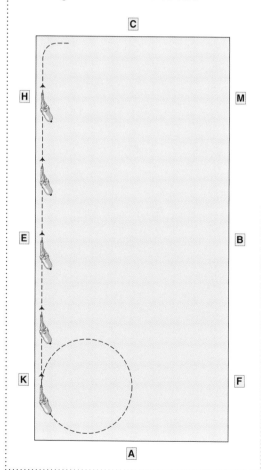

The exercise

❏ In trot, as you come through the end of your long side, ride a little shoulder-fore through the short side.

❏ Coming out of the corner, straighten up and then ride a diagonal MXK, haunches in. Keep a lot of impulsion coming off your inside leg. Use the outside leg to keep the haunches in.

❏ Return to the track. Resume trot and ride shoulder-in through the opposite short side.

❏ Repeat the exercise through FXH.

What you should be looking for

As you come out of the corner, keep your horse pointed at the letter you are aiming for. Make sure your horse is bent towards the letter, and that the shoulder and the front legs are going towards that letter – and then think of the haunches in.

What can go wrong?

If your horse's haunches drift to the inside too much, you are probably sitting on the wrong seat bone and affecting his ability to bend around your inside leg. Try to keep your weight on your inside seat bone.

Moving on

Shorten the diagonal and make the angle a little deeper and therefore a little more difficult for the horse. Make sure you achieve more collection.

EXPERT TIP

That forward desire and the impulsion needs to stay aggressively off your inside leg – this gives the horse the freedom he needs and also the desire to go forwards, and keeps the half-pass expressive.

'I think what happens often in the half-pass is that we get so caught up in going sideways and in getting the horse from A to B, the horse loses the desire to go forwards.'

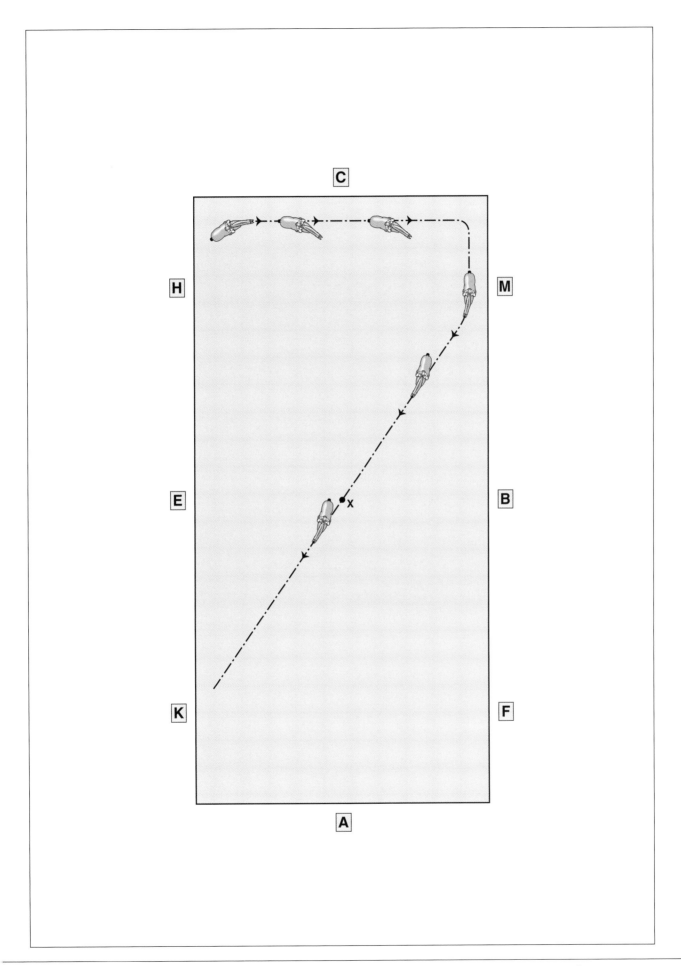

'Pirouette canter' to prevent anticipation

'We get great pirouettes on our schooling exercises and then we go in our test and everything falls to pieces because the horse anticipates the movement. This exercise helps tremendously.'

'I call this the "pirouette canter" without actually doing the pirouette! You take the horse back so he thinks: "Oh my God, we're going to do a pirouette," – and then go straight out.'

The exercise

❏ Working in your canter, once you have your horse warm, come out of the corner on to a long side and on to a diagonal.
❏ Using half-halts, take the horse back in preparation for a pirouette, but then ride straight out.
❏ Do this again by X, and maybe towards the end of the diagonal.
❏ On reaching the track, do a flying change or hold the counter canter, according to the level of your horse.

What you should be looking for

Your horse should feel very manageable and you should feel in control of every single one of his steps.

Double check

Shorten up the canter a little bit, go a little forwards, take the tempo back, go a little forwards. Try to maintain the impulsion. Try to collect the horse without letting him get behind you.

What can go wrong?

Your horse can start to anticipate this exercise! And what happens in anticipation is that they get a little crooked. They throw their haunches in a little bit or out a little bit. Now as a rider, you have to stay sharp. With some horses you will have to go slightly shoulder-in, but if they tend to lean in too much, go slightly, slightly haunches-in, but very, very little – almost not visible. Then straighten immediately.

Moving on

1. Take this exercise on to the centre line, and ride the exercise where you have your pirouettes in the test.
2. Shorten the diagonal, and try bringing the horse back to you once or twice on the short diagonal. This will really put your horse on the spot! Think of the small pirouettes. Make sure your horse comes all the way back, perfectly prepared for a good, small pirouette.

'Really reward your horse for thinking and staying with you and in front of you and for not anticipating the turn.'

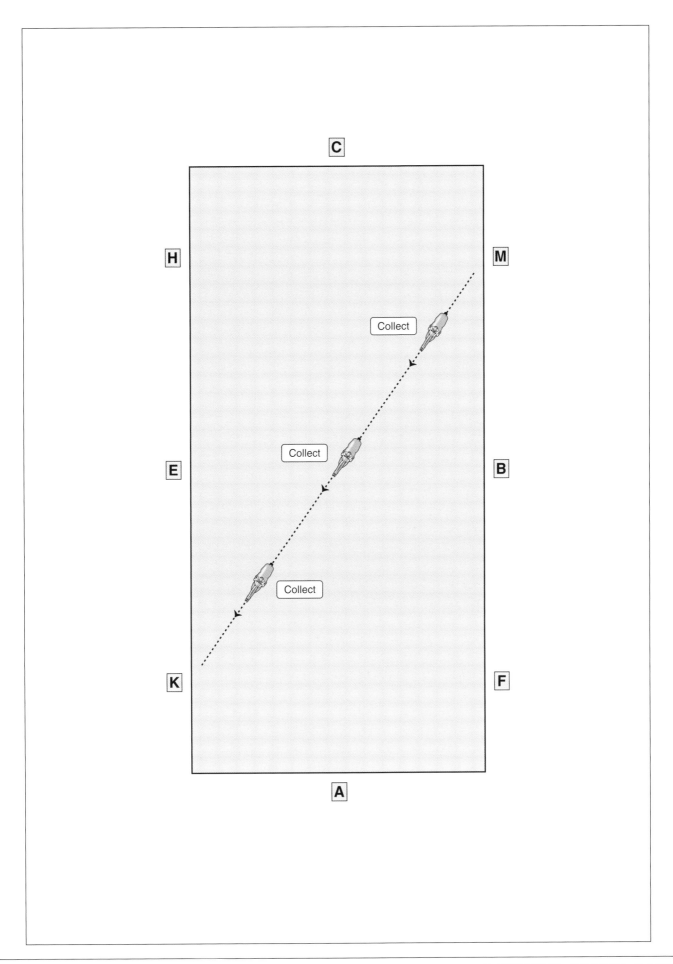

70

Flexing for fluency

'I like to use this exercise when I can get out of the dressage arena and work in a field with a bit more space. I call it half-pass with less bend!'

EXPERT TIP

Make sure you have your forwardness established first, and be subtle. This is a very subtle and soft kind of riding.

The exercise
❑ This exercise incorporates a little leg-yield into the half-pass.
❑ Working in trot, as you come out of the turn from the short to the long side, prepare half-pass.
❑ Then, after a few strides, very slowly change the bend to almost a leg-yield, and then back again.
❑ Repeat this whilst you continue in the half-pass. This is not a neck bend, but works on suppleness through the jaw, asking the horse to be supple on both sides. On reaching the opposite long side of the school, straighten up and ride forwards.

What's being achieved
This exercise helps to keep the fluency in the half-pass by keeping the horse supple to both sides.

What you should be looking for
Ask for the change of bend very, very slowly, without taking anything away from the trot or from the rhythm. There should not be much change in the feeling of the bend around your leg. This should be almost non-visible, and shouldn't interrupt the gait of the horse.

> ### PREPARING FOR HALF-PASS
> 1. Check your rhythm, straightness and self-carriage.
> 2. Increase the impulsion slightly.
> 3. Prepare your horse by the use of half-halts.

'This exercise gives the half-pass that last little bit of extra elasticity.'

What can go wrong?
If you take this to the extreme and start flexing your horse to left and right you will end up with a shorter neck and the horse coming back too much. If you make it too strong he will lose the desire to go forwards.

Moving on
You could try riding the exercise in canter.

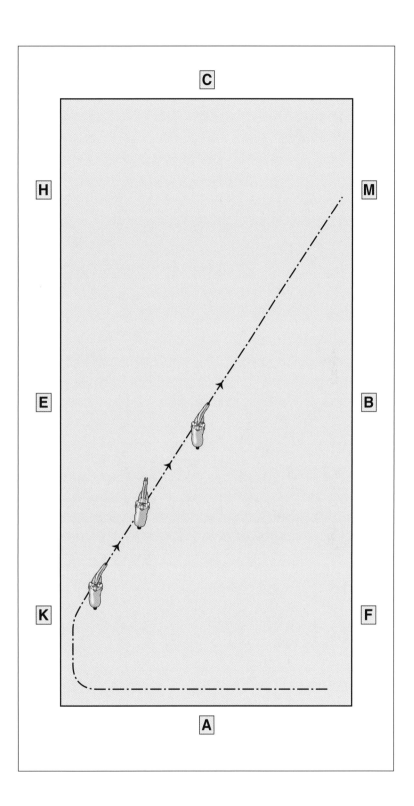

Playing around with half steps

'Some horses get a little scared when you ask them for more energy from behind whilst half-halting and not allowing them to go forwards as much as they would like.'

EXPERT TIP

Some horses will find this phase of their training easier from the trot, some from walk. Regardless, you need to find the exercises that work for your horse.

The exercise

❏ Begin by working on trot/walk transitions to get your horse in front of your leg and prepared to think forwards.

❏ Now, in walk, ask for a little more collection. This will give you and your horse the idea of the half step.

❏ After a few strides in the half step, if your horse starts to get slightly worried, make the aids for turn on the haunches, allowing him to go sideways a little.

❏ Now let him go forwards a little more, and then take him back a bit again and repeat the process for just a few strides.

What's being achieved

Often, when a horse first comprehends the idea of the half step, he starts to come too far under with the quarters, without really understanding enough about what is required of him. This exercise will help him grasp the degree of collection needed for the half step and piaffe, without losing the desire to go forwards. As he is going somewhere, it is easier for him to understand.

What can go wrong?

Your horse starts turning for himself and not staying straight. If this happens, repeat the exercise, concentrating on communicating 'forwards' to your horse. You must always be working at making your horse go forwards.

HALF STEPS

When a horse is ready to begin learning piaffe and passage under the rider, having either been taught the preliminaries in hand, or by a very sensitive rider, his trot can be collected to a point where it is known as 'half steps'. These should only be ridden for a short period and followed by an active collected or working trot. Once half steps can be performed without loss of rhythm, he is ready to begin piaffe.

'This exercise helps the horse start to understand the feel of the half steps. It makes him almost think he's doing a turn on the haunches. If, when going into a turn on the haunches, he begins to get a little hot and has the desire to trot on, you can regulate this, keeping in the half steps.'

Piaffe/passage ... and relax

'After the piaffe or passage, we can go to the extended trot or the canter or something quite easily, but to go to a good, regulated extended walk takes practice.'

The exercise
- ❏ This exercise can be done from piaffe or passage.
- ❏ From the movement, make a transition to walk. Try to keep the horse a little rounder through the transition, and then let him stretch into an extended walk.
- ❏ Practise this in different places around the arena, picking the horse up again after the extended walk.

What's being achieved

The horse knows that once you walk after the piaffe/passage, if you allow him to, he may stretch and relax the back. If you find that your horse is tight afterwards, work on leg-yielding in walk with the idea of stretching to make the back loose.

What you should be looking for

1. Regularity of gait.
2. Clear steps in the passage.
3. A four-beat walk.

THREE TIPS FOR EXTENSION IN WALK

1. Remember, in extended walk, although you are lengthening the reins and moving your hands forwards, it is important not to give up the contact. You must be able to alter the length of the stride or change the direction when you want.
2. Your horse must be allowed his natural nodding movement if he is to take long, ground-covering strides.
3. When making the transition back to a collected or medium walk, this must not be done with a backward movement of the hands. Your horse needs to be ridden forwards into a gentle contact, taking more weight on to the hindquarters and shortening from behind.

'In the Grand Prix, you see lots of points lost because the horse is tight, and by the time he starts to do a good extended walk, half the diagonal is over!'

Playing with trot/piaffe/ passage transitions

'In the Grand Prix, piaffe and passage have to be ridden across the centre line on a serpentine. It is so important for your horse to get to that place with enough energy and confidence that they aren't afraid of the spot. This exercise will help, and can be adapted to prevent your horse anticipating any type of serpentine transitions, whatever level you are riding at.'

The exercise

To avoid anticipation and maintain confidence, work through working trot, piaffe and passage on the serpentine, but not necessarily across the centre line.

To get you started

❏ Ride a five-loop serpentine in trot. Once you have crossed the centre line for the first time, prepare and then, over a few steps of passage, ride piaffe just before the next loop.

❏ Ride forwards in trot, through the loop, cross the centre line and into collected trot through the next loop.

❏ Cross the centre line, and at the corresponding point to the previous piaffe transition, prepare for piaffe but keep the piaffe slightly forward for a few strides.

❏ Ride through the loop, cross the centre line, then prepare and ride a few strides of piaffe just before the final loop.

❏ Complete the serpentine in collected trot.

Now use this idea and work through working trot, piaffe and passage on the serpentine but not necessarily on the centre line. Use the changes of pace to correct your horse. For example, if he has a problem holding passage and anticipates the transition back to piaffe, go into a collected trot and then back to passage. If he tends to get a little slow in the passage, work on piaffe/trot/piaffe transitions.

What's being achieved

Confidence is the main goal of this exercise, which helps stop your horse anticipating transitions. It is important that any transition is approached with energy and confidence and that, in anticipating the transition, your horse doesn't get tense, lazy or misbehave.

'You see so many horses piaffe and passage in the warm-up arena like a million dollars, and then when they come to that particular exercise everything falls apart.'

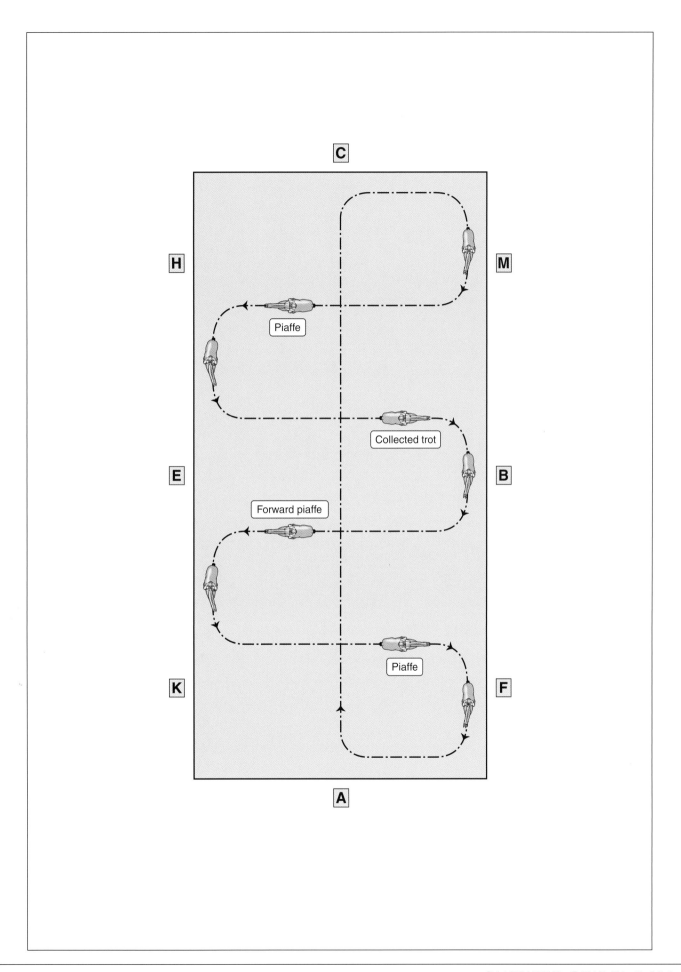

OLIVER TOWNEND

Oliver has consistently been in the rankings since he began his international competitive career in eventing, and has successfully brought on horses since his early experience at the Horse of the Year show with a 14.2hh pony called Cool Mule. However, the 23-year-old landed well and truly in the limelight following his four-star debut at Badminton in 2005, finishing in 12th place, having completed a clear round across country on his own Topping. And with Flint Curtis in 2006 he was third at Badminton, and 11th at the World Equestrian Games at Aachen.

The son of 'horsey' parents – his mother showed side-saddle at county level, and his father competed in three-day eventing, and bought and sold horses – Oliver began riding at the age of seven. His logical approach to training a horse over jumps is reflected in his practical exercises, and in his philosophy of allowing the horse to learn from its own mistakes and successes. This formula proved effective in producing Gold Ringer, on which he came sixth at Windsor CCIJ** in 1999, to Grand Prix level show jumping and advanced eventing.

Part of the World Class Potential Squad, Oliver set up his own yard in Market Harborough, Leicestershire, after three years as stable jockey for Kenneth Clawson, and has gained a good reputation for getting results from difficult horses.

Q: What's the best piece of advice you've ever been given?
Keep relaxed and positive, and be consistent.

Q: What do you do when you hit a training 'brick wall'?
Go back to basics.

Q: How do you identify your training problems?
I keep things simple, and concentrate on basics. And every so often I work with a trainer.

Q: And what are you working on at present?
Position and relaxation. And breathing!

Q: What is your training passion?
Training horses to come through to top level.

Q: Whose performance do you watch?
Marcus Enhing, show jumper, Carl Hester, dressage, and A P McCoy.

Q: And who do you most admire in the equine world?
My dad, my girlfriend and A P McCoy.

Q: And what do you look for when you get on a horse for the first time?
Attitude, ability and type – but as long as they want to do the job, it doesn't really matter.

Q: Can you recall your last equine 'magic moment'?
Every day in the school when the horse goes well.

CONTENTS

Helping a drifter to straighten up

'This exercise using V-poles encourages straightness in horses that veer to one side or another. We use V-poles a lot.'

The exercise
- ❏ Set up an upright at a height that your horse is comfortable and confident with.
- ❏ Rest two jump poles in a V-formation at the outside edges of the fence, resting on the top bar. Start off with them quite wide, and bring them in as necessary to achieve the desired result.
- ❏ If your horse is drifting in one particular direction – left or right – over the fence, have the pole quite high on that side, so it protrudes above the fence, to encourage the horse to keep straight through his shoulder and come up through his forearm.

What's being achieved
The V-poles help both horse and rider concentrate on the straightness of the horse's shoulders over the fence, and focus his attention on the centre of the fence.

What can go wrong?
If you find your horse is spooked by the V-poles, widen them out to begin with.

Moving on
Replace the upright with a parallel and move the V-poles to the back of the parallel. This will bring your horse closer in to the fence and help him stay square through his shoulders.

A HORSE OR RIDER PROBLEM?

Is your horse still jumping crookedly? Ask yourself if it is the horse's physical status that is causing the problem, or your riding:

- ❏ Are you doing enough flatwork on both reins to help both sides of his body develop symmetrically? Or could he benefit from some focused work on his weaker side?
- ❏ Are you sitting evenly in the saddle, or are you putting too much weight on one side or the other?
- ❏ Are you allowing evenly with the reins?
- ❏ Is your horse sound? Or is he suffering from arthritis, or just rather stiff?

'I use this exercise to straighten up Flint Curtis who I took to Badminton and the World Equestrian Games at Aachen in 2006.'

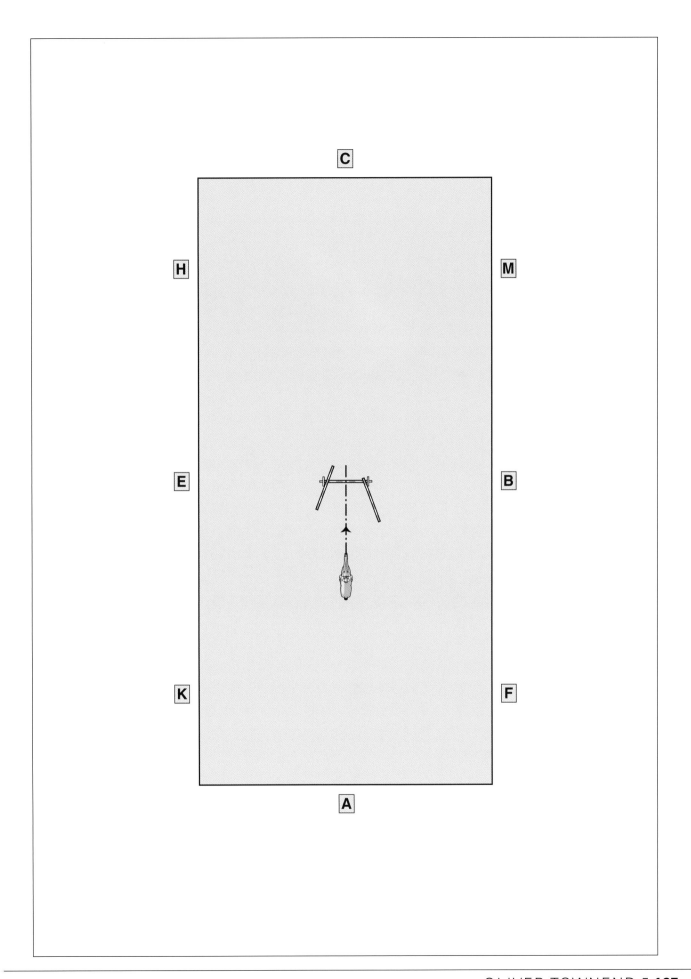

Feeling the stretch

'If you have a horse that jumps over his shoulder a little bit, this exercise gets him stretching the knees and forearms out in front of him, rather than folding over the shoulder.'

The exercise

❏ Set up a small upright fence about 70cm (2ft 3in) high. Behind the fence, at a distance of about 30cm (1ft), place three ground poles on pole raisers.

❏ Have these ground poles spaced quite close to each other to start off with – about 30cm (1ft) apart – and bring them out gradually (to a maximum of 1.5m (5ft). Your aim is for the horse to jump the fence and all three ground poles behind.

❏ The further you take the poles away from the back of the fence, the higher the fence has to go.

❏ Jump the fence in canter.

'This is my favourite – think like you're creating a water fence, or something like that.'

What's being achieved

This exercise encourages a horse to bring his knees and forearms out in front of him as he jumps.

What you should be looking for

Jumping is about confidence for both horse and rider, and it is important for you to be well balanced, secure in your position, and to have an allowing rein contact for this exercise.

What can go wrong?

If your horse isn't reaching far enough out, or the front fence isn't high enough, there's a chance he may clip the ground poles. Ride into the fence with a little bit more rhythm, or reduce the distance between the ground poles again, so you don't lose the horse's confidence.

Moving on

Raise the fence and widen the distance between the raised poles.

> ### AN ALLOWING REIN CONTACT
>
> Any horse will go better if his head is not restricted by the rider's hands and rein contact. Experienced riders are able to maintain contact with their horse's mouth and to follow the natural extension of the horse's head and neck over the jump, allowing the hands forwards by simply relaxing the arms. This is a skill that all riders should be working towards, but in the meantime it is as well to have the confidence to slip the reins, without throwing them away – a skill in itself. Both require balance and a secure leg.

Tramlines

'This exercise helps horse and rider to keep straight on their approach to, and departure from, a fence. Begin with a jump at a height your horse is comfortable and confident with.'

The exercise

- ❏ Lay two poles on the ground, just in from the wings, on the approach to the fence and at right angles to it, and two more on the landing side.
- ❏ Start off with the poles quite wide apart, and gradually bring them in closer together, as necessary. (Don't, however make the poles on the landing side too close together as your horse might risk clipping them.)
- ❏ Trot or canter to the jump repeatedly until your horse is maintaining a straight line.

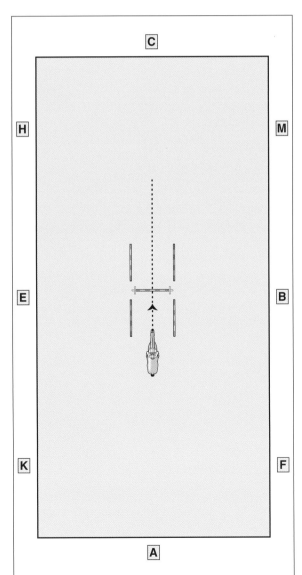

What's being achieved

The poles form a channel along which the horse must approach the fence. Once in the air, the landing poles encourage him to make a better shape over the fence, and to be careful where he puts his feet on landing.

What you should be looking for

Don't over-ride or over-steer your horse. Just put him on a straight course to the fence and let him work out for himself what he's meant to be doing.

What can go wrong?

The most common problem with this exercise is that the horse concentrates too much on the ground rails. Keep repeating the exercise and if the problem persists, lower the fence to the floor and then gradually raise it back to its original height.

Moving on

V-poles correct straightness *over* the fence, whereas these 'tramline' poles correct straightness *to* the fence. We often put the two together, tramlines, V-poles, tramlines, away.

'Combine this with the V-poles and you are giving the horse every opportunity to learn to jump a fence in a correct technique.'

Concentrating on the canter stride

'This exercise teaches the horse to land and keep his canter stride dead level; this will help him maintain rhythm and balance between fences that are built on a related distance.'

The exercise

❑ Set up a cross-pole with a placing pole.
❑ This is followed by six or seven ground poles, all about 3 to 3.5m apart (10 to 12.5ft) (depending on your horse's stride)…
❑ …and then the same distance to a small upright fence.
❑ Take the grid in canter, keeping your rhythm even.
❑ Stay relaxed, allowing your horse to work things out.

What's being achieved

Your horse will need to concentrate on synchronizing his front and back legs to take the poles cleanly. You also need to keep him straight, and to keep him going forwards, otherwise he will find it hard to maintain a level, rhythmic canter stride.

What you should be looking for

This exercise looks deceptively simple. However, cantering a line of poles like this is difficult for the horse as he has to stay balanced, and the rider has to remain in balance with his horse through the extremes of extension and collection required for this pace.

What can go wrong?

Your horse speeds up through the exercise, in which case see 'Moving on' below, for a way to teach the horse to be less impetuous.

Moving on

You can make this slightly more difficult for the horse by raising the ground poles on pole raisers.

Also, if you have a horse that is a little bit bold and it lands over the first fence of a line and runs down the line, you can 'play illusions' with him and shorten the last distance – bring the last fence back towards the ground pole a little bit. This will oblige him to shorten himself, and teach him to back off.

'This exercise will teach your horse to become level between the fences in canter and not to increase his stride pattern.'

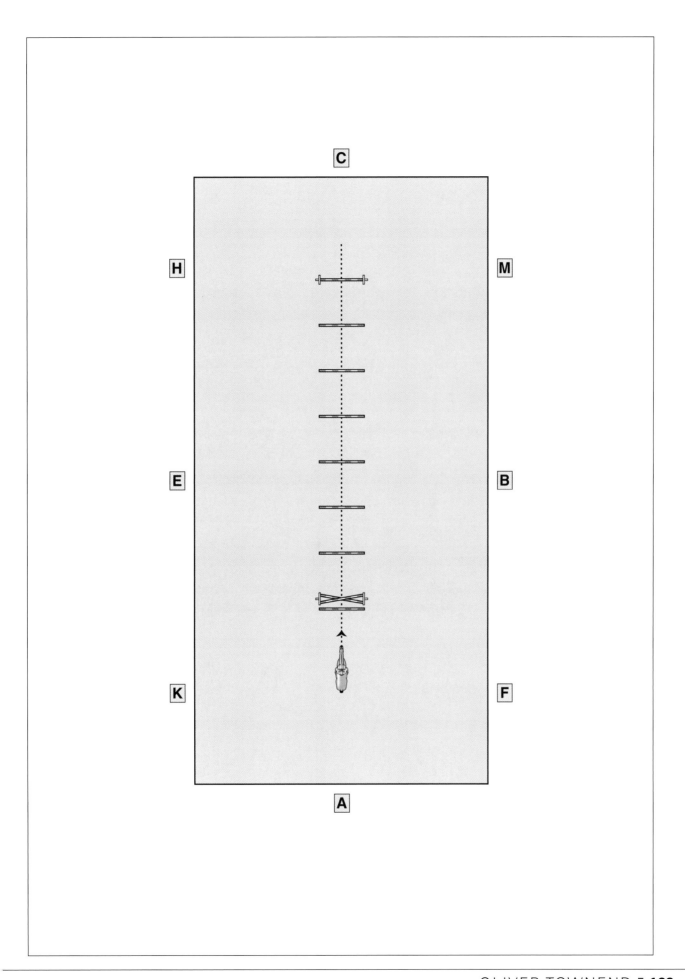

EXERCISE
78

Grids

'In this exercise we are teaching the horse to open and shut down his strides quickly.'

EXPERT TIPS

Here are five tips for riding grids:

1. *Look up and ride towards a point past the last jump.*

2. *Double check: is your weight in your heels, and is your leg position secure?*

3. *Don't forget to allow the reins to go with your horse's head and neck.*

4. *Maintain your rhythm throughout the grid.*

5. *Don't interfere with your horse once you've set him up for the grid, but allow him to learn for himself the lessons that it presents.*

The exercise
- ❑ Begin your grid with a cross-pole.
- ❑ Three open canter strides (15–16m approx) away from the cross-pole, set up two uprights to form a bounce (3.3--3.6m between them);
- ❑ then have a comfortable two strides (11–12m approx) to a decent parallel.

What's being achieved
The variations in distance between the fences in this particular grid encourage the horse to lengthen and shorten his stride, and the parallel fence asks him to be very quick and accurate in judging the height and position of the top poles.

What you should be looking for
Come quite forwards to the cross-pole, then have three open canter strides, and then the bounce itself is quite short, so you're really teaching the horse to adjust his stride; then he will have to move forwards again to get the two strides to the last fence.

What can go wrong?
Your horse clips the front pole of the parallel: continue the exercise until he works it out. This will also encourage him to stretch out over the jump and make a good shape. Your horse gets strong and wants to take control after the parallel: quietly and firmly, with low hands, pull him up a few times after jumping the fence, until he accepts, lands and waits.

Moving on
Grids are a fundamental aid in the training of a show jumper, whatever level it is competing at, and can be used to address almost any problem with horse or rider.

'This exercise teaches the horse to be quick athletically, and to shorten very quickly when necessary – to be quick on its feet.'

170 ▌ OLIVER TOWNEND

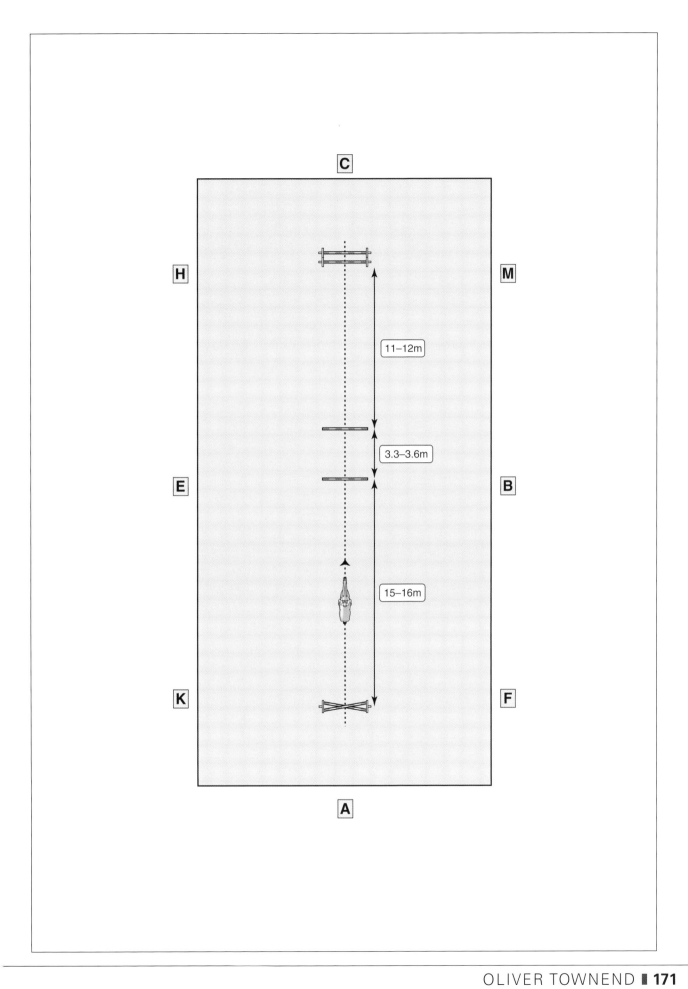

EXERCISE 79

Tackling narrow fences

'Barrels (empty 50-gallon drums) are great for practising narrow fences, as you can use them either on their side or on their end. Jump the barrel backwards and forwards, backwards and forwards until the horse clocks on.'

The exercise

❏ Set up a barrel as a narrow jump, probably on its side to begin with, then on end as the horse gets the idea of jumping something so narrow. (When it is on its side, tuck a ground pole against it on each side to stop it rolling if the horse knocks against it.)

❏ Start off by putting a show-jumping wing on each side of the barrel, and some poles on the ground on the approach as 'tramlines' (see diagram).

❏ As you progress and the horse gains in confidence, move the jump wings wider and wider apart so that you end up with just the tramlines on the ground.

❏ Only move the jump wings away when your horse feels 100 per cent straight in the way he jumps.

What's being achieved

This exercise helps the horse learn to focus on the jump and to keep going forwards however narrow and unusual it may seem to him, so that a run-out does not even occur to him.

The tramlines and wings make life easier for the rider, but it is still important to keep the leg on, and a firm, consistent rein contact so the horse doesn't lose impulsion and straightness: if he isn't going forwards enough he will be harder to keep straight, and if he wavers he is much more likely to run out. In this exercise you are looking for obedience to the leg and contact, and trust in the rider.

What can go wrong?

The most usual evasion is that the horse runs out, but this is generally lack of confidence – such a narrow fence looks unusual and he doesn't trust you that it is really safe to jump – and not just him being naughty. If you feel that a single barrel on its side will be too narrow to begin with, use two, end to end. (Remember the ground poles on each side to prevent them rolling.) If, when you move the wings away, he still runs out, try using V-poles (as in Exercise 74) on each side of the barrel – either propped on the wings, or on the barrel itself – to keep him focused and straight.

Moving on

With the barrel standing upright, place a tyre on top. This makes quite a decent fence, and it is a good test that the horse is really focusing on what he is doing.

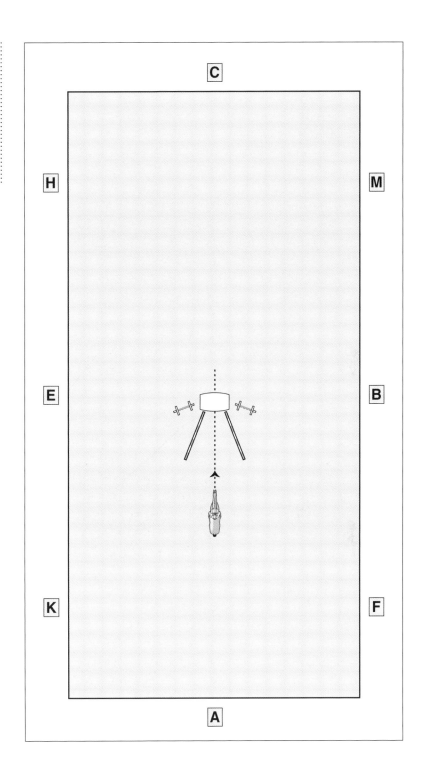

Maintaining rhythm through turns

'If you have a horse that struggles to hold its rhythm, especially a young horse, trotting poles can be very useful. Most horses tend to lose their rhythm through a corner or turn, and using trotting poles on a circle will help them maintain it.'

The exercise
❑ Begin by placing three poles on a 20m circle in your arena or schooling area, with the centre of each pole on the track (*see* diagram).
❑ When your horse is comfortable with those, and can successfully maintain an even rhythm and bend over the poles, increase the number to five (1).
❑ Ride this in trot in both directions, keeping to the exact centre of each pole.
❑ You could also set three poles through a corner of the arena and ride the exercise, to improve the horse's rhythm through corners and turns.

What's being achieved
The horse must adjust his stride whilst maintaining the bend.

What you should be looking for
Pay attention to occasions when your horse may try to fall in through a shoulder or out through his quarters on a circle, and the relationship that this has with the position of the poles. This tendency may be reflected in his performance on turns to a jump, and can be anticipated and prepared for if you are aware of it. Be sure your shoulders are following his shoulders around the arc of the turn.

What can go wrong?
You may find that your horse is particularly stiff through turns in one direction. Put some additional work into that rein to help him become as supple in that direction as he is in the other.

Moving on
Once your horse is comfortable over five poles on a 20m circle, try the exercise over three poles on a 10m circle (2).

WORKING ON CORNERS
Even the more experienced horses can develop the habit of cutting corners, whereas the youngsters and novice riders tend to lean out in the turn. Here's a simple exercise to help: place a jump as near to the corner of your arena or training area as is safely practicable (3), clearly allowing enough space on each side to ride past it, as well as to jump it! As you come around the arena decide, well before your approach, whether you are going to pass to the left, or to the right, or take the jump. Keep varying your route. This jump can also be incorporated into other exercise work, if you have sufficient space – for example you may be working on a circle at the opposite end of the school, so you could leave your circle work and take the jump, and then return to the circle work. The point is, that it will get your horse listening to your aids.

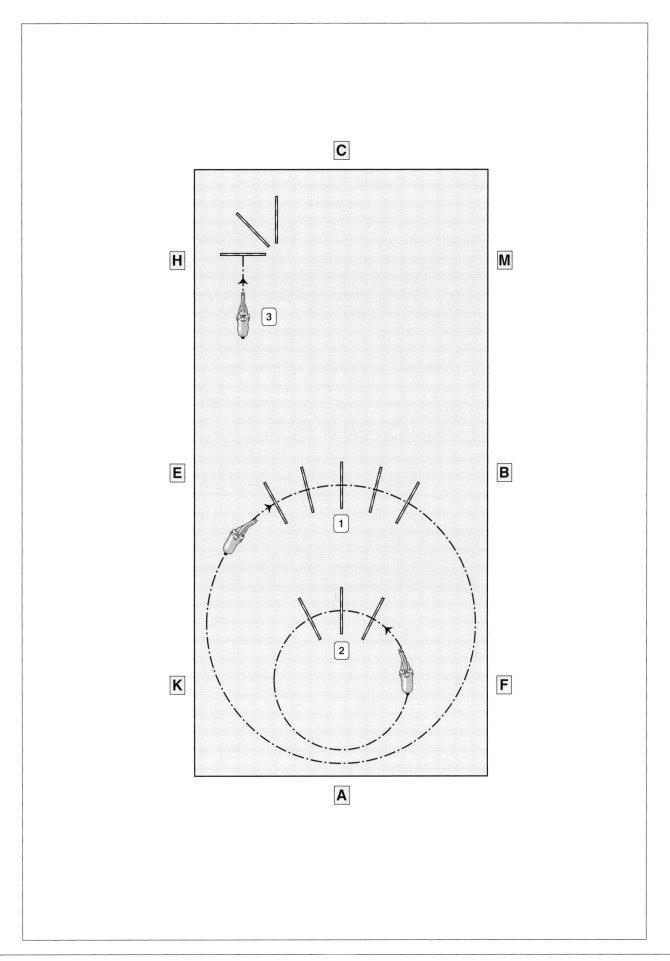

EXERCISE

81

Dealing with rushing

'I use this exercise to help a horse that has been ridden inconsistently into fences, and has got into the habit of rushing. After a while he learns to land from a jump and to wait for you to tell him where he is going, and this habit makes him steadier in his approach to the fence, too.'

The exercise

❑ Arrange three uprights, all exactly the same, in the shape of a fan, seven strides away from a cross-pole, as shown in the diagram. Keep the fences to a comfortable height, based on your horse's level of experience.

❑ Jump the cross-pole, and canter towards the fence in front of you. If your horse grabs the bridle and goes to run at the fence, you can turn him away and jump one of the other fences.

❑ Every time he goes to grab the rein and take you to one fence, you take him to one of the others.

What's being achieved

The height of these fences should not be a challenge for your horse. One of the reasons a horse rushes is apprehension about a jump – your horse needs to be able to take these comfortably. Only increase the height when you are sure he is listening to your directional aids.

What you should be looking for

Most horses rush fences because they are worried about the jump. This could be because they have been over-faced in the past, ridden into jumps inconsistently by a nervous rider, or punished for not having adequate ability. All are quite major problems, and will need patience and consistent training by a confident rider if they are to be overcome. Here are some suggestions as to what you are aiming for:

❑ Don't let everything go once you are over a jump, keep your horse listening to you and work on getting him to relax.

❑ Think very carefully before resorting to a stronger bit to deal with rushing. This rarely works in the long term and can make the problem worse.

❑ Use circles before and after a fence to focus your horse on your aids.

❑ Concentrate on building up your horse's confidence, using repetition and gradual progression to help.

What can go wrong?

If your horse pulls you into a fence that is not the one you are intending to jump, pull up in between the cross-pole and the uprights until he learns to jump and wait for you.

Moving on

Try shortening the distance between the cross-pole and the uprights.

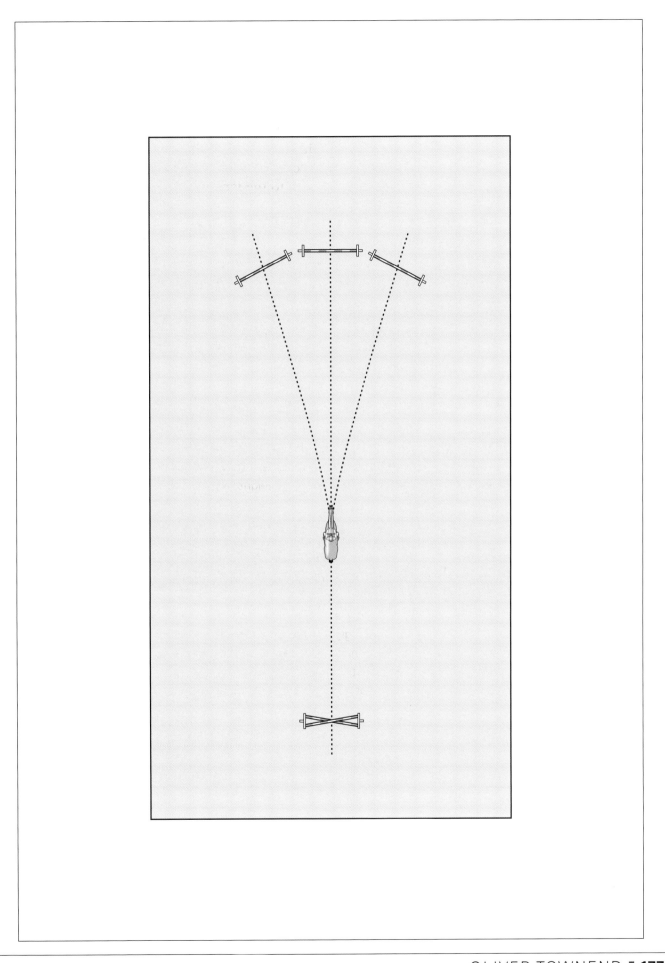

Tackling corners

'Start with the corner very, very small – almost no angle at all so the horse can jump straight over the centre to get him started.'

The exercise

❏ Using barrels, wing stands (at the far end of the corner) or plastic jump holders, set up a very small corner with almost no angle at all so that your horse can jump straight over the centre to get him started. Keep this at a height with which he is more than comfortable, and ride the fence in canter.

❏ Once he is happy with this, open the 'wings' out.

❏ When he is taking this absolutely 100 per cent straight, widen the corner further by opening up the 'V'. As you open the 'V', you will take the jump more towards the point of the corner. If your horse starts to feel like he's looking one way or the other, you can always move him back down the fence again.

What you should be looking for

It is especially important to maintain your rhythm and keep a good rein contact until you have actually taken off.

What can go wrong?

Corners on a downhill are particularly difficult as horses are encouraged to run out by the slope. If you find yourself in this position, keep your seat in the saddle and lift the horse's head a little higher. Also, it may sound obvious, but go a bit slower than normal.

Moving on

You can also use barrels or a fence filler in the middle of the corner so as to make the fence more difficult.

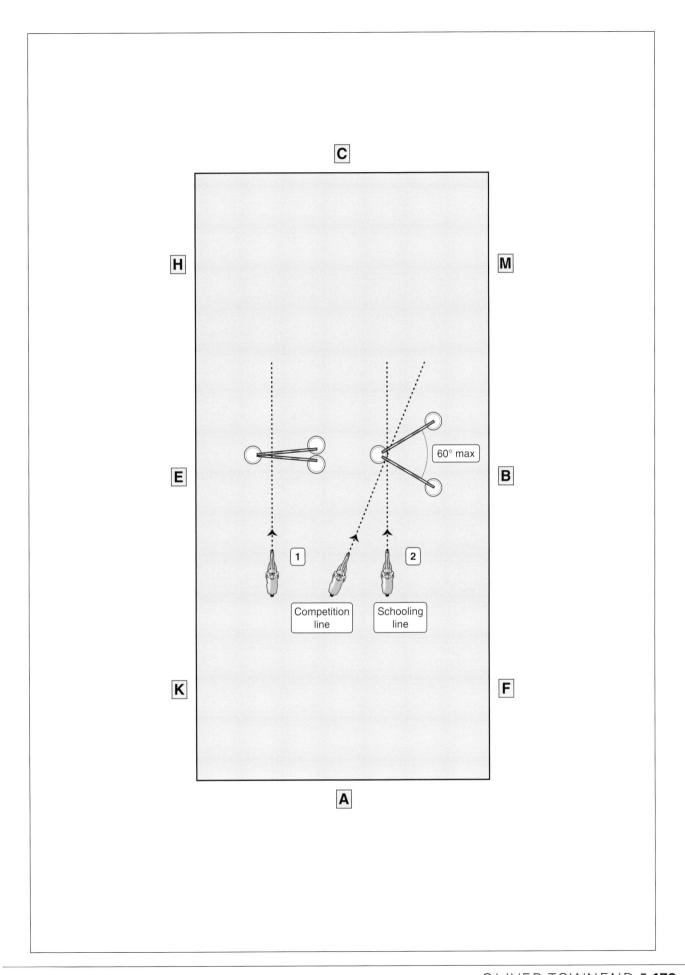

60° max

1

2

Competition
line

Schooling
line

ISOBEL WESSELS

In the course of her career Isobel Wessels has spent time training with the best around the world – in England at Porlock Vale, in Vienna with the Spanish Riding School, and in South Africa where she became South African Champion and an Alternative Olympics gold medal winner (when SA was not allowed to compete internationally) – and then judging the best: she is a British List 1 and international judge. This depth of experience and knowledge is reflected in the exercises that she shares with us here, yet her ability to keep things simple and inspiring all at the same time is the common denominator. 'I think my strength is that I am trying to give the rider exercises that improve their techniques and make it easier for the horse,' she understates.

She grew up in Somerset where she discovered her deep love of horses, gained qualification at Porlock Vale, and then took a job in Vienna to find out more about dressage. Through her connections there she found a place in South Africa, where she achieved great competitive success as well as training many of the top riders who, likewise, became national champions. It was here that she met and married her husband Justin.

The couple returned to England, and Isobel won many national titles with several different horses including Leopardo; she trained him to international level at Grand Prix, and was a member of the Olympic Potential Squad with him. At this point in her career she began judging, and this preoccupation has taken her all over the world. For the last four years she and her husband have lived in Germany, and since losing the ride on Leopardo she has concentrated on judging. 'Being able to judge the best horses in the world can be as inspiring as riding.' She now has another horse almost ready to compete at Grand Prix level – the sixth she has trained during her career – and Isobel, Justin and the horses are returning to the UK.

Q: What's the best piece of advice you've ever been given?
From Georg Wahl, Spanish Riding School: in every transition push the knees down and the toes up – don't clamp.

Q: What do you do when you come up against a brick wall in training?
I go back to the scales of training (see page 8–9), make it as simple as possible, and start from that point again.

Q: What's your training formula?
The scales of training once again. I preach this formula, eat it, sleep it, drink it, and judge it!

Q: How do you identify a problem in your own performance, and how do you work on it?
I go a lot by my feeling. If I am not getting a good feeling, I go back to basics to get that feeling back, and then I proceed.

Q: Aspiring riders will watch you ride and learn from your techniques. Whose performance do you watch?
Isabel Werth, Anky van Grunsven, Hubertus Schmidt, Heike Kemmer, and lots of very good riders who are not so famous.

Q: What would be the three pearls of wisdom you'd like to pass on to anyone with equine ambitions?
Train for something else, do it for fun, and have something you can go back to. Be able to keep your conscience absolutely clear. Never do anything you regret, that is unfair to the horse, the client or yourself. Watch good riders riding as much as you can and learn everything.

Q: Good training is based on communication with the horse. Is this true or false?
True, but you must listen to your horse, ride within his capabilities, and only push him gradually, even if it takes him some time.

Q: Whom do you admire most in the equestrian world?
Stephen Clarke, he has done so much for the sport. He rides beautifully and he's a good example.

Q: Whatever level of rider we are, we all have those magic moments when we feel really connected with our horses and the situation. Can you describe the last 'magic moment' that you had?
Today, in the arena, just my horse and me, and feeling the whole horse moving in perfect swinging rhythm, chewing on both sides of the bit. It was lovely, warm and sunny, and the birds were singing!

CONTENTS

Transitions on a large circle

'I feel that this is a very good exercise to stop riders kicking and pulling all the time, which is a thing I hate.'

The exercise

❏ Work on a 20m circle – your horse must be moving straight, with impulsion and a correct bend, in a good, active working trot, swinging over the back.

❏ Start with a very simple transition: ask the horse to come back to walk for one or two steps and immediately go forwards, in front of the leg again. Repeat as often as you can. After a while you will just have to think about it, and your horse will come back to you. As you repeat this exercise, work on your aids becoming absolutely minute.

❏ The same thing can now be done with trot/canter transitions. Remember the horse must remain supple, through and in front of the rider. After a while, because the horse knows what is coming next, the rider has the chance to achieve the reaction from smaller and smaller aids. Repeat this on both reins.

What's being achieved

This improves the suppleness and the connection through from behind, through the whole body into the reins, and helps to put the horse more in front of the legs and in front of the aids of the rider. Thus the horse becomes much more attentive, on the aids and quicker to react in the hind legs.

What you should be looking for

The main thing I feel with this exercise is that it makes the horse react more and more in the hind leg. So, when you ask the horse to make a transition it starts behind the rider in the hind leg, and not on the forehand going away from the hind leg with the horse becoming on the forehand. This happens because the rider is sitting in a balanced way in the middle of the horse and, through the repeated exercise, is actually learning to use the seat and the weight aids.

'Before I begin any schooling, whether it's in my personal training or training of rider and horses, I feel really strongly that the horse should always be properly warmed up.'

What can go wrong?

The main thing that can go wrong is that the transitions are ridden too abruptly and the horse doesn't therefore work over the back, so the rider is riding backwards rather than riding the hind legs forwards to the front. When I have a rider that does this, I always tell them to think of the hind legs stepping through under the body towards the reins, and allow it to happen, and then they stop blocking the horse and they become much more activating and motivating.

Moving on

If you make the trot/walk/trot for two or three steps only, and gradually eliminate the walk steps, you have the half-halt. Rather than telling somebody to make a half-halt, which makes them pull the reins and slow the horse down, I tell them to think they are going to come back to walk, and then trot on. It's something that riders of all levels can do, it is straightforward, it is not easy to do it perfectly, but that's the challenge.

'When the transitions feel really easy and good and fluent, then the horse is in front of the leg, it is in self-carriage, and it is a happy athlete underneath you…'

Understanding the lateral aids

'For this exercise, your horse needs to be a little bit deeper and rounder than he would be, perhaps, in a test or competition situation.'

The exercise

- On a 20m circle have the horse in a working trot, going nicely forwards, through and round.
- On two opposite points of the circle, make a small 10m circle in from the bigger circle. As you complete the first quarter of this small circle, give the inside rein away and hold the horse with your inside leg to the outside rein.
- Now try to maintain the rest of the circle like that, and only retake the inside rein coming back towards the big circle again.
- Rejoin the main circle and ride the horse a little bit more forwards into both reins, and then repeat the exercise again.

What's being achieved

This exercise teaches the rider to ride from inside leg to outside rein and to stop the tendency to turn the horse with the inside rein. The rider has to turn the horse with the outside rein, the body, and the closing of the legs. It helps the rider to stay more upright, because if they lean or collapse too much they cannot do this without the inside rein.

What you should be looking for

You are trying to develop exactly the same evenness on both sides of the horse. If it is very straight on the left side and rather banana-like on the right, you have to do a lot on the left and get the horse really bending and flexing. Then, when you come on to the right rein, the horse is slightly straighter than he was at the beginning.

What can go wrong?

The rider uses too much inside rein and there is too much inside bending, which means the horse falls out through the outside shoulder. Then the rider is actually unable to make the circle at all, let alone without the inside rein aid. To rectify this, the rider must ride the horse actively forwards on the big circle and put the horse into both reins a little bit, so the neck is not over-flexed to the inside. There should be a uniform bend throughout the body. The rider should then ask for the exercise again without using too much inside rein. The other thing that I have sometimes seen happening is that the rider tries to neck rein the horse. In this case the rider needs to keep one hand on each side of the wither and to ride the horse a little more forwards into both reins, and should then start to turn the horse more with the body and the outside rein.

Moving on

A horse fully on the aids could make all four small circles 'within' the larger circle. The size of the smaller circle can also vary according to the level of the horse: if it is an advanced horse it could be a 6m circle, but if it is a less experienced horse it should be a 10m circle. And for those who have a more balanced horse, the same thing can be done in canter.

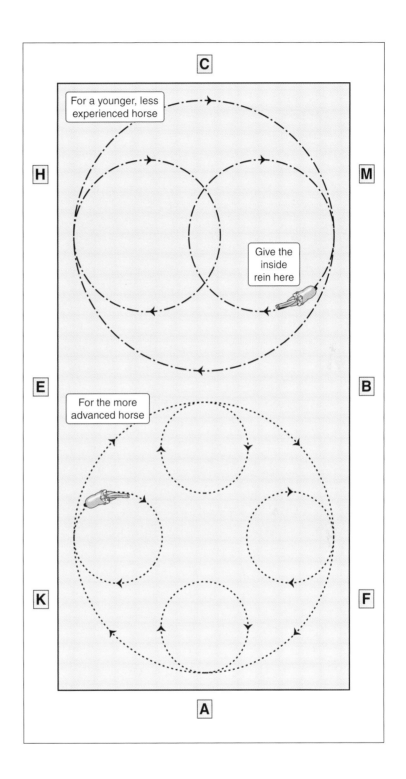

For a younger, less experienced horse

Give the inside rein here

For the more advanced horse

Easy half-pass on a spiralling circle

'I have found that when many riders start half-pass they think "I have got to do it now", and get really, really tense, so they start off with a backward rein. I use this exercise to teach them the feeling for half-pass, and because the circle is a never-ending line, they can start and finish when they are ready, so they feel more confident and don't block the horse.'

The exercise

❏ Begin this exercise in its simplest form, spiralling in and spiralling out from a 20m circle down to an 8m circle.

❏ When you have done that a few times, you and your horse should be able to spiral in and leg-yield out, with the inside hind leg of the horse stepping under the body in the direction of the outside rein.

❏ Now try a little bit of easy half-pass. On the large circle, create a bend with a little bit of shoulder-fore, and then come in for four or five strides to make the circle smaller. As soon as your horse starts to fall in, leg-yield out again.

❏ Repeat this exercise on both reins until you are able to half-pass in and then leg-yield out freely.

What's being achieved

❏ As you ride the leg-yield, you are creating a bending and a lowering of the hindquarters which helps the horse to stretch and use his back more.

❏ You get him into the outside rein, so he becomes suppler through the rib cage.

What can go wrong?

Once again, the horse can become too bent one way and not enough the other. The rider really has to keep control of the bend and the shoulders, and be sure the horse really is giving through the body to develop this uniform bend. If you find that the exercise is going wrong, you can always go back to its most simple form, or change the rein and freshen the horse up by going straight ahead a little bit. You don't have to stay there until it is perfect – simplify or intensify it according to the way your horse is feeling or the level of his training.

EXPERT TIP

After a while the rider can come in and out, in and out, taking as many or as few strides as they want, and they will get the feeling for controlling the shoulders and keeping the movement supple and fluent. I've taught many riders half-pass through this exercise, and it is not so tough on the horse.

'I think it is essential that the horse really learns to give as much as physically possible through the rib cage for lateral work.'

'This is quite a good exercise for horses that get really sour if they have to repeatedly do things at a certain point.'

Moving on

I do the same exercise in canter, too. That leg-yield out helps the horse to give through the rib cage and to really supple up and come around the inside leg. You get the feeling that the horse is really being ridden from behind to the front. To do this in canter, the horse must accept the half-halt and take the weight back. It is really difficult to do this if the horse is a little bit on the forehand. Sometimes in the canter, the horse gets a little bit tense in the leg-yielding part because being flexed one way and moving the other is quite difficult for the horse to achieve. The solution is to take more time and keep the horse deep and round and supple, so he hasn't the time to tighten the back and come hollow against the hand. Gradually, as the horse understands, it becomes easier and easier – especially if you ride the exercise in canter after you have just done it in trot, and the horse understands the turning and the moving away from the leg.

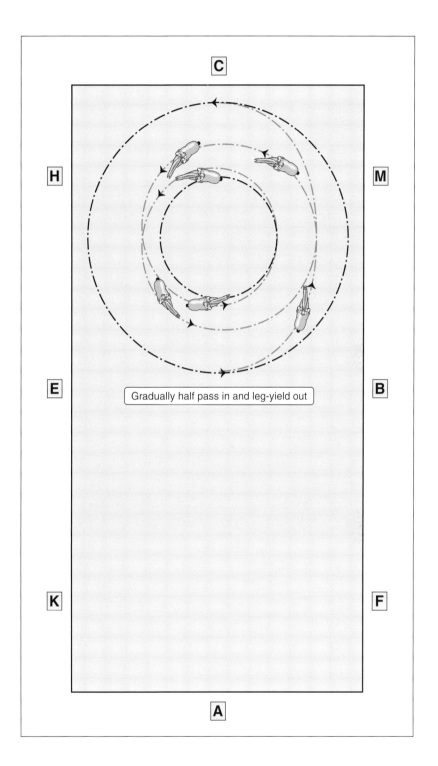

Gradually half pass in and leg-yield out

Getting a feeling for half-pass

'I found this way of learning the half-pass for the rider and horse who are not too experienced. You get the feeling of the horse coming through the rib cage before you ask for the half-pass, and it seems to flow much easier.'

The exercise

❏ Ride through the corner in trot, coming on to the long side. Position your horse on to the diagonal, and then change the flexion and leg-yield away from the corner marker towards the middle of the centre line. If you are leg yielding to the left, the right leg is on the girth, motivating the horse's inside right hind.

❏ From this halfway point, go back to the wall in half-pass. You will find out after a while which side of your horse needs more bending, and which a little bit less.

What's being achieved

❏ Whilst leg-yielding, the rider is really making the horse give through the rib cage and wrap himself around what would then be the inside leg, so the body of the horse is made supple so that in the changeover to half-pass the horse is easier to bend/flex.

❏ In the leg-yield, the rider has got the inside leg and the outside rein, so when the half-pass starts the horse is already 80 per cent there and you just bend him a little bit more and he moves back to the wall easily. Horses always gravitate towards the wall anyway.

What you should be looking for

On the left rein, if the horse has moved off the wall, he is flexed a bit to the right, and more or less parallel through the body. He's moving to the left, supple and flexed at the poll to the right, and in the left rein from the rider's right leg and into the outside rein. Then there should be a supple changeover to half-pass back to the wall.

What can go wrong?

The horse falls or drifts to the side, losing his balance, going on to the shoulder. The rider must straighten him up and get him a little more upright and into both reins and then come again, because most horses will wobble a bit in the beginning.

'If you tell a rider to ride a half-pass, they immediately take the inside rein, the horse tilts the neck, tilts the head, and becomes stiff.'

Moving on

For a horse and rider who are already reasonably established, you can do this the other way round. You can half-pass off the wall and leg-yield back, and then do another half-pass if you have room.

'The best half-pass is the one after the little bit of leg yielding – because the horse is bent around the leg and giving through the rib cage, and there is a more supple and loose-moving frame and the horse is not falling against the inside leg.'

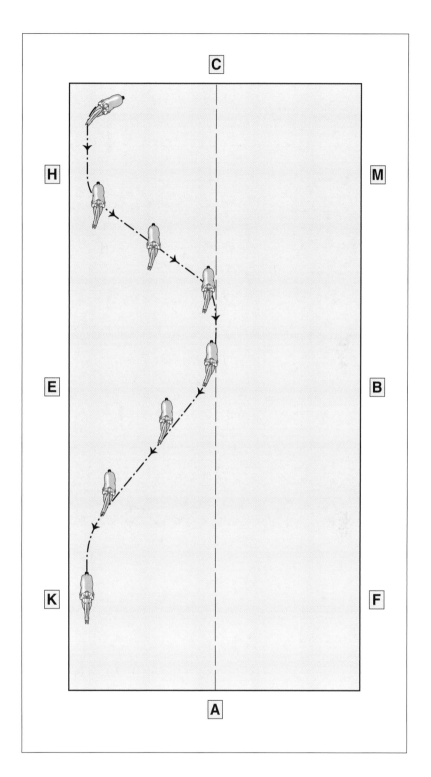

On and back within the pace

'I think this exercise is particularly useful in canter. In that pace a lot of people don't ride with enough impulsion, and you have to encourage them to feel confident enough to ride a lot more forwards and to bring the horse into a good balance.'

The exercise

❑ On a big circle, or using the long side, wherever you feel comfortable, in a normal working canter, bring your horse back with a little half-halt so he takes his weight back on the hind legs.

❑ From there, push him forwards to really react behind, go more over the back, and cover more ground.

❑ Then bring your horse back again to a collected canter, with as clear a transition as possible without blocking the horse.

❑ Now, within the canter ask for lots of transitions from a bigger working canter to a collected canter, a medium canter and then a pirouette type of canter. If the horse is too tense and becomes high and tight, then these transitions will be easier on a curved line or with a horse in a deeper frame.

What's being achieved

❑ These exercises make the horse really responsive to, and in front of, the rider's leg, with really good reactions in his hind legs.

❑ The horse develops quite a lot more impulsion and spring through these exercises, and his whole body starts to be motivated.

❑ He will learn to accept and respond to the half-halt more quickly, and to take his weight back.

'What I always say to anybody doing these transitions is that the exercises should never be grinding on and on. You should do them with feeling, short and sweet, activating and efficient, and always with rewards. When your horse comes back with a good understanding of the half-halt, pat him with the inside rein, so that you give the inside rein away a bit, and then the horse feels he is allowed through and it makes him relax even more.'

What you should be looking for

The horse should be on the hind legs from the half-halts, and then ridden forwards into the medium stride and back again, so he learns to keep his weight and balance on the hind leg.

What can go wrong?

The obvious problem with this exercise is that the horse becomes very hurried, and loses his balance when his forearm or front legs are going away from the hind legs. The whole of the horse's frame and his ability to use that frame should be involved in this exercise. The horse becomes a bit longer and rounder and more collected, and in this way one avoids the loss of balance.

Turns on a serpentine

'Everybody hates the walk pirouette, but I think it is one of the best exercises of all time because it has this wonderful effect of closing the horse's hind legs.'

The exercise

❏ This exercise can be as simple or as complicated as required, according to the level of the horse.

❏ In an active medium walk (not too collected), ride a serpentine to the long sides of the arena. As you come to the track to make the serpentine loop, ride – according to the level of the horse – either a half circle, thinking like a walk pirouette, a very large half pirouette, or a proper half pirouette.

❏ As you go across the width of the school, allow the horse to stretch forwards and then collect again, and repeat the turn at the next loop.

❏ Your horse will start to get the feeling and as he naturally improves and collects a little bit more, you can ask for a little bit more.

What's being achieved

The horse shouldn't be crossing and stepping sideways, he should be actively stepping forwards under his body, his hind feet in the direction of his ears. If he does this and stays through over the back and into the reins, quite often if you push him to stretch, you will find that the walk becomes really round and more supple through the body, and the horse really swings. And because he is in a good way through the back, you can collect him and ask him again, and in this way you can keep on making him stretch and collect.

What you should be looking for

❏ As you make the turns, be sure the quarters don't fall out. Don't push them in too much, but don't let them fall out, either.

❏ If you are near a mirror and you watch the horse as he turns you will see how 'closed' he is. You can imagine him just sitting down and piaffing out of this.

What can go wrong?

The most common mistake is losing the quarters too much to the inside or outside. Alternatively, the horse loses the correct walk rhythm, or stops walking altogether and backs off. In this case, you can turn the pirouette into a normal turn, ride the horse more forwards into the hands, correct the basic fault, and then ask again. This time, however, make the turn a little bit bigger so the hind legs of the horse are continually motivated and stepping through. And when he does that and gives, you can 'allow' the horse through and let him stretch, and he then finds it easier and easier.

EXPERT TIP

You can make this exercise extremely complicated and do many pirouettes, as small as possible, or you can make it dead simple for a very young horse and just think of a turn.

Moving on

Begin with a simple half circle and progress to a proper walk pirouette, increasing the number of turns as you do so. This is a great exercise to set you up for a piaffe (*see* Exercise 92).

'If riders were to ride more pirouettes in walk, they wouldn't hate them so much!'

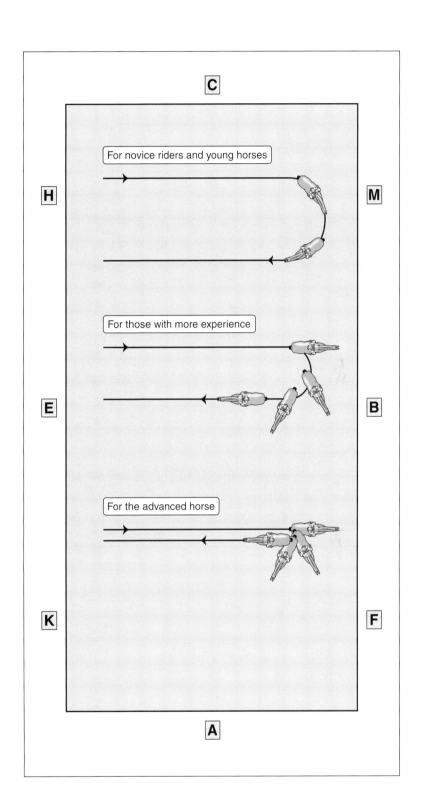

For novice riders and young horses

For those with more experience

For the advanced horse

Straightening your horse

'This is a good exercise for horses that, on the long side or through the corners, are constantly falling in against the inside leg of the rider.'

EXPERT TIP

Lengthen and then collect back your horse just before a corner. Because the horse is expecting you to do the small circle, he will be ready to come back to you, but you need not always make the circle. Sometimes, just pat him with your inside hand and then proceed through the corner. You will find you can ride a real cracker because, again, you have the inside leg and the outside rein.

The exercise

❏ Come out of the corner in canter, and at the beginning of the long side, make a small inward circle at the corner marker. It can be anything from 6m to 10m, according to what your horse is comfortable with.

❏ As you come out of the circle on to the track, ride a little shoulder-fore so the neck is just about straight but there is a little bit of flexion at the poll to the inside. You should be able to see the corner of the eye and nostril, and the rest of the horse is more or less straight. That slight shoulder-fore means that the shoulders are a little to the inside of the quarters so the horse is, in fact, dead straight.

❏ Now develop a little bit of lengthening, not too much to start with…

❏ …and then bring the horse back and immediately make another small circle.

❏ You can continue doing this for as long or as short a time as you like.

What's being achieved

I find this a very good exercise for teaching the rider to keep the horse between the inside leg and the outside rein – to keep the horse straight and in good balance. This straightness, and the ability to stay upright, also helps the horse to develop a better canter stride.

What you should be looking for

The straightening effect of the shoulder-fore before the small circle sets the horse back on his quarters, and if the rider makes these clear transitions it really develops the ability to expand and compress the canter.

What can go wrong?

If the rider does not have the horse between the inside leg and the outside rein, the horse tends to fall through the corner and is unable to make a circle of any description.

If the horse tightens a little at the beginning of this exercise he may be a little bit stiff on one rein and disunites behind. In this case, I always tell people to sit still and correct and ride just the canter – just ride the aids again and try to make him correct himself, so you don't have to bring him back into trot. He learns to jump himself back into a good canter again. This will also help later on when you do flying changes.

Moving on

❑ Start a bit bigger and gradually close down the circles.

❑ Gradually develop the extension and make clearer transitions back, keeping the horse absolutely straight with just a tiny bit of flexion of the poll to the inside. After a while, if you ride the medium canter without the two small circles, you will find that the horse begins much straighter and more 'through' and in balance, and comes back in the same way.

'Whenever you come up against a brick wall in your training, go back to the scales of training. Make it as simple as possible and start again – rhythm, looseness, acceptance of the bit, impulsion, straightness, collection.'

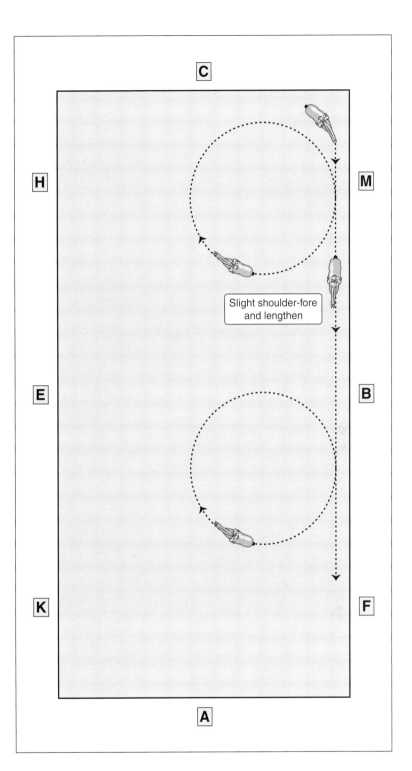

Slight shoulder-fore and lengthen

EXERCISE

90

Developing the canter pirouette

'I use this exercise to help the rider get the feeling of starting pirouette work without blocking and restricting the horse.'

<table>
<tr><td>

EXPERT TIP

It helps here to have a mirror or some 'eyes on the ground' for this exercise, to make sure the horse's shoulders are on the centre line and the quarters a little bit to the inside, and that the line is quite straight.

</td><td>

The exercise

❏ At this stage in his development, the horse is much more collected, with more weight on the hind leg. He should still be working on the deep side, nicely over the back, so that he can work through the frame without tightening his back or lifting his neck, because pirouette work needs the horse to give in his back and to come through with the hind legs.

❏ From the long side, riding a little quarters-in, make a turn on to the centre line, approximately half way down, keeping the quarters in.

❏ Proceed on the centre line, still with the quarters in, and then turn again and rejoin the long side, all the time feeling that the hind legs are a little bit to the inside. Your horse should be supple around your inside leg, going nicely over the back, and jumping with the hind feet as far forward under the body as possible.

❏ Once you are comfortable with this, start to make it a little bit more difficult by making the turn a little bit tighter. From the centre line, now turn on to the quarter line instead of on to the long side, so it is now a 5m turn.

❏ Then turn back on to the centre line. The exercise should be ridden equally on both reins, and in between the horse should be ridden straight forwards, and allowed to stretch neck and back.

</td></tr>
</table>

What's being achieved

I have found it is much more successful with some riders than a working pirouette because riders tend to go on and on and on in the working pirouette. Sometimes I will ask a rider to count how many strides they are doing on this working pirouette. We often find they are there for much too long and do thirty-odd strides, bringing the horse to its knees. Exercises should never grind on and on.

What can go wrong?

The most common problems are (a) losing control of the shoulders and, consequently, the ability to turn, or turning too much; and (b) the canter becomes rather stiff and the horse tries to raise the croup instead of sitting. In both these cases the rider needs to make things a little bit more simple for a moment.

If the horse gets very slow behind, try to ride the slight quarters-in with more like a working canter, so the horse is striding a little bit more and not working backwards. The collecting process shouldn't make the horse come back at the rider, he should keep a forward tendency. There has to be something to collect, there has to be something bursting out, otherwise you haven't got anything to collect and when the rider is concentrating a lot they can lose that bit of the recipe. What I would normally suggest to overcome it is to ride a little bit more forward, keep everything fluent, don't ask repeatedly too many times, and don't ask the horse to go sideways too much, either.

The pirouette shouldn't be a contortion, it should be a feeling of the horse bending around the leg, and then the shoulders coming around the hind legs. At the end of the day, the quarters are just behind the front legs, they should never be leading, so if the rider exaggerates things too much, the basis is lost, and you have to go back to being simple again.

Moving on

You can intensify the turns even more so they become a half 2m or 3m circle, but it is then more or less a half pirouette. The advantage here is that you have a line of straightness in between each turn so you have time to make the horse supple, and improve on the forward tendency.

'When you ask a rider to make a pirouette, they can get so tense and start pulling the horse around; this makes things easier because you are talking about turning rather than pirouette.'

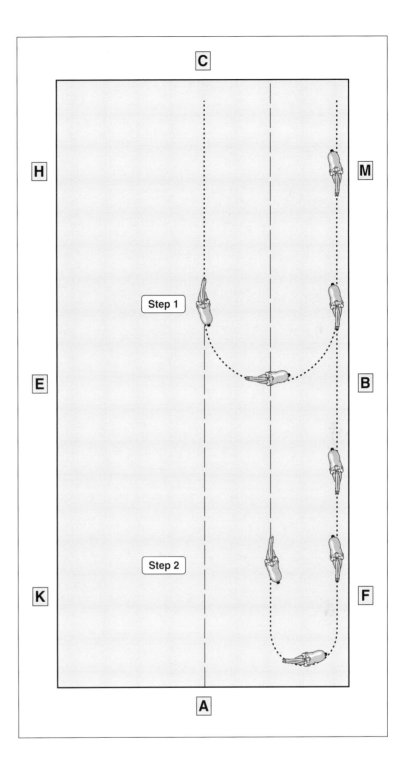

EXERCISE 91

Working on half-halts to develop the passage reaction

'If you repeat this exercise often enough, and the horse is swinging enough, you get this lovely feeling of lift.'

The exercise

❑ On a circle in trot, with your horse correctly bent, loose and supple with lots of impulsion, closer to a working trot or working semi-collected, bring him back with a series of half-halts so the energy gravitates upwards and over the ground, rather than into the ground. You will get the beginnings of the moment of suspension that you need for the passage.

❑ When the horse does this, he needs to be encouraged to stay as deep and round as possible so the back swings, because if you do this and the horse hollows the back and uses the neck in an upward way against you, the energy is blocked from coming through. It is very important that the passage is developed from here and not from a false tightening, dwelling type of feeling. Try for three or four strides at any one time in the beginning.

❑ When the horse starts to give you that lift and feel, then you reward him, you let him relax a little and then go forward again – not on the forehand, but in the same balance and a little bit more forward.

❑ Pump up or refresh the energy again, and then repeat the exercise. And if you repeat it often enough, and the horse is swinging enough, you will find that just when you are thinking of using your seat, he comes back to you and you get this lovely feeling of lift.

❑ Repeat the exercise on both reins.

What's being achieved

You use the impulsion from the working or collected trot and the swinging in the back to get the element of the passage. It's only a reaction to start with, and the horse should be instantly rewarded and allowed forward. Then you repeat it again and after a while he really likes it. Obviously some horses have the talent for it and others not, but even a limited horse learns quite a lot from this exercise.

What you should be looking for

You have to feel and think the rhythm of the passage, think bigger and slower, trying to keep your horse as round and soft as possible.

'This is not a slow trot with the horse holding himself and blocked – which of course is a very, very negative thing. One sees it a lot and it has got nothing to do with passage at all.'

What can go wrong?

The main faults are that the hind leg gets much too slow and, quite often, becomes straight or pushes out behind, so the horse is no longer 'closed'. You'll notice the lifting in the neck and blocking in the back – the horse is suddenly in a different position. He may also try to go with irregular steps – long and short.

Moving on

The passage reaction should be developed in the same round way as any other transition or half-halt, so the horse really works over the back; and as the horse strengthens – and this exercise does require a lot of strength – then you can ask for even more. Try working the exercise at various points around the school – out of a circle on to a straight line, for example. Keep 'through' in a genuine way. The connection has to be secure. And your horse has to be fresh and forward in front of the leg. This 'reaction' should become like a gear change so you can just put the horse in that gear and off you go.

An exercise to get the piaffe reaction

'The piaffe is all about reaction, and if your horse really does react as easily as this from standing still, it will be even easier out of walk or when there is some motivation. After a while they just love it because they're always getting patted.'

The exercise

❏ This might sound easy, but it is actually quite difficult. Your horse has to be a horse that really stays 'through' to do this exercise.

❏ With your horse on the long side of the school in a proper collected walk, bending the joints and through to the bit, ride into a halt. The horse remains through, straight and soft.

❏ Remain still for a moment or two, and then take both legs a tiny bit back and ask the horse to react in the hind leg, bearing in mind what he has learnt from all the other transitions. As soon as he moves his hind legs, immediately give the reins and pat him.

❏ Now let him walk again, and then stand still and give the leg aid again, and as soon as he reacts, lighten your aids. He may stay reacting for a little bit longer, but pat him again and as soon as he reacts, take the pressure away.

❏ He will learn to spring from the lightest leg aid for himself.

What's being achieved

The horse is learning to close behind and wait in front. His hind legs need to be quick and very reactive to get a good piaffe, and because you are not restricting the horse in any way, he feels he can go a little bit forward, so he keeps the regularity and suppleness. However, some just don't learn it this way, and others learn it really easily.

What you should be looking for

You want the feeling that when you give him the aids, whatever your aid is, he moves the hind legs (and obviously the front legs move as well), and he stays through and on the bit and straight, but he just reacts in the hind legs and gives you the beginning of that quicker feeling that the piaffe needs.

'I have had one or two horses where I could literally stand still and ask and they would piaffe on the spot, and then I just pat them.'

What can go wrong?

This exercise isn't easy, and you may need help from the ground a little bit – perhaps somebody there to occasionally just touch a hind leg will help, so that the horse gets the feeling of the rhythm as well as the reaction after a while. It is difficult for the horse: if your horse backs off and goes backwards or goes crooked or comes above the bit, all these resistances are because he feels trapped or is unsure. You will probably find that you have to go a little bit more forward and do it again. Remember, he may react incorrectly, but better that than no reaction at all.

Moving on

If you can get this reaction, your horse is really in front of you and it is possible to learn to do the piaffe with very small aids. I think the piaffe is no big deal, it is a very natural thing for the horse to do, so you have to play on the horse's tendencies. Try to come back to the basis of the smallest aids possible with the horse reacting quickly. Because I always do this transition work a lot from the very beginning, when it comes to this stage, I think I have already got this understanding with the horse and it is not so complicated.

'If you get used to sitting and doing too much, obviously in the end the horse does nothing, the rider is doing a lovely piaffe and the horse is doing nothing at all.'

GUY WILLIAMS

The rosettes wall at Guy Williams' home in Chilham, Kent is a truly memorable sight. Regularly placed first or second at national championships and in Grand Prix classes, Guy is ranked 14th on the British Show Jumping Association (BSJA) list, has regularly been leading rider at his local Kent County Show, and was a Nations Cup team member in 2005.

Having started on ponies at gymkhanas and graduated to top class competition at Wembley, Guy is a good example of how the BSJA competition ladder works at its best. His down-to-earth approach to getting the best out of his horses has endeared him to owners and pupils alike. His ambition is to build up a good string of horses and to 'be there' at the 2012 London Olympics.

Q: What's the best piece of advice you've ever been given in regard to training horses?
Keep yourself in the best company and your horses in the worst.

Q: What do you do when you come up against a training brick wall?
Climb over it or get around it.

Q: Name three things that you look for when you begin to train a horse.
Temperament, carefulness and braveness.

Q: How do you identify problems in your own performance, and how do you work on them?
I demand a lot from myself. I am self-driven and I have to win. I think that helps me – I'm always picking faults!

Q: Who coaches you?
I've got lots of people that criticise me! But I'd advise everyone, don't be afraid to ask for help.

Q: If I asked one of your pupils 'What's the thing that Guy goes on about the most', what would it be?
Stay straight and sit up in the body.

Q: What would be the three pearls of wisdom you'd like to pass on to anyone with equine ambitions?

Be patient, work hard, marry someone rich.

Q: Whom do you admire most in the equestrian world?
John Whitaker or Nick Skelton for coming back after major injury and getting to the top of the game again.

Q: Do you have a formula for goal setting?
Definitely. Within a year I know what I want. I want every year to be better than the year before.

Q: Whatever level of rider we are, we all have those magic moments when we feel really connected with our horses and the situation. Can you describe the last 'magic moment' that you had?
My best moment was when I won the Horse of the Year Grand Prix in 2004. It was a cheap horse, the owner's first – she had never owned a horse before. I didn't have enough money to buy him so she bought him for me. He's called Loro Piana Hamlet, he's very naughty and I've still got him.

CONTENTS

Cross-poles with a bounce

'My first three exercises are for working with young horses. This is how I'd start a young horse jumping. It's very simple.'

The exercise

❑ Set up a cross-pole in the middle of your arena at a height of approximately 30cm (12in) to start with.

❑ Place a ground pole about 1.5–2m (5–6½ft), or three human strides, each side of the cross-pole.

❑ Ride over the ground poles aiming for the middle of the cross-poles in a good forward trot.

What's being achieved

You will need to adjust the distance of your bounce poles from the jump to teach your horse to shorten before and after jumping the fence. He should be looking to see where he is placing his feet after the jump, and this will help him to make a correct shape over the fence.

What you should be looking for

❑ You are aiming for your horse to bounce into the cross-pole and out again on the other side. Check that the distance between the ground pole and the cross-pole suits your horse's stride, and shorten or lengthen them as necessary. You may need someone on the ground to do this for you, and to adjust your poles.

❑ Don't allow your horse to rush.

What can go wrong?

Your horse runs to one side and knocks the cross-pole: as your jumps get higher you need to stay straight, and that's what cross-poles do – they help you keep your horse straight. So it is important that you are able to keep your horse between leg and hand at this stage. Think of your legs and hands forming a tunnel that directs and guides the horse to the point at which you want to jump – the middle. If your horse tips the pole, don't panic, but allow it to learn for itself where it is supposed to make the jump.

Moving on

Begin in trot and progress to canter. (Don't forget to adjust the position of the ground poles.) Start with the cross-pole small, and as you get better, build it up.

Add additional ground poles before or after the fence, depending on whether you want to slow your horse down coming into the cross-pole or on landing.

'Young horses rush jumps and try to take them miles too fast. This exercise helps them understand the basics, and starts to work on containing their stride.'

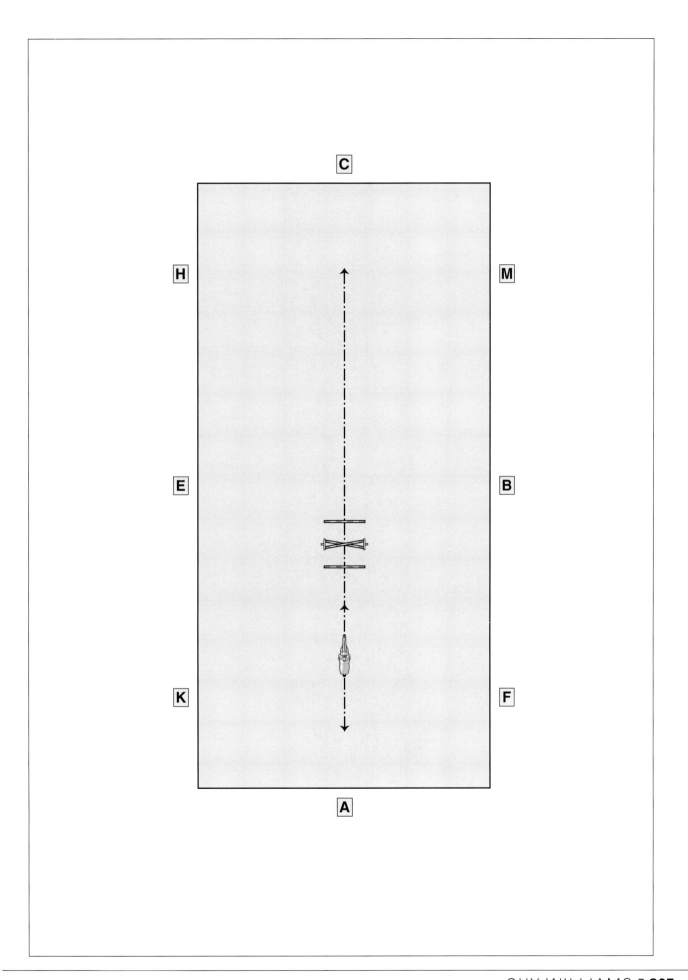

The cross-pole

'This exercise is similar in principle to my first, and teaches the young horse to jump an oxer.'

The exercise
❏ Use two cross-poles to make an oxer. Set them close together to begin with.
❏ Place a ground pole a canter stride in front and behind the oxer. Once again the cross-poles will help to keep your horse over the centre of the fence.
❏ Ride this exercise in canter, and from both directions.

What's being achieved
This exercise works in the same way as Exercise 93, but it can also be used to teach the horse to stretch over the fence (*see* Moving on).

What you should be looking for
Make sure that your horse comes into this fence straight, and goes over it straight. He should be using his shoulders and picking up his hind legs behind. He should also be looking at the ground pole on landing to help with his shape over the fence. You want him to land inside the pole!

What can go wrong?
If your horse swings his legs, haunches or shoulders to either side he will knock a pole. This will teach him that he cannot do this, and in that way will help him to straighten up for landing.

Moving on
❏ Once your horse is comfortable with the oxer at a narrow width, gradually increase the distance between the two cross-poles, and raise the ends. Keep the same distance from each side of the oxer to the ground poles.
❏ Make the cross-poles into two uprights at the same height as the X of the cross-poles. It will be easier for your horse to do this than to try an ascending oxer (a cross-pole in front of an upright), as the top of his arc will be in the same place.

'This fence encourages a horse to use his shape properly from the word go.'

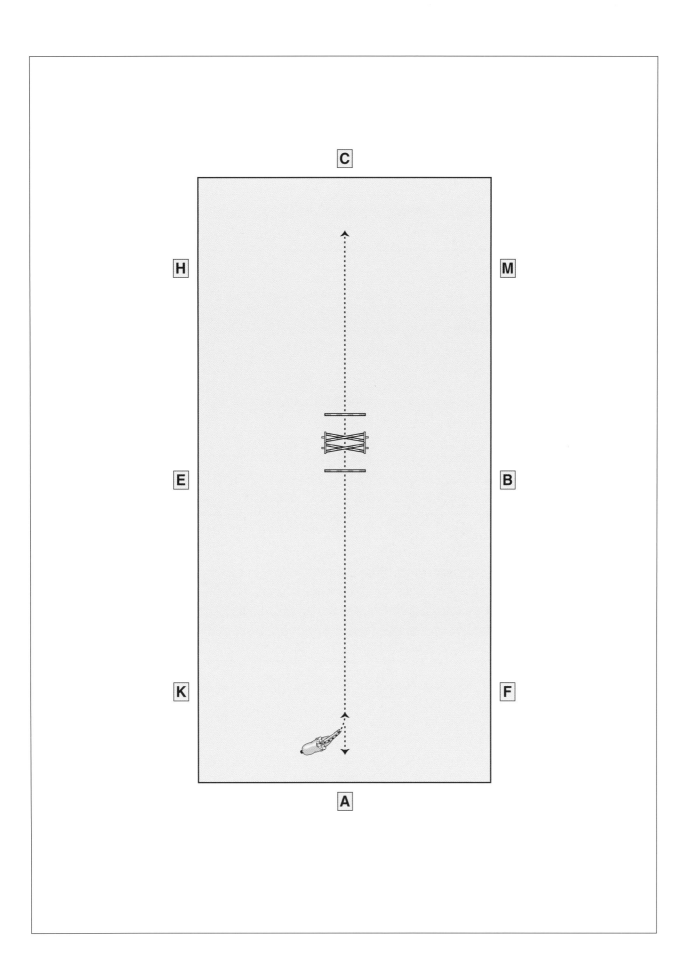

An easy grid

'This is my final exercise for young horses – this one gets them used to jumping more than one fence.'

The exercise

❏ Set up a grid beginning with a ground pole 1.5–2m (5–6½ft) or three of your strides from a cross-pole, followed by another ground pole and then an upright, all the same distance apart.

❏ Establish your horse in an even-rhythm trot. Aim for the centre of the cross-pole, and make sure you keep him straight through the grid.

❏ You can then use this exercise to teach your horse to lengthen or shorten his stride, either increasing the distance between each element if you have a short-striding horse, or shortening the distances if you have a horse with a great big stride.

What's being achieved

Your horse will have to concentrate all the way through this exercise, as he needs to be careful about where he is placing his feet; he should remain in an even rhythm throughout the grid.

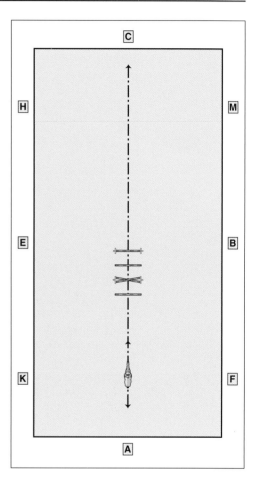

What you should be looking for

Concentrate on feeling the shape your horse is making over the fence. He should be using his shoulders, not throwing away a hind leg, not landing too far over any one element, staying straight, not going flat, and keeping round in the back.

What can go wrong?

Your horse wants to rush down the jumps and won't wait, and consequently he keeps pushing the poles or kicking the vertical. To teach him to slow down, keep jumping the grid and let him learn. Keep soft in the hand, pick him up a little bit, and stay calm.

Moving on

Build the upright into an oxer, or add an oxer and try the grid in canter, checking your distances between elements carefully, first.

Five bounces

'Think of a soldier running through a row of tyres: this is the horse's equivalent!'

'My older horses jump down a row of bounces like this at least once a week to keep them supple.'

The exercise

❏ Build a row of three bounce fences approximately 3m (10ft) apart, at a height that your horse will be comfortable with. Start at 80–85cm (31–34in); for the more advanced horse work up to 1m (40in), but do not exceed this. Begin in trot and ride down the centre of the bounces.

❏ Once your horse is comfortable with three jumps, you can add a fourth and then a fifth.

What's being achieved

This exercise teaches a horse to use his shoulders and to be more agile. It will also make him quicker behind, and in his reactions. At the same time it slows down a horse that likes to rush his jumps, as he cannot run down that line!

What can go wrong?

Don't overface your horse: keep the height of the fences comfortable for him. If he knocks them down, check that your distances are correct, and then come in at them again. Don't punish him if he clips a pole – this is how he learns. Remain calm. Do not add extra fences until he is happy with three.

Moving on

Add extra jumps to increase from the original three to five, and raise the height of the jumps; however, do not exceed 1m (40in). Ride the exercise in canter, and always check your distances.

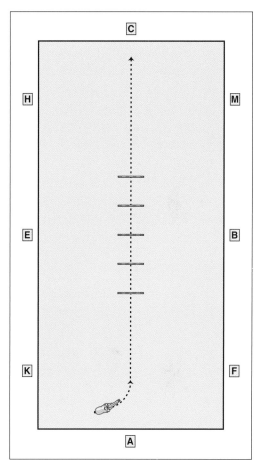

EXERCISE 97

Bounces with a 'V' into a jump

'I don't like a horse to "screw" over a fence, evading to one side or the other. This exercise helps put a stop to that.'

The exercise

❏ Build a vertical jump at a height with which your horse is comfortable. Place two ground poles on the vertical in a V-shape.

❏ Place a bounce pole on the ground in front of the vertical and another behind, both at a distance of 1.5–2m (5–6½ft) or three of your strides.

❏ Begin by cantering straight into this jump. As your horse becomes comfortable jumping at the centre point, move the V-poles out to the sides of the jump.

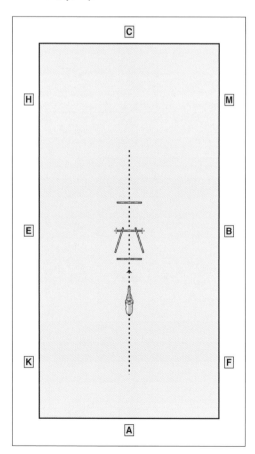

TACKLING EVASIONS

Why did your horse try to evade the jump?

❏ Was it your indecision and lack of commitment?

❏ Or did *he* take the decision and run out at the last moment?

Once you've established that there is no good physical reason why your horse ran out, the next thing to ask yourself is whether it is a question of confidence – yours or his. Are you overfacing yourselves? Do you need to take a step backwards, working with smaller challenges until both of you are confident enough to move forwards once again? Is the issue one of steering? (In which case *see* David O'Connor's Exercise 49.) Take some time to analyze the answers to this question, and break the problem down into small, achievable chunks, seeking professional help if necessary.

What's being achieved

This exercise teaches a horse to use its shoulders and jump in the correct shape. It also helps to keep a horse straight, and stops him 'screwing' over a fence.

What you should be looking for

You are looking for a good shape over the vertical, which is encouraged by the ground pole on landing and by riding a straight line into the fence. The bounce pole gives your horse something to think about before the fence.

What can go wrong?

Your horse may try to evade the jump, but the bounce before and the V-poles leading to the jump will help to keep him on course. You must ride forwards into this fence.

If your horse is inclined to run off to one side or the other over a jump the bounce pole on the other side will help.

Moving on

Try approaching the fence on a curve, and gradually tighten the curve as you would if you were approaching a fence in a jump-off.

Combination of oxers

'This is quite a difficult exercise, and tests a horse's scope.'

'Don't make the course bigger than you are really comfortable popping over.'

The exercise

❏ Begin with a ground pole on the ground, and set three oxers in a line, and then a ground pole at the end. Each should be about 90cm (3ft) high to start with (or of a height that your horse is comfortable with), and with two canter strides (to suit his length of stride) between.

❏ Once your horse is comfortable with this line of jumps, you can change the distances between the two outside oxers to lengthen or shorten his stride.

What's being achieved

This will teach your horse to keep its shape down a distance. It will have to use its whole body down the line. It has to be good in the shoulder to jump the front rail, and quick behind for the back rail.

What you should be looking for

Make sure that your horse is jumping straight and maintaining that straightness. If he is jumping across the oxer at an angle, the oxer becomes wider.

What can go wrong?

If your horse is really in trouble with three oxers, begin with one oxer with two ground poles to get his confidence, and then gradually build up to three. Make sure that the height of the oxers is not overfacing him, and that the distance between the jumps is correct for his length of stride and ability.

Moving on

Gradually increase the height of the oxers, but do not exceed 120cm (3ft 11in).

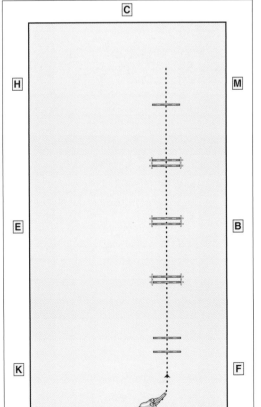

V-pole with an oxer

'Your horse will jump the front rail and then hover for a minute over the fence – it's quite a different feeling.'

EXPERT TIP

If you have a horse that rushes an oxer, it will find it can't rush over this exercise.

The exercise

❑ Set up a small oxer at a height your horse is confident with. Place V-poles on the front and back of the oxer, as shown in the diagram.

❑ Ride this exercise in trot or canter until your horse is going over the fence in a straight line. Keep your eye on the middle of the fence and make sure your horse is going straight.

❑ This exercise can be ridden on both reins.

What's being achieved

This is a good exercise for horses that 'don't jump' back rails, or that are not very good behind, allowing their hind legs to drag, rather than 'throwing them away'. It is also good for horses that don't stay straight in the air. The horse has to stretch and hold its shape over the oxer.

EXPERT TIP

You will need to do this exercise with a trainer or somebody watching, to see how wide you need to have the oxer.

What you should be looking for

Try not to use too much hand to 'steer' your horse into the jump. He needs to learn for himself where he should be jumping. As you jump over this fence you will get quite a different feeling, as the horse 'hovers' for a minute as he works out where to put his legs on landing.

What can go wrong?

If your horse is jumping this like an upright, make it wider – he has to be pushing himself a bit. If he clips the back rail at the first few attempts, don't rush to lower it because he needs to make the mistake to learn to pick up his back feet.

Moving on

Move up a pace and try making the spread of the oxer wider.

'This exercise works more on the back end than the front.'

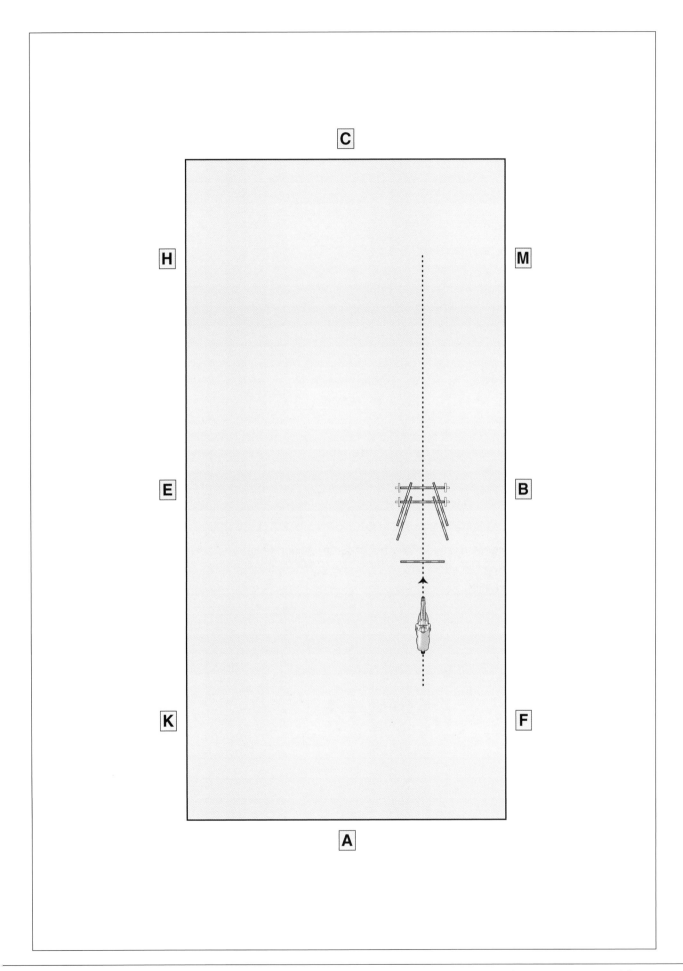

A jump on a figure-of-eight

'This is good practise for graded horses working on jump-offs.'

The exercise

❏ Set up an upright in the middle of your school or arena where you will have enough space to ride a figure-of-eight over the jump.

❏ Ride a figure-of-eight in canter, making sure that you are straight on your approach and landing (*see* diagram).

❏ Every third or fourth jump, ride a circle rather than continuing on the figure-of-eight.

What's being achieved

It is important to get your horse turning and bending to ensure he can keep his balance, and to get him off the forehand. He won't know which way you are turning on landing, and will learn to land and wait for your instruction on which way to turn.

What you should be looking for

Make sure that you are straight over the jump.

What can go wrong?

Your horse will 'screw' over the fence, trying to go off to one side or the other, and knock the fence down. If this is the case, forget about your circles for the moment and try the following exercise: lay two ground poles on either side of the fence at an angle of 70° to the fence. If your horse has a preference for an angle at which to run out, begin in that direction (so if your horse tends to run out to the left, come into the jump from right to left. Once you are happy with this, stop and change the angle to the opposite direction.

Moving on

You could try making the turns and circles tighter and tighter, or you might change the fence to an oxer to make the exercise more demanding. However, don't be tempted to put more fences on the circle for this exercise as it will give your horse too much to think about and will possibly confuse him. The point of repeating the exercise is consistency, and this is how the horse will learn.

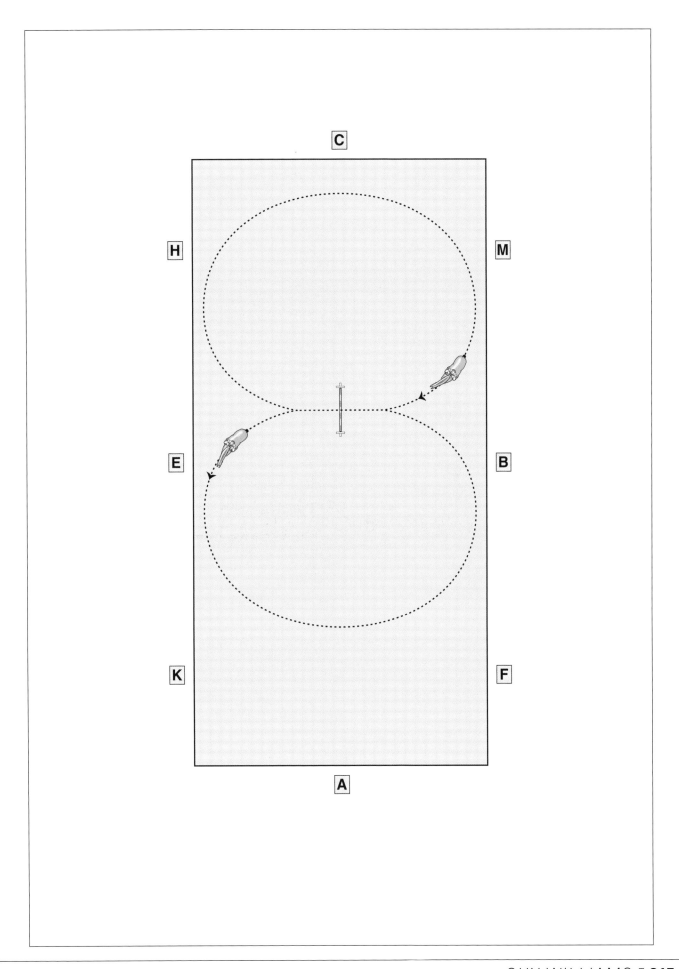

Sorting out changes of direction

'When I'm in the ring my horses all listen for me to tell them exactly which way I want them to go.'

The exercise

❑ Place an upright fence in the middle of the sand school, and approach it in canter on a dead straight line.

❑ Once over the jump and upon reaching the end of the school, the horse will usually indicate which way it wants to turn.

❑ As soon as you have an indication which way your horse wants to go, bring him to a halt and then strike off again, turning him in the opposite direction.

❑ Repeat this exercise until your horse waits for your guidance upon landing.

What's being achieved

This exercise teaches the horse to listen to your aids, and to wait for your instructions after a fence.

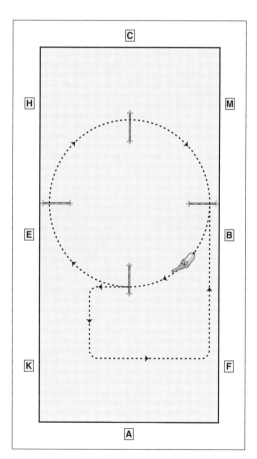

What you should be looking for

This exercise should become seamless, and your horse should remain in rhythm throughout the change of direction.

Moving on

Try this exercise:

❑ Place four uprights on a 20m circle with three canter strides (15 or 16 of your strides) between each.

❑ Jump these fences on a circle first of all, which is good practice at jumping on a bend.

❑ As soon as you land after one fence, decide whether you are going to remain on the original circle for the next, or if you will circle away in the opposite direction and rejoin the original circle over the next fence, going in the other direction (*see* diagram).

'New horses run off all the time; this exercise teaches them to land correctly right from the word go. That is, he will land and shorten his stride and wait for you to tell him where to go.'

EXERCISE INDEX